Portrait of the Central Wales Line

Portrait of the Central Wales Line

Martin Smith

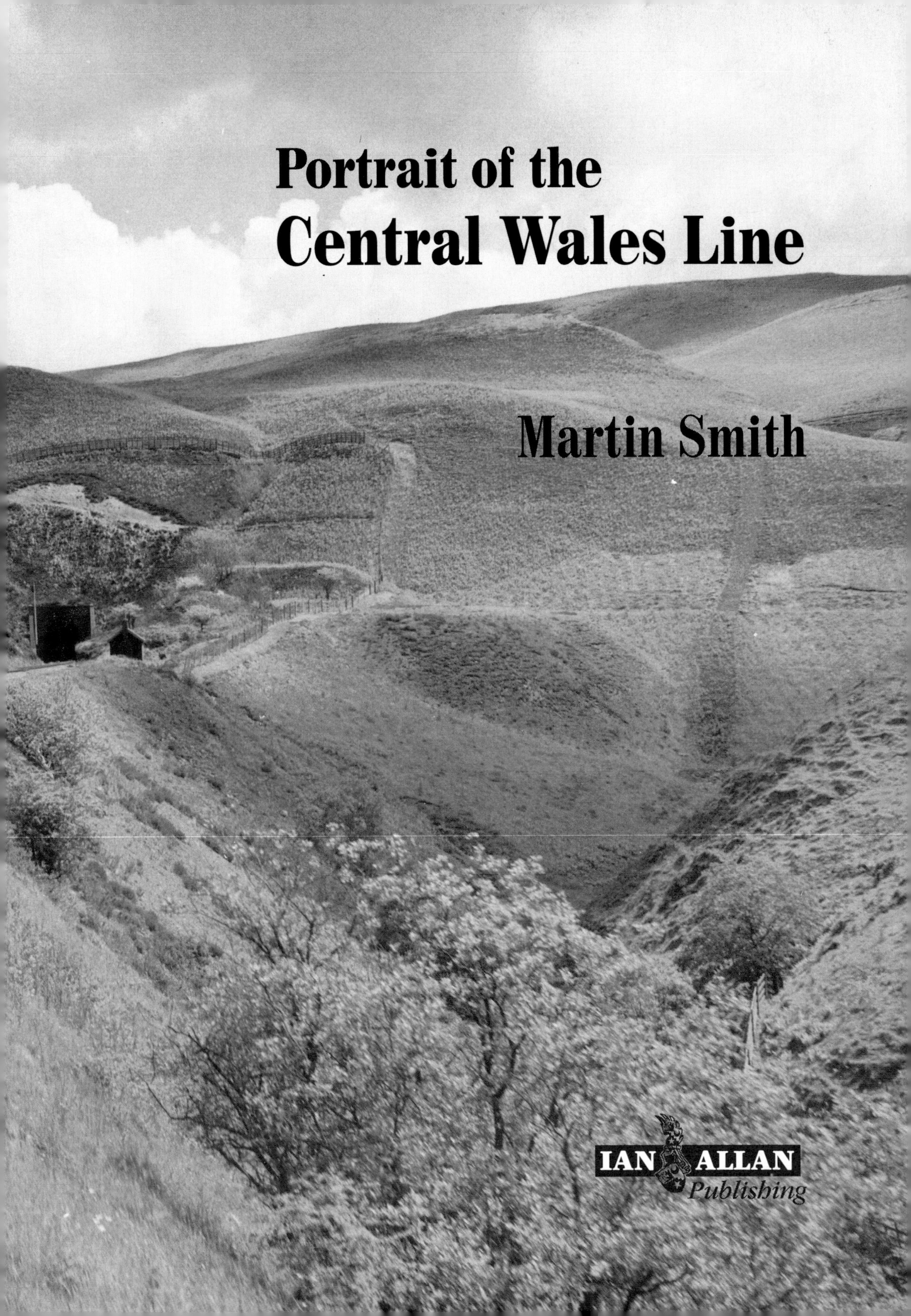

IAN ALLAN Publishing

First published 1995

ISBN 0 7110 2346 8

Published by Ian Allan Publishing

an imprint of Ian Allan Ltd, Terminal House, Station Approach, Shepperton, Surrey TW17 8AS.
Printed by Ian Allan Printing Ltd, Coombelands House, Coombelands Lane, Addlestone, Weybridge, Surrey KT15 1HY.

Bibliography

Much of the information for this book was gathered from official railway company records which are now housed at the Public Record Office, Kew. Some additional information was gleaned from the following:

A Celebration of the Heart of Wales Railway, Nigel & Sue Bird/HOWLTA, 1994
The Central Wales Line, Tom Clift, Ian Allan 1982
Clinker's Register, C. R. Clinker, Avon-Anglia 1988
History of the Great Western Railway, MacDermot & Clinker, Ian Allan 1964
LMS Engine Sheds, Vol. 1, Chris Hawkins & George Reeve, Wild Swan 1981
Locomotives of the GWR, RCTS
A Regional History of the Railways of Great Britain, Vols. 11 & 12, Peter Baughan/D. S. M. Barrie, David & Charles 1980
Track Layout Diagrams of the GWR and BR (WR), R. A. Cooke 1994
Welsh Railways Archive (The journal of the WRRC)
Various public and working timetables, Bradshaw's, and assorted railway magazines of impressive vintage.

Half title page: The Llanelly Railway was the first company to construct a component of what eventually became the Central Wales line. The LR's Llanelly Dock–Pontardulais section opened to mineral traffic as early as 1839, and later passed to GWR control. After the closure of the Pontardulais–Swansea section of the Central Wales line in June 1964 trains to and from Shrewsbury were re-routed via the old LR line to Llanelly, and so it might be argued that the LR section became a part of the Central Wales line only by default. On the approach to Pontardulais from Llanelly, trains pass through a short tunnel before entering the station. The platform and station buildings are seen in the mid-distance, but by the time this photograph was taken in June 1972, Pontarddulais station (as it was then spelt) was a mere shadow of its former self.
Andrew Muckley

Acknowledgments

The biggest thanks of all are undoubtedly due to Mr Bryan Wilson (of the Welsh Railways Research Circle), who not only provided a wealth of detailed information from his own researches, but also gave advice and assistance in exceedingly generous helpings. A very very nice man!

Considerable thanks are also due to my ever-patient wife, Micky, who, despite sharing my love of Central Wales, has asked if my next book can include place-names which contain a few more vowels.

Sincere thanks are also due to: Ben Ashworth, Hugh Ballantyne, Peter Bennett (Welsh Industrial & Maritime Museum), Nigel Bird, Richard Casserley, Ray Caston (Welsh Railways Research Circle), I. C. Coleford, Hugh Davies, John Davies (Dyfed Record Office), Geoff Dowling (photographic printer extraordinaire!), Alun Edwards (Powys County Archives), Paul Gilson (Welsh Railways Research Circle), Chris Hawkins, Mr J. V. Hughes (West Glamorgan County Library), Derek Huntriss, Alan Jarvis, Rex Kennedy, Norman Lee (LNWR Society), Michael Mensing, Brian Morrison, Denzil Penberthy, Bill Peto (GWR Society), Ann Pritchett (Shropshire Records and Research Unit), Leslie Sandler, Richard Strange (Steam Archive Services), Malcolm Took, Bob Tuck, Peter Waller, Ron White, and the staff of the Public Record Office, Kew. While we're at it, let's also mention the Coleford menagerie — Oswald and Judy (the mutts), and Pudding and The Butler (the moggies) — without whose 'assistance' this book would have been finished a whole lot quicker!

Martin Smith,
Coleford, Somerset.
November 1994.

Author's note: *For anybody with an interest in the railways of Wales, membership of the Welsh Railways Research Circle is one of life's great bargains. Details from the Membership Secretary (Mr Ray Caston), 22 Pentre Poeth Road, Bassaleg, Newport, Gwent NP1 9LL. I've done the plug, Ray.... now can I have my pint of Felinfoel, please?*

Title page: No matter who owned which part of the Central Wales line, one of the things that could never change was the magnificent scenery. When it came to the approach to Sugar Loaf Tunnel from the south, did it really matter whether one was travelling in LNWR six-wheelers or LMSR or BR corridor stock? This picture was taken from the 10.25am Swansea (Victoria)–Shrewsbury train on 10 June 1960. *Hugh Ballantyne*

Front cover: Sugar Loaf Summit, May 1964.
A. Jarvis

Back cover: Swansea (Victoria) station, May19
A. Jarvis

Craven Arms, August 1962. *Colour Rail*

Contents

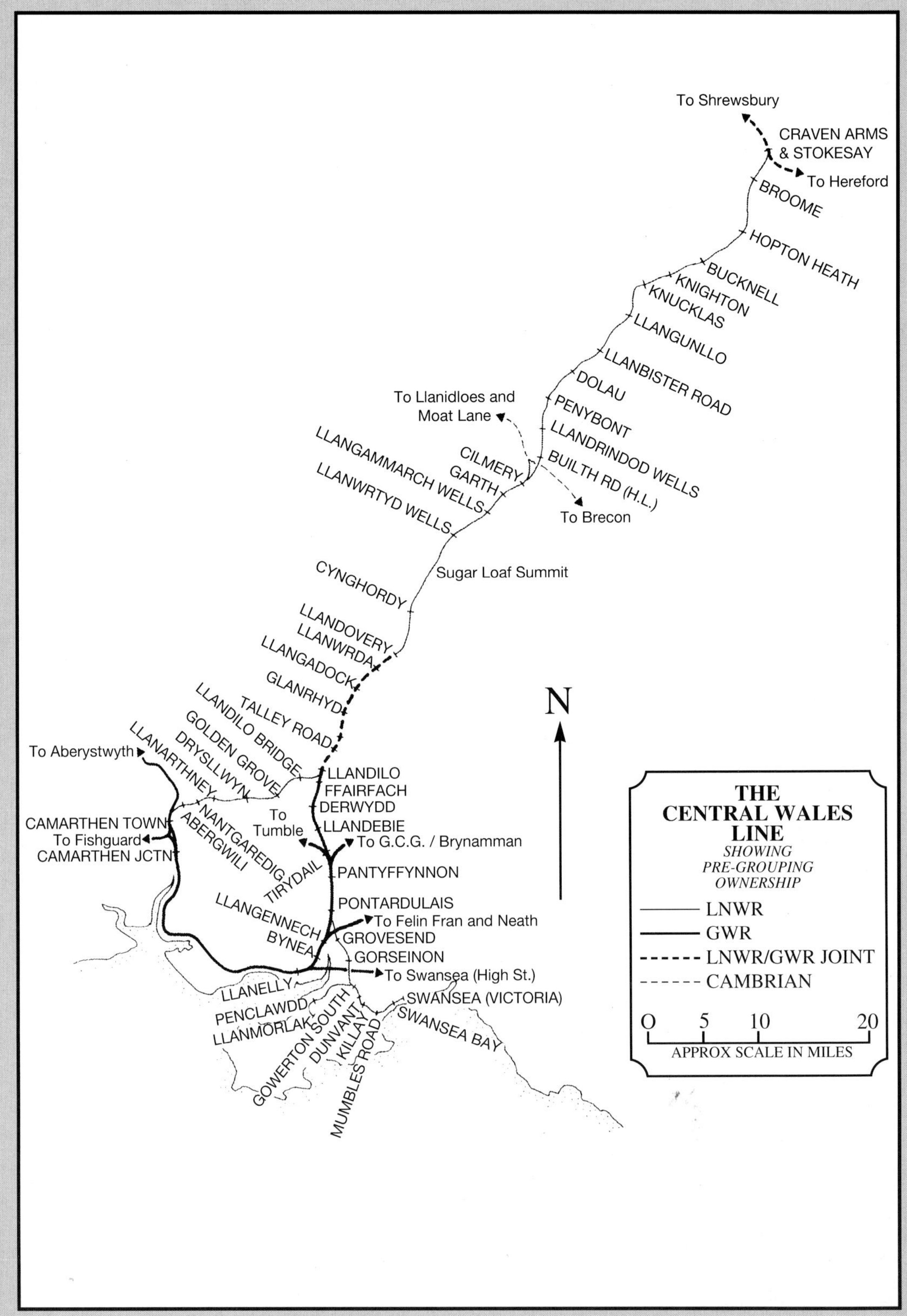

THE CENTRAL WALES LINE
SHOWING PRE-GROUPING OWNERSHIP
LNWR
GWR
LNWR/GWR JOINT
CAMBRIAN
0 5 10 20
APPROX SCALE IN MILES
N
To Shrewsbury
CRAVEN ARMS & STOKESAY
To Hereford
BROOME
HOPTON HEATH
BUCKNELL
KNIGHTON
KNUCKLAS
LLANGUNLLO
LLANBISTER ROAD
DOLAU
PENYBONT
LLANDRINDOD WELLS
To Llanidloes and Moat Lane
BUILTH RD (H.L.)
To Brecon
CILMERY
GARTH
LLANGAMMARCH WELLS
LLANWRTYD WELLS
Sugar Loaf Summit
CYNGHORDY
LLANDOVERY
LLANWRDA
LLANGADOCK
GLANRHYD
TALLEY ROAD
LLANDILO BRIDGE
GOLDEN GROVE
DRYSLLWYN
LLANARTHNEY
NANTGAREDIG
ABERGWILI
To Aberystwyth
CAMARTHEN TOWN
To Fishguard
CAMARTHEN JCTN
LLANDILO
FFAIRFACH
DERWYDD
LLANDEBIE
To Tumble
To G.C.G. / Brynamman
TIRYDAIL
PANTYFFYNNON
PONTARDULAIS
To Felin Fran and Neath
LLANGENNECH
BYNEA
GROVESEND
GORSEINON
To Swansea (High St.)
LLANELLY
SWANSEA (VICTORIA)
PENCLAWDD
LLANMORLAIS
GOWERTON SOUTH
DUNVANT
KILLAY
MUMBLES ROAD
SWANSEA BAY

Introduction

The Central Wales line, which connects Shrewsbury and Swansea — albeit via Llanelli these days — is one of Britain's very few predominantly-rural railways which is still operative. It is a truly delightful line, much of its route passing through superb scenery, and it has always been highly regarded by railway enthusiasts.

The line's widespread appeal was, arguably, best summed up by Allan Brackenbury in the SLS Journal of August 1980: '(it) possesses characteristics of both a trunk route and a country branch line, without being either. In Britain, no genuine branch line is 90 miles long, and no serious contender for main line status would, even in its heyday, have more than half its route single track.' Couldn't put it better myself!

Despite the line's charisma, its fascinating history, its one-time purpose as an LMS route to the GWR stronghold of South Wales, and its still-vital use to many communities, it has received relatively little coverage in the railway press. Lines of a vaguely similar nature such as the Somerset & Dorset, the Midland & Great Northern and the Stainmore line have been covered extensively. Could that possibly be because they are now only memories, whereas the Central Wales line has the temerity to remain open?

The fact that the line is still operational is partly due to the efforts of HOWLTA — the Heart of Wales Line Travellers' Association. Since its formation in 1981, HOWLTA has made commendable efforts to secure the line's future but, despite enjoying a high public profile, HOWLTA has failed in one particular aspect. While it refers to the route as the 'Heart of Wales line', to most railway enthusiasts it will always be the Central Wales line.

The days of LMSR 0-8-0s, '8Fs' and 2-6-4Ts struggling up the steep gradients at Sugar Loaf and from Knighton to Llangunllo have now passed — so have the days of the delightful LNWR 2-4-2Ts, the famous 'Coal Tank' 0-6-2Ts and, later, GWR 0-6-0PTs working sedately on the archetypically rural branch between Llandeilo and Carmarthen. Victoria station at Swansea has also disappeared, as has much of the heavy industry once associated with the southern section of the line. Freight trains — once an essential ingredient of Central Wales operations — are no more. Although this book records events over the past thirty-odd years, the emphasis is unashamedly on the bygone days. Hopefully, it will rekindle a few memories of a magnificent line as it was in its heyday.

Author's note: For much of this book, the Anglicised spellings of place-names are used for example, Llanelly instead of Llanelli and Llandilo instead of Llandeilo. This has been done simply because the Anglicised versions were in common use for most of the line's existence. The Welsh spellings took over from the 1960s and, therefore, these are used only in the chapter dealing with that period.

One of the best-known features of the Central Wales line is the ferocious climb to Sugar Loaf Summit. Not only is the surrounding scenery magnificent but, in pre-diesel days, ascending locomotives could be absolutely guaranteed to display all-out effort. With most workings, there was the added bonus of another engine working hard at the rear of the train. Here, it's '8Fs' front and back on a goods train ascending the 1 in 60 to the entrance to Sugar Loaf Tunnel. The date is 30 October 1961. *B. J. Ashworth*

Above: Another well-known feature of the Central Wales line is Knucklas Viaduct, which carries the railway some 75ft above the Heyope Valley on 13 arches. On 16 May 1964, 'Black Five' No 45406 was photographed crossing the viaduct with the 11.45am Shrewsbury–Swansea train. *B. J. Ashworth*

Below: Standard '5MT' 4-6-0s were used extensively on the Central Wales line in the 1950s and early 1960s. On 5 June 1964, No 73090 approaches Llangunllo with a Swansea (Victoria)–Shrewsbury train. *Derek Cross*

Right: Through goods workings on the Central Wales line ceased in August 1964. Just two months earlier — on 10 June — '8F' No 48347 was photographed pulling away from Builth Road (High Level) with a northbound goods.
B. J. Ashworth

Below: The Central Wales line is widely remembered as an ex-LNWR/LMSR route, but much of the southern section was also used by the GWR. Although the entire line passed to the Western Region in 1948, ex-GWR engines were almost totally excluded from through workings. Nevertheless, they took over some of the local and shunting duties and, of course, retained their traditional turns between Llandovery, Llandilo and Llanelly. At the risk of offending LNWR and LMSR devotees, this book devotes proportionate space to GWR matters. Kicking off for the GWR team, we have 0-6-0PT No 9621 waiting at Llandovery on 3 September 1963 before working to Llanelly.
Andrew Muckley

Left: Despite evading the chop, the Central Wales line has, for the last 30 years, never had the luxury of a totally secure future. Nevertheless, as one of the most scenic routes in Britain it has justifiably attracted considerable attention, and in the last couple of years has hosted steam-hauled specials. On 6 June 1993, preserved '4MT' 2-6-4T No 80079 and 'Black Five' No 44767 worked double-headed on the line, this picture being taken near Sugar Loaf Tunnel. Fittingly, the two preserved engines are representatives of types which worked the line regularly in steam days. Compare this picture to the earlier one, which was taken 33 years earlier from almost the same viewpoint — the lineside hut is still there, but the trees are rather more luxuriant. Another difference between the two pictures is the presence in this one of a helicopter (top left of frame). The contraption was, apparently, carrying a film crew, but its antics incurred the wrath of many lineside cameramen and questions were subsequently asked about whether the pilot actually had permission to fly so low. *B. J. Ashworth*

Below: Unlike many cross-country railways, the Central Wales line remains open today — albeit with a partly-amended route. During the 1980s the line benefited from a degree of investment, part of the ongoing improvements being the refurbishment of Llandrindod station. With work to the buildings on the up platform (on the left) still underway, Class 150/2 'Sprinter' No 150265 waits with the 11.02 from Pembroke Dock to Crewe on 25 August 1990. 'Sprinter' No 150269 (on the right) forms the 12.08 from Crewe to Tenby. The services shown here are, incidentally, a reactivated form of the 1963 services between Shrewsbury and Pembroke Dock, although the 1963 workings operated via the Llandilo–Carmarthen branch. *Brian Morrison*

The Background

The Central Wales line wasn't built by one single company, nor was it built in one go. Far from it. The line was, in effect, an amalgam of five (or, arguably, six) separate railways, although three of those were, admittedly, backed by the London & North Western with the intention of forming a direct through route between Shrewsbury and South Wales. That said, the original section of what eventually became the Central Wales line opened more than six years before the LNWR was even formed.

The Shrewsbury-Swansea line took shape over a period of no less than 28 years, and a summary of who did what, in conjunction with whom, and when, is given in the Table below. Let's look at each of the concerns in turn.

The Llanelly Railway

The Llanelly Railway or, to give it its full title, the Llanelly Railway & Dock Co, was one of the first public railways in South Wales. The company was incorporated in August 1835 and was, in effect, a reconstituted version of the Llanelly Dock Co, which had been incorporated in June 1828 and had constructed, among other things, a horse-worked branch to Dafen.

The LR, which was a standard gauge company, opened its 6¼-mile section of line between Llanelly Dock and Pontardulais on 1 June 1839, locomotive haulage being used from the outset. Somewhat ironically, that pioneering line was adopted for the diverted course of the Central Wales line in 1964 — more of which later. On 10 March 1840 the LR opened its extension to Pantyffynnon and Cwmamman (Garnant) for goods traffic, and on 6 May 1841 Pantyffynnon became a junction when the Mountain Branch to Duffryn (later renamed Tirydail) and Cross Hands opened. The LR's original intention of extending along the Loughor Valley from Duffryn to Llandilo was put on ice.

The LR had been incorporated to carry mineral traffic, but by May 1841 (if not before) a passenger carriage was attached to each train. The passengers were conveyed at their own risk and had to contend with a lack of regular train timings and an absence of stations; the assumption, therefore, is that the carriages were intended primarily for workmen and their families.

The LR nevertheless expected a 'passenger line' standard of efficiency from its staff, the company's working instructions of 1842 insisting that:

'*The Engine driver, under penalty of five pounds* (several weeks' wages in those days), *must keep his Engine going regularly at as near eight miles per hour as possible, and in no case to exceed that rate without a written order from the Superintendent of the Company, and if time should unavoidably be lost he must not increase his speed to regain it without a special order...He is to keep himself clean, and take care that the fireman is so also*'.

Summary of opening dates and ownership of the Central Wales line

Section of Line	Owning Company	Opened throughout	Leased by LNWR	Taken over by LNWR
Pontardulais-Pantyffynnon[1]	Llanelly Ry	10.3.1840	-	-
Pantyffynnon-Duffryn[2]	Llanelly Ry	6.5.1841	-	-
Duffryn-Llandilo[2]	Llanelly Ry	27.7.1857[3]	-	-
Llandilo-Llandovery	Vale of Towy Ry[4]	1.4.1858	25.6.1868[5]	-
Craven Arms-Knighton	Knighton Ry	6.3.1861	22.6.1863	25.6.1868
Knighton-Llandrindod	Central Wales Ry	10.10.1865	17.10.1865	25.6.1868
Pontardulais–Swansea	Llanelly Ry	14.12.1867[3]	1.7.1871[6]	28.7.1873
Llandrindod-Llandovery	Central Wales Extension Ry	8.10.1868	30.4.1866	25.6.1868

Notes: [1] continued to Cwmamman (Garnant).
[2] Duffryn renamed Tirydail in July 1889.
[3] dates for opening to passenger traffic; mineral traffic carried earlier.
[4] worked by Llanelly Railway.
[5] leased jointly with Llanelly Railway.
[6] worked (NOT leased) by LNWR from date shown.

Left: Until the closure of the Swansea section of the Central Wales line in 1964, the services between Llanelly and Pontardulais route were mainly locals. On 25 July 1962, 0-6-0PT No 8749 emerges from the tunnel at Pontardulais with the 5pm from Llanelly. *Leslie Sandler*

By 1846 the LR's four locomotives had fallen into such a poor state of repair that the company had to employ horse traction. Locomotive haulage was reintroduced in 1847 but, by then, the LR's poor financial position had started to become painfully apparent. In 1849 the LR approached the South Wales Railway with a view to selling out, but the SWR (which opened through to Llanelly in October 1852) didn't want to know.

In May 1850 the LR introduced a formal passenger service between Pontardulais and Duffryn (Tirydail), horse-drawn buses connecting at each end to provide a primitive form of 'road/rail' service between Swansea and Llandilo. The LR could therefore boast that it had reached Llandilo, but the road-borne manner of its arrival there was a little different to that which had been originally envisaged.

By then, the LR's financial position was healthier. Most of its existing lines were relaid with new rails of 70lb/yd (the original rails having been 42–50lb) and were partially equipped with semaphore signals. Furthermore, a line was laid to the SWR station at Llanelly, LR trains using a standard gauge platform alongside the broad gauge SWR station. The LR station at Llanelly Dock nevertheless remained in use until September 1879.

By October 1856 rails had been laid into Llandilo. The Duffryn (Tirydail)–Llandilo section was opened to mineral traffic in January 1857 (some sources give the date as the 20th, others the 24th), and passenger services commenced on 27 July. The first link in what later became the Central Wales line was therefore complete, but the Llanelly Railway's involvement with the line was far from finished, as we shall see later.

The Vale of Towy Railway

The Vale of Towy Railway was incorporated on 10 July 1854 to construct an 11¾ mile-long railway from the (then unbuilt) LR line at Llandilo to Llandovery. The VoTR was authorised to lay mixed gauge rails if it thought fit or if required by the South Wales Railway — in the latter case the SWR was to foot part of the bill.

The Vale of Towy's line between Llandilo and Llandovery was inspected for the Board of Trade by Capt Tyler on 16 January 1858. He was not particularly impressed. One aspect which concerned him was that:

'*On certain bridges and viaducts* (which were all built of timber)*, the unevenness of the planking has been compensated for by thin wedges inserted under the bottom of the rail; and rather longer dog spikes are used in these cases, where the rail is sometimes as much as 3 inches from the planking, and where consequently the spikes are uncovered to the same extent'.*

Capt Tyler recommended that the '*...means of securing the rails to the planking be improved*', and that: '*...to prevent undue oscillation to engines and trains passing over the viaducts, it is desirable that means of stiffening some of them should be adopted'.* Further criticisms were that: '*...lamps are required at the public road level crossings, and a stationary buffer is wanted at Llandovery*'.

A reinspection the following month revealed that the viaducts had indeed been strengthened, but none of the other improvements had been effected. It took a third inspection before permission to open the railway was granted and public traffic finally commenced on 1 April, (1858).

It appears that Capt Tyler's concern about the viaducts was not wholly unfounded, as in 1872 one of the viaducts over the River Towy near Llandovery was found to be so badly decayed that the railway had to be diverted via a new 15-span timber viaduct. In November 1889 a second deviation was opened —

Right: Some of the Llanelly Railway's routes were taken over by the LNWR, and some, including the Llanelly–Llandilo 'main line', by the GWR. Pantyffynnon was the point where the ex-LR branch to Gwaun-cae-Gurwen (known as GCG) diverged from the Llandilo line. The latter is visible on the left, and the branch (complete with an 0-6-0ST in the sidings) on the right. One little mystery — the signal post to the left of the hotel has no signal arms. A case of photographic touching-up, perhaps — but why? An alternative explanation is that, as the Pantyffynnon signalboxes were renewed or replaced in 1892, the picture might possibly have been taken as a 'record' shot just before the work had been fully finished. For those with remarkable vision, the GCG branch signalbox may just be discernible behind the signal to the right of the telegraph pole. This box was also installed in 1892 — it replaced the original box which was on the opposite side of the branch line and beyond the crossing. *Lens of Sutton*

Centre: The Llanelly Railway reached Llandilo in 1857 and, after the completion of the Central Wales line throughout in 1868, Llandilo became an important station on the line. Here, Fowler 2-6-4T No 42385 — an archetypal Central Wales line engine — waits at Llandilo with the 7.40am Shrewsbury–Swansea train on 25 July 1962. The engine's shedplate is 87D (Swansea East Dock), the ex-LMSR shed at Paxton Street in Swansea having closed in 1959 and its successor, the ex-GWR shed at Landore, having closed to steam in 1961. *Leslie Sandler*

Lower right: Llanwrda station, on the Vale of Towy section, had staggered platforms, the up (northbound) platform being seen here in the foreground. This picture was taken on 7 July 1958, some six years before the passing loop was lifted and the down platform dispensed with. There is a pleasing combination of signals — an LNWR lower quadrant on the left and an LMSR upper quadrant by the box on the right. The top half of the signalbox, incidentally, is of LMSR origin, which indicates a partial rebuild between 1923 and 1948. *H. C. Casserley*

Above: Shrewsbury's 'Black Five' No 45190 enters Llangadog station with a Swansea-bound four-coach train. The station was one of only two passing places on the old Vale of Towy section (the other being at Llanwrda), and until 1958 its name was spelt 'Llangadock'. *Andrew Muckley*

this time via a new four-span steel girder viaduct.

The VoTR was leased to and worked by the Llanelly Railway from the outset, the LR formally securing a 10-year lease on the line on 2 August 1858. The VoTR formed the second section of the future Central Wales line.

The Knighton Railway

Some distance to the northeast, across the Wales/England border in southwest Shropshire, matters were in hand for what became the third component of the Central Wales line. On 21 May 1858, the Knighton Railway was incorporated to construct a line from Craven Arms to Knighton.

Craven Arms was a small community which took its name from a public house. A standard gauge railway from Shrewsbury to Ludlow via Craven Arms had been opened by the Shrewsbury & Hereford Railway on 21 April 1852 and had been extended southwards to Hereford (Barrs Court Junction) on 6 December 1853. It was a strategically-important line, and on 1 July 1862 was jointly leased by the GWR, the LNWR and the West Midland Railway. The WMR became part of the GWR empire on 1 August 1863.

The Knighton Railway opened its line as far as Bucknell on 1 October 1860, but only to goods traffic, the trains being worked by the contractor, Thomas Brassey. The line was completed through to Knighton early in 1861, and was inspected for the Board of Trade by Capt Tyler on 18 February:

The Knighton Railway.—July, 1866.

Miles.	UP TRAINS.	WEEK DAYS. 1 Goods. 1, 2.	2 1, 2, 3.	3 † Goods.	4 1, 2.	5 1, 2, 3.
		A.M.	A.M.	A.M.	P.M.	P.M.
	Craven Arms ......dep.	5 0	8 5	10 50	2 40	6 45
3	Broome	5 15	8 12	11 5	2 47	6 52
5¼	Hopton Heath	5 25	8 17	11 15	3 0	6 58
8¼	Bucknell	5 35	8 25	11 30	3 8	7 5
12½	Knighton ....arr.	5 50	8 40	11 50	3 20	7 15
	Do. Depart for Llandrindod	...	8 45	12 5	3 25	...

† No. 3 Up Goods leaves Craven Arms at 11.5 a.m., on Thursdays, and conveys Market Passengers between Craven Arms and Knighton.

Miles.	DOWN TRAINS.	1 1, 2, 3.	2 1, 2, 3.	3 Goods.	4 Cattle. 1, 2.	5 1, 2, 3.			
		A.M.	A.M.	A.M.	P.M.	P.M.			
	Knighton, Arrive from Llandrindod.	...	9 40	11 45	3 15	...	...	...	...
...	Do. ....dep.	6 20	9 45	12 0	3 25	8 15	...	...	...
4¼	Bucknell	6 35	9 55	12 15	3 35	8 27	...	...	...
7¼	Hopton Heath	6 47	10 2	12 26	3 43	8 33	...	...	...
9½	Broome	6 55	10 10	12 35	3 50	8 40	...	...	...
12½	Craven Arms ......arr.	7 5	10 20	1 5	4 5	8 48	...	...	...

Knighton Railway — working timetable for July 1866. *Courtesy: Bryan Wilson*

'This is a single line, 12¼ miles long, extending from the Craven Arms Station of the Shrewsbury and Hereford Railway to Knighton; and forming the first section of the Central Wales Railway. It will for the present be worked as a branch of the Shrewsbury & Hereford Railway, but it is intended, eventually, after its extension to Llandovery, to become a through route, via Llanelly, to Milford Haven. Land has therefore been purchased, and the works have been constructed, with a view to the line being doubled at a future period.

'The permanent way is laid with double-headed rails, weighing 75lbs to the lineal yard, secured at the joints by means of wrought-iron fishplates, and 4 screw-bolts and nuts. The chairs, which weigh 22lbs each, are fastened to the sleepers by wrought-iron spikes ⅞" in diameter. The sleepers are of Larch, 9 feet long, and 10" x 5" in section, and are laid transversely, 2'3" apart at the joints, and 3' at other portions of the rails.

'The gradients are severe, two miles and three-quarters being laid on inclinations of 1 in 80. The curves are generally moderate, but there is a curve of 10 chains radius at the Craven Arms which the trains should in all cases pass over at slow speeds.

'It was originally intended to form a junction at the Craven Arms, but this idea has been wisely given up for the present, and the Knighton Railway runs into that station now on an independent line of rails.

'There are 8 bridges under, and 5 over the railway, all of small spans, ranging from 12 to 31 feet, and constructed either with cast-iron girders or

LLANELLY & VALE OF TOWY
RAILWAYS.

LLANELLY, LLANDILO, LLANDOVERY & CWMAMMAN

On and after NOVEMBER 15th, 1858.

UP-TRAINS.

Distance	Starting from	1, 2, & 3 Class	1, 2, & 3 Class	1, 2, & 3 Class	Fares 1st Class s.	d.	2nd Class s.	d.	3rd Class s.	d.
	Llanelly ...	8.40	1.45	5.0						
1	Dock ...	8.45	1.50	5.4	0	3	0	2	0	1
2	Bynea	8.50	1.55	5.12	0	9	0	6	0	3
4	†Llangennech ...	8.55	2.0	5.18	1	0	0	8	0	5
7½	Pontardulais	9.5	2.10	5.25	1	6	1	2	0	7
	*Garnant *depart*	8.50		5.10						
	Cross Inn ..	9.10		5.35						
13	Cross-Inn *arrive*	10.0		5.50	2	0	1	10	1	1
17	*Garnant ..	10.25		6.15	3	3	2	3	1	5
13	Llandebie ...	9.30	2.35	5.50	3	3	2	3	1	3
16½	†Derwydd Road...	9.40	2.45	5.55	3	6	2	7	1	4½
19	Fairfach	9.50	2.55	6.5	4	0	3	0	1	7
20	Llandilo ...	9.55	3.0	6.10	4	0	3	0	1	8
24	†Glanrhyd ...	10.5	3.10	6.20	4	9	3	7	2	0
25½	Llangadock ...	10.10	3.15	6.25	5	2	4	0	2	1½
27½	Lampeter Road ...	10.15	3.20	6.30	5	6	4	3	2	3½
31½	Llandovery ...	10.25	3.30	6.40	6	3	4	8	2	7

DOWN-TRAINS.

Distance	Starting from	1, 2, & 3 Class	1, 2, & 3 Class	1, 2, & 3 Class	Fares 1st Class s.	d.	2nd Class s.	d.	3rd Class s.	d.
	Llandovery ...	8.55	2.40	6.40						
3½	Lampeter Road ...	9.5	2.50	6.50	0	9	0	7	0	3½
6¼	Langadock ..	9.10	2.58	6.55	1	2	0	11	0	5½
7	†Glanrhyd ...	9.15	3.0	7.0	1	6	1	2	0	7
11	Llandilo ...	9.25	3.5	7.10	2	3	1	9	0	11
12	Fairfach	9.30	3.10	7.15	2	6	1	11	1	0
14½	†Derwydd Road	9.40	3.20	7.25	2	10	2	3	1	2½
16	Llandebie ...	9.45	3.30	7.30	3	6	2	6	1	4
	*Garnant *depart*	8.50		7.0						
	Cross Inn ...	9.10		7.25						
20	Cross-Inn *arrive*	10.0		7.40	4	3	3	3	1	8
24½	*Garnant ...	10.25		8.5	4	9	3	8	2	0
24	Pontardulais ...	10.15	3.55	7.55	4	9	3	6	2	0
26½	†Llangennech ...	10.22	4.2	8.2	5	3	4	0	2	2
28	Bynea	10.28	4.8	8.8	5	6	4	2	2	4
30½	Dock	10.36	4.16	8.16	6	0	4	6	2	6½
31½	Llanelly ...	10.40	4.20	8.20	6	3	4	8	2	7

* *Garnant Passengers will be set down or taken up at Gellyceidrim or Cross Keys, if required.*
Cross Inn Passengers by Middle-day Trains will be set down or taken up at Pantyffynon.
†The Trains will stop at Llangennech, Derwydd Road, and Glanrhyd by signal only; Passengers wishing to alight must give notice to the Guard at the next Station of their intention.

Above: The Knighton Railway was opened throughout in 1861. A little over a century later — on 2 September 1963 — Knighton station still appeared to be in good structural condition, although a clue as to its then ownership is provided by the WR lower quadrant signal just beyond the bridge. The signalbox on the left was built in 1872, was equipped with a new frame in 1907, and survived until December 1965. This view looks towards Swansea. *Andrew Muckley*

brick arches on masonry abutments. The work has in all cases been economical, but it appears to have been substantially performed; and the cast-iron girders are sufficiently strong by calculation, and yield moderate deflection. (The use of cast iron for sections of bridges which were subjected to tension was, at the time, on the wane. Wrought iron, although more expensive, had started to take over as it coped far better with tension and bending. After the partial collapse of a cast iron bridge at Norwood in 1891, the use of cast iron for bridge girders was effectively barred, and the Board of Trade stipulated that ALL cast iron structures should be replaced as soon as practicable.)

Capt Tyler continued *'I observed that the gate-posts at one of the public road level-crossings required to be shifted to a greater distance from the rails; and this alteration was ordered to be carried out on the same (Saturday) afternoon. I found, also, that indicating signals had not been supplied to the junctions. These are now to be added, and there are locks up in them, by means of which they may be kept securely fastened during the passage of the trains. Two temporary water tanks are to be immediately removed. The clocks are stated to be ready for fixing on the outside of the stations, though they are not put in their places.*

'Considering the length of the line, the circumstance that it is being extended, and that a further portion of it will be opened in a few months, as well as that it is worked by a six-wheeled tank engine (an 0-4-2ST, in fact), *I have not thought it*

Above: An unidentified LNWR 'Special DX' 0-6-0 allegedly enters Bucknell station, but the solid stances of the station staff and the interest shown by the engine driver suggest that this was a posed shot. The station was on the Knighton Railway section, which opened between Craven Arms and Knighton in 1861. The picture was taken before March 1906 as, in that month, the signalbox seen here was replaced by a box on the far side of the level crossing. *Lens of Sutton*

necessary to require that engine turn-tables should be supplied.'

Capt Tyler concluded by stating that, subject to the railway company making the necessary improvements and supplying the customary certificate confirming the use of only one engine in steam (or two coupled together), the opening of the line for passenger traffic could be sanctioned. Public services commenced two days later on Wednesday 6 March, the trains being worked by the contractors (Messrs Brassey & Field, as the firm had, by then become) until 1 July 1862, when the LNWR effectively took over. That was, incidentally, the same day as the GWR/LNWR/WMR joint lease of the Shrewsbury & Hereford Railway came into effect.

The Central Wales Railway

In corporate terms the Central Wales Railway was responsible for only a 19½-mile stretch of line, but the unsung company eventually had its name adopted for the entire route between Craven Arms and Swansea. The CWR was incorporated on 13 August 1859 to construct a railway from Knighton to Llandrindod, the latter's more-familiar title of Llandrindod Wells not appearing in the timetables until January 1876.

The CWR opened the Knighton–Penybont (Crossgates) section of its line to goods traffic in October 1864, but the railway was not completed through to Llandrindod until October 1865. The ceremonial opening took place on 10 October, and public passenger traffic commenced seven days later.

On 21 May 1863 a Bill was passed enabling the CWR to enter into a form of amalgamation with the Knighton Railway. A further Bill of 22 June recognised agreements made between the Knighton Railway, CWR and LNWR, whereby the LNWR undertook to provide locomotives, rolling stock and maintenance facilities. However, the LNWR's lease on the CWR did not come into effect until 17 October 1865 — the day passenger services on the CWR commenced.

Pontardulais to Swansea

The southernmost — albeit not the last — link in the chain between Craven Arms and Swansea was the Pontardulais–Swansea section, which had complicated, albeit interesting, origins. In October 1860, the Llanelly Railway received a proposition from Thomas Savin, the well known and respected railway engineer who worked a number of the railways he had constructed in Mid-Wales. Savin suggested that the LR promote three new lines and that he should not only build and work all three, but also lease and work the LR's existing lines. The three new lines in question were from Llandilo to Carmarthen, from Llandovery to Brecon, and from Pontardulais to Swansea.

At an early stage, however, it became apparent to all concerned that the leasing bill was unlikely to

Above: The LMSR '8F' 2-8-0s made their debut on the Central Wales line in 1937 and were a familiar sight on the route until 1964. A rather grimy No 48328 approaches Knucklas Viaduct from the south on 5 June 1964. It seems that the notice by the fence on the right had not been changed for at least 41½ years although, perversely, the notice on the gate has clearly received attention.
B. J. Ashworth

Below: In this superb period picture, a pair of 'Coal Tank' 0-6-2Ts haul a Shrewsbury-bound train into Llandrindod Wells station. Although the photograph is undated, it must have been taken before May 1909 as No 2 signalbox (on the down platform) has not yet been built. The caption inscribed on the picture (in contemporary postcard fashion) states that the train is a Euston express — perhaps technically correct, but not a little misleading! *Courtesy: LNWR Society*

Above: The Pontardulais-Swansea section opened to passenger traffic on 14 December 1867, and was doubled throughout by May 1893. At Pontardulais, the Swansea trains had their own two platforms while GWR trains on the Llanelly–Llandilo route also had two platforms to themselves. The Llanelly platforms can be seen on the extreme right. Fowler 2-6-4T No 42385 waits at the up Swansea platform at Pontardulais with an empty stock working; don't be fooled by the engine's headlamp — this is NOT a conventional passenger working! Note the Siphon G behind the engine and, for whatever reason, a WR 0-6-0PT at the rear of the train. *Leslie Sandler*

Left: Llandrindod station (later renamed Llandrindod Wells), which opened to passengers in October 1865, once befitted an important spa town. Its up platform was taken out of use in 1955 and, although the buildings on the down platform seem to have been very well maintained, a gaping maw alongside the disused and somewhat herbaceous platform takes away much of the gloss. The up platform was, however, reinstated in 1986. Here, well-scrubbed 'Black Five' No 45143 enters Llandrindod Wells with a Swansea-bound train on 16 May 1964. *B. J. Ashworth*

Lower left: The Central Wales Railway opened the Knighton–Penybont section of its line to goods traffic in October 1864, a temporary goods station known as Cross Gates initially being provided at Penybont. The permanent passenger station was built on the same site and opened for business in October 1865. Penybont was one of the many delightful stations on the Central Wales line; it was the sort of unpretentious station where a stranger would be unsure whether he or she was on a main line or a rural branch. Here, 'Black Five' No 45190 enters Penybont with a Shrewsbury–Swansea train on 3 September 1963. Note the oil lamps on the up platform. *Andrew Muckley*

gain approval. Savin therefore withdrew from the deal stating that he didn't want to proceed with the new lines unless he could lease and work the LR's existing lines as well. Nevertheless, the idea of extensions had been sown, and the LR subsequently promoted the Llandilo-Carmarthen and Pontardulais-Swansea lines itself (the Llandovery-Brecon line having been dropped), and Savin agreed to build them.

The LR obtained the necessary Act on 1 August 1861. The contract for the construction of the lines was agreed in July 1862, but NOT with Thomas Savin. The agreement was made instead with Messrs Watson & Overend, who undertook to build and work the lines (the contract stipulating the provision of nine locomotives, 35 passenger carriages and 389 goods trucks) and to lease the lines, on their completion, to the LR.

The proposed terminus at Swansea was on the low level, a few chains west of the South Docks, and extended to the boundary of the Swansea Harbour Trustees' lines; an agreement with the SHT regarding shipping traffic was anticipated. In 1862 the LR obtained powers to extend its line to the SHT's high level railway, which would permit through traffic to and from the authorised Swansea & Neath Railway. Powers were also obtained to extend the Carmarthen line into Carmarthen itself by means of a separate standard gauge line terminating near the Market Place.

The contractors were at liberty to apply for Parliamentary permission to alter the proposed routes, and in 1863 they obtained powers for three revisions. These were an improved approach to Swansea, a branch to the south side of Swansea Docks and, on the Carmarthen branch, a reversion to the original arrangement whereby running powers over the Carmarthen & Cardigan Railway (by means of a third rail) would be obtained and exercised instead of laying a separate standard gauge line into Carmarthen.

All looked promising, but that state of affairs did not last for long. The contractors were forcibly wound up in April 1866, but at least the Carmarthen branch was, by then, operational and, furthermore, the works on the Pontardulais-Swansea line were at an advanced stage. Mineral traffic to and from Swansea South Docks had been accommodated as early as December 1865, but there was still a good deal of work to be undertaken before passenger traffic could be accepted.

The LR had to pick up the threads which had been left by the contractors. The on-going problems included fending off legal actions for trespass, various landowners being distinctly unhappy about having a railway on land which still hadn't been paid for. Matters were eventually resolved, but it took until late 1867 before the Swansea section was in a fit state to handle passenger traffic.

The Pontardulais-Swansea line was inspected for the Board of Trade by Col Rich on 3 December 1867:

'These lines are single, except that portion between the Junction with the dock line at Swansea and the St Helens Junction which is about a mile from Swansea. A separate line is also laid alongside the Passenger line for the Goods traffic, from the Junction with the Dock line to the Low Level Station at Swansea.

'Land has been enclosed for a double line throughout, and the Bridges and Viaducts have been constructed for a double line. The greatest gradient is 1 in 45, and the sharpest curve (which is on the low level line) has an 8ch radius. The gauge is 4ft 8½ins, but the formation and girders have been laid for carrying a broad gauge line as well.

'The permanent way consists of a flat bottom or contractors' rail, which weighs 72lbs per lineal yard. It is laid in lengths of 21ft, is fished and fixed with fang bolts and wood screws to transverse sleepers which are laid at an average distance of 3ft apart. The sleepers are semi-circular, 9ft long, and 9" x 4½". Four rectangular sleepers are placed in each length of rail on the curves. The line is ballasted with gravel, broken stone, and sand. Turntables are provided at Swansea and at Llandilo, to which station on the Llanelly Railway it is proposed to run Passenger Trains. The Stations are Swansea, Killay, Gower Road, Loughor Common (Gorseinon) *and Pontardulais on the main line* (other stations were added later)*, and Penclawdd on the Branch.*

'The work consists of 4 viaducts, three of which have stone abutments and wrought iron girders, and one which has one opening with wrought iron girders, and 43 brick arches.

'There are 19 under-bridges, 10 of which have wrought iron girders on stone abutments. Two have cast iron trough girders, and the rest have brick arches on stone abutments and brick arches.

'There are three level crossings of public roads authorised on the line from Swansea to Pontardulais.'

Col Rich recommended that the line be sanctioned for opening, but nevertheless advised that: *'The Gates* (of the level crossings) *require stops to prevent their being opened outwards, and the blocks of wood which have been placed as stops in the middle of the public roads should be removed... Double cover plates should be added to the joints of the upper plates of the bottom flanges* (on the wrought iron bridges)... *the points and signals at the entrance to Swansea Station should be arranged on the locking principle.'*

Public passenger traffic on the Pontardulais-Swansea section commenced on Saturday

Above: After the opening of the Pontardulais–Swansea section, much of the area through which the line passed became increasingly industrialised. One of the communities to see major industrial development was Gorseinon, as is evidenced here by the plethora of chimneys and factory roofs near the station. The large premises seen behind the train are those of the Grovesend Steel & Tinplate Works. The line through Gorseinon remained open for coal traffic until 25 May 1984 — almost 20 years after the cessation of passenger services. The unprepossessing nature of the station's passenger facilities might, perhaps, be seen as a reflection of the freight-orientated nature of local activities — indeed, the local Swansea-bound train (photographed on 2 September 1963) seems not to have brought in or picked up too many passengers. *Andrew Muckley*

Left: Killay signalbox was at the south end of the station just beyond the down platform. It closed in 1938 and was replaced by a ground frame. Unfortunately, this picture is undated. *G. A. Davies Collection*

14 December 1867 and services on the short branch from Gower Road (later Gowerton South) to Penclawdd started on the same day. The main line passenger terminus at Swansea was, however, still in a sorry state and was not really completed until January 1882.

The Central Wales Extension Railway

The CWER was the final link in the Central Wales chain and the third to have the overt support of the

Left: The terminus of the line at Swansea (Victoria) was never the most glamorous of premises, and the removal of glazed sections from its roof during and after the war did little to help cosmetic appearances. In this early 1950s picture, ex-LNWR 'Coal Tank' 0-6-2T No 58880 prepares to take out a Pontardulais local. *P. Ransome-Wallis*

Below left: Despite its usually gloomy appearance, Swansea (Victoria) could look almost welcoming in summer sunshine and after a lick of paint. On 10 June 1960, 'Black Five' No 45283 waits to leave with the 10.25am to Shrewsbury and ex-GWR 0-6-0PT No 4650 shunts in the sidings. The elevated line (on the right) was owned by the GWR, and continued across the entrance to North Dock, over the River Tawe, and connected with other GWR lines near the Prince of Wales Dock. *Hugh Ballantyne*

LNWR. The CWER was incorporated on 3 July 1860 to construct a railway between the CWR at Llandrindod and the Vale of Towy Railway at Llandovery. The first sod for the CWER was cut at Llandovery on 15 November by Mrs Crawshaw Bailey, the wife of the well-known industrialist whose activities in South Wales, in particular, have been well documented elsewhere.

Despite its LNWR backing, the CWER was slow to construct its line, and in April 1866 an extension of time had to be obtained. Although the Llandrindod–Builth Junction (renamed Builth Road in May 1889) section was presented for inspection by the Board of Trade on 9 August 1866, the inspecting officer, Col Yolland, refused to sanction its opening. This did little to help matters.

Col Yolland was dissatisfied with, firstly, the placing of a station on a gradient steeper than 1 in 300, secondly, the lack of hand-rails or fencing adjacent to the underbridges near Builth Junction station and, thirdly, the absence of a turntable at Craven Arms. Although the CWER didn't actually reach Craven Arms, the CWER, CWR and Knighton Railway were effectively part of the same line, as was explained by Col Yolland in his report:

'*...the whole of these lines, belonging to three distinct Companies, are to be worked by the London & North Western Railway Co as one continuous line, and the proper place for Engine Turntables are at the Craven Arms and Cwmbach* (in contemporary BoT reports, Builth Road/Junction was referred to as Cwmbach — a third identity!). *The Central Wales Co gave an undertaking dated the 17th Nov. 1865 to procure the erection of an Engine Turntable at the Craven Arms Station within 8 weeks. That undertaking has not yet been fulfilled.*'

The matter of turntables, particularly the siting of the turntable at Craven Arms, had generated a flurry of correspondence between the LNWR and the Joint Committee, the latter administering the Shrewsbury & Hereford Railway which owned the main line through Craven Arms. From Alexander Mackintosh of the LNWR on 27 June 1866 — *'There is an undertaking to the Board of Trade to put down an Engine turntable at Craven Arms Station, and the table itself is ready for delivery'*; from Robert Johnston of the Joint Committee on 12 July — *'I have marked* (on a tracing) *where I think it would be most convenient to put down the Engine table, for then it can be used both by the Knighton and Bishops Castle Engines'*. (The Bishop's Castle Railway — one of Britain's delightful little rural lines — opened through to Craven Arms on 1 February 1866); from the LNWR on 14 July — *'The proposed site for Turntable will suit us, only the ground is much excavated at the place, and I thought it desirable to leave that space for Extra Sidings when required...the Turntable has been ordered for some time, and Messrs Cowans Sheldon (the makers) of Carlisle are anxious to deliver'*.

The problem of the turntable was eventually resolved and the CWER finally opened the section as far as Builth Junction (Builth Road) on 1 November 1866.

However, the company soon received another setback. The Board of Trade inspection report on the section between Builth Junction and Garth — or Maes-cefn-y-ffordd as it was referred to — was issued on 6 November and it brought depressing news. The inspecting officer, Capt Tyler, remarked that the lineside fencing was incomplete, the abutments and wing walls of the viaduct over the River Wye showed signs of settlement, there were no clocks (visible from the line) at the stations, the connecting rods of some points were too short, extra joists were required to support the platform at Builth Road and the sides of the cuttings near one of the tunnels needed trimming. The result was that permission to open was refused.

In view of the CWER's corporate and physical connections with the mighty LNWR, and also the importance of the line to the latter company, it might sound surprising that it presented a poorly-finished line for inspection, but that situation was far from unique. For example, the Princetown Railway in Devon had a close allegiance with the GWR but, at Yelverton, it presented for inspection a mixed gauge line where the third rail for standard gauge workings had been laid on the wrong side! But we digress...

The requisite work on the CWER was not completed until the following year (1867) and passenger services started operating as far as Garth on 11 March. The line was extended to Llanwrtyd on 6 May 1867 and the final section to Llandovery opened to public traffic on 8 October 1868.

The ceremonial opening of the CWER had taken place on 1 June, but it seems that those concerned with the railway had a healthy appetite for free dinners. The *Carmarthen Journal* of 26 June 1868 included a report of a further beanfeast on 23 June:

'Wales is no longer the isolated Principality of former times. A new era has been inaugurated in its history by the opening of the Central Wales Extension Railway down to Llandovery.

'The auspicious event was fittingly celebrated by a grand dejeuner at the Town Hall at Llandovery on Tuesday last (ie 23 June).

'The advantages which will almost certainly result to Wales from the new and most direct railway communication to the North of England are almost too many to recount here. In the past, Wales and the Welsh have worn too much of foreign characteristics in the eyes of the population residing in the remainder of the British Isles. Intercourse has been very restricted and only comparatively few Englishmen have visited the land of mountain and of flood. A great change is now likely to commence...'

With the opening of the CWER to traffic, the Central Wales line was effectively complete and provided the LNWR with access to Swansea. Earlier, the LNWR had courted the Llanelly Railway with a view to obtaining running powers over the latter's Vale of Towy Railway southwards from Llandovery and also over the rest of the LR system including, importantly, the then-uncompleted Pontardulais-Swansea section. The courtship had worked. In 1867 the LNWR was granted running powers over the LR, and on 25 June 1868 the lease on the VoTR was renewed jointly by the Llanelly Railway and the LNWR. Another important event of 25 June was the LNWR's formal amalgamation of the Knighton, Central Wales, and Central Wales Extension Railways.

Above: Named, simply, Llanwrtyd when it was opened by the Central Wales Extension Railway in May 1867, the station was retitled Llanwrtyd Wells (LNW) in 1876, if not before. As evidenced by this period view (which looks north towards Craven Arms), it was a passing place with two platforms. The original station building is now in commercial use. *Lens of Sutton*

The inaugural public service between Craven Arms and Swansea comprised four trains each way, the journey times for the 95¾-mile trip being between four and five hours. Special fares were available, those between Shrewsbury and Swansea being 36s 3d (£1.81) first-class and 26s 0d (£1.30) second-class return. Third-class single tickets were 8s 10d (44p).

The LNWR's involvement with the lines from Craven Arms had not amused the Great Western Railway. The GWR had rightly viewed a potential standard gauge link between Shrewsbury and South Wales as competition and had approached the Board of Trade in an attempt to stop the LNWR's expansionism. The GWR had failed, defeat having been formally conceded on 3 November 1866 in a letter from the GWR's solicitor to the BoT:

'Referring to your letter of the 28th ult to the Secretary of this Company, on the subject of a proposed Agreement between the London and North

Western and the Central Wales Extension Railway Companies, I am now instructed to inform you that, satisfactory arrangements having been come to between this Company (the GWR) *and the London and North Western company, this Company will not further trouble the Lords Committee of the Privy Council for Trade on the subject of such Agreement, their objections to which may be considered as withdrawn.'*

The running powers and leases gave the LNWR access to not only Swansea, but also Llanelly and Carmarthen. The LR's branch from Llandilo to Abergwili Junction — on the Carmarthen & Cardigan Railway's Carmarthen-Pencader line — had opened to mineral traffic in November 1864 (some sources state 1 November, others state the 14) and to passenger traffic on 1 June 1865 (also quoted as 29 May). The C&CR-owned section onwards from Abergwili Junction had been constructed to the broad gauge, a third rail having been laid by the Llanelly Railway for its own use.

The Carmarthen branch was constructed and worked on behalf of the LR by the contractors, Messrs Watson & Overend. The first carriages used on the branch were inscribed with the name of the Mid Wales Railway, another concern worked by the same contractors. Predictably, the MWR was not particularly happy about 'their' rolling stock being requisitioned, but legal actions were nevertheless avoided. The contractors' provision of 'secondhand' rolling stock instead of new vehicles for the Carmarthen branch was, perhaps, a hint of what was just around the corner — indeed, the LR's involvement with Messrs Watson & Overend was to cease rather abruptly, as we shall see later.

Below: Builth Road was the point where the Central Wales line crossed the Mid Wales (Brecon-Moat Lane) line. The Central Wales line station was on the high level — in the early days it was sometimes referred to as Cwmbach although, officially, until 1889 it was named Builth Junction. The northbound Central Wales train is hauled by '8F' No 48354, while the Mid Wales train on a Moat Lane working is in the charge of '2MT' 2-6-0 No 46516. The date is 29 August 1962 —just four months before the Low Level station closed. *B. J. Ashworth*

Left: 'Black Five' No 45422 arrives at Builth Road (High Level) with the 12 noon Shrewsbury-Swansea train on 21 April 1962. Eagle-eyed readers might be able to make out the GWR-style signal and disc to the left of the rear carriage. *Michael Mensing*

Centre left: The Llandilo-Carmarthen branch was served by ex-LNWR motive power until Nationalisation, but early in 1948 the Western Region introduced pannier tanks on the line. On 6 September 1963, 0-6-0PT No 7439 waits at Llandilo Bridge before continuing its journey from Carmarthen to Llandilo. *Andrew Muckley*

Below left: GWR motive power on the Swansea end of the Central Wales line — who would have thought it in the 1870s? As already evidenced, ex-GWR locomotives were commonplace on the Pontardulais–Swansea section in the 1950s and early 1960s but, that said, the '5600' class 0-6-2Ts were used only infrequently. Here, No 5602 pauses at Gowerton South before continuing with a one-coach Pontardulais-Swansea (Victoria) local in September 1963. On the far side of the level crossing, the mineral wagons stand on the remains of the disused Llanmorlais branch. *Andrew Muckley*

CARMARTHEN BRANCH.

Distance from Abergwilli Junction. Miles	UP TRAINS. Week Days.		1 PASSENGER	2 PASSENGER. SO	3 Local Goods. S	4 PASSENGER	5 Local Goods. SO	6 PASSENGER.	7 PASSENGER	8 Goods C	9 PASSENGER	10	11 Fish.	12 PASSENGER.	13 Goods or Cattle. C	14 Fish. C
			a.m.	a.m.	a.m.	a.m.	a.m.	p.m.	p.m.	p.m.	p.m.		p.m.	p.m.	p.m.	p.m.
—	Myrtle Hill Jct.	dep.	...	...	...	...	...	...	...	...	...	...	5 35	...	...	7 10
1½	CARMARTHEN †	dep.	6 15	8 5	8 45	10 10	11 0	12 45	2 55	3 25	4 35	...	[illegible]	6 55	7 10	7 20
—	ABERGWILLI JC. †	arr.	...	...	8 50	...	11 5	...	...	...	...	...	Conditional on Saturdays.	...	—	...
		dep.	[illegible]	[illegible]	9 0	[illegible]	11 15	[illegible]	[illegible]	[illegible]	[illegible]	...		[illegible]	[illegible]	[illegible]
¾	Abergwilli	„	6 21	8 11	X	10 16	X	12 51	3 1	Cattle.	4 41	...		7 1	—	—
4½	NANTGAREDIG †	arr.	...	8 18	9 20	...	11 35	...	...		...	...		...	...	...
		dep.	6 29	8 23	9 40	10 23	11 55	12 56	3 8		4 48	...		7 8	—	—
6¼	LLANARTHNEY †	arr.	...	...	9 50	...	12 0	...	...		...	...		...	—	...
		dep.	6 35	8 29	10 10	10 29	12 20	1 4	3 14	[illegible]	4 54	...	[illegible]	7 14	—	—
8	Dryslwyn	„	6 39	8 32	X	10 32	X	1 7	3 18	...	4 58	...	...	7 18	—	—
10½	GOLDEN GROVE †	arr.	...	—	10 25	...	12 35	...	...	...	...	...	See	...	—	—
		dep.	6 45	8 38	10 45	10 38	12 55	1 13	3 24	[illegible]	5 4	...	note.	7 24	—	—
13	LLANDILO BRIDGE †	„	6 52	8 46	[illegible]	10 45	[illegible]	1 20	3 32	...	5 10	...	...	7 30	—	—
13½	C. V. JUNCTION †	„	[illegible]	[illegible]	[illegible]	[illegible]	[illegible]	[illegible]	[illegible]	[illegible]	[illegible]	...	[illegible]	[illegible]	[illegible]	[illegible]
—	LLANDILO †	arr.	6 55	8 50	11 10	10 48	1 15	1 23	3 35	4 10	5 13	...	6 9	7 33	7 55	7 51

Distance from Carmarthen Valley Junction. Miles.	DOWN TRAINS. Week Days.		1 Mixed Good and PASSENGER.		2 PASSENGER. SO	3 PASSENGER.	4 Local Goods.	5	6 Light Engine.	7 PASSENGER.	8 Light Engine.	9 PASSENGER.	10 Light Eng. C	11 Mixed Goods and PASSENGER.
			a.m.		a.m.	a.m.	p.m.		p.m.	p.m.	p.m.	p.m.	p.m.	p.m.
—	LLANDILO †	dep.	7 45	...	9 35	11 25	12 30	—	1 45	2 40	4 10	5 35	8 5	8 25
—	C. V. JUNCTION †	„	7 46	...	[illegible]	[illegible]	[illegible]	...	[illegible]	[illegible]	4 11	[illegible]	[illegible]	[illegible]
½	LLANDILO BRIDGE †	„	7 48	...	9 38	11 28	[illegible]	—	...	2 43	—	5 38	...	8 28
3¼	GOLDEN GROVE †	arr.	...	...	—	...	12 55	...	...	...	...	...	—	...
		dep.	7 56	...	9 45	11 34	1 20	...	[illegible]	2 49	...	5 43	After working No. 13 Up.	8 36
5¼	Dryslwyn	„	8 3	...	9 50	11 40	...	...	...	2 55	...	5 49		8 43
6¾	LLANARTHNEY †	arr.	...	...	–	...	1 30	...	...	...	...	5 52		...
		dep.	8 8	...	9 53	11 43	1 40	...	[illegible]	2 58	...	5 53		8 47
9½	NANTGAREDIG †	arr.	8 14	—	—	—	1 50	...	...	3 5	...	...		...
		dep.	8 18	...	9 59	11 49	2 7	—	[illegible]	[illegible]	...	6 0	...	8 53
12¼	Abergwilli	arr.	8 23	...	10 4	11 55	2 17	..	—	3 15	...	6 6	—	8 58
		dep.	8 25	...	10 6	12 0	2 25	—	...	3 18	...	6 10	—	9 1
13⅝	ABERGWILLI JC. †	arr.	...	—	—	—	2 30	—	...	—	...	...	—	...
		dep.	[illegible]	...	[illegible]	[illegible]	[illegible]	—	[illegible]	[illegible]	[illegible]	[illegible]	[illegible]	[illegible]
—	Carmarthen Yd.	arr.	8 29	—	...	...	2 45	—	...	—	...	...	8 35	...
		dep.	8 32	...	[illegible]	[illegible]	...	...	...	...	...	...		...
—	CARMARTHEN †	arr.	8 35	...	10 15	12 5	...	...	2 10	3 23	4 35	6 19	...	9 12

Nos. 1 and 11 Down, must not exceed 25 miles an hour.

Any wagons from or to Carmarthen and Newcastle Emlyn and Manchester and Milford Lines must be exchanged at Abergwilli Junction.

Engine and Break Van for working 5.35 p.m. Fish Train from Myrtle Hill Junction will leave Carmarthen Town at 4.55 p.m. for Myrtle Hill Junction G.W., arriving there 4.57 p.m.

No. 7 Down—Engine and men for working this train will leave Llandovery (S) attached to 12.5 noon Passenger from Craven Arms, and return working No. 11 Up (S).

No. 8 Down—To work Goods Train if required.

No. 13 Up—To be put back and follow No. 14 if latter is running.

Above: LNWR Working timetable for the Carmarthen branch, February 1913 until further notice. *Courtesy: Bryan Wilson*

Chapter 2
The Route

Author's notes:
1) This chapter is NOT intended to describe the line at any specific point in time, although it largely ignores the changes which have been implemented since the mid-1960s — these are discussed in Chapter Six.
2) For reasons stated elsewhere, this chapter uses the Anglicised spellings of place names.
3) The mileages quoted are taken from Western Region WTTs — older WTTs often listed different mileages.
4) 'Down' means towards Swansea, 'Up' being towards Craven Arms.

Doubling of Central Wales line — summary of dates

Note: Several sections remained single.

? 1871	Central Wales Junction (Craven Arms)-Knighton
10.5.1871	Llanbister Road-Penybont Junction
15.2.1876	Gower Road (Gowerton)-Killay
29.5.1876	Penybont Junction-Llandrindod No 2
29.5.1892	Killay-Swansea Bay (St Helens Junction)
28.5.1893	Gorseinon-Pontardulais
11.2.1894	Gorseinon-Gowerton
2.6.1907	Pantyffynnon South-Tynycerig
15.12.1907	Tynycerig-Pontardulais North

When describing the physical attributes of the Central Wales line, it is tempting to intersperse the description with frequent (and totally warranted) references to the area's scenic and historic attractions. That temptation will, however, be resisted, and the emphasis will therefore be on railway matters. It is hoped that the residents and the many devotees of Central Wales will understand the lack of flowery and poetic superlatives, however justified they might be. Having made the apologies, let's proceed with the nitty-gritty.

To outward purposes the Central Wales line starts at **Craven Arms station**, on what was originally the joint LNWR/GWR Shrewsbury-Hereford line. Craven Arms station — which is 19½ miles from Shrewsbury station where most of the Central Wales train services originate or terminate — was renamed Craven Arms & Stokesay in July 1879, but reverted to its original title on 6 May 1974.

In its heyday, Craven Arms station was smart and spacious. Of its three platform roads, that on the

Below: An afternoon Shrewsbury-Swansea train, headed by 'Black Five' No 45145, leaves Craven Arms on 31 March 1962. The locomotive's livery of lined black might well have appealed to LNWR traditionalists! *Hugh Ballantyne*

The who-owns-what at Craven Arms taken from the RCH Junctions Diagrams book for 1903. *Courtesy: I. C. Coleford*

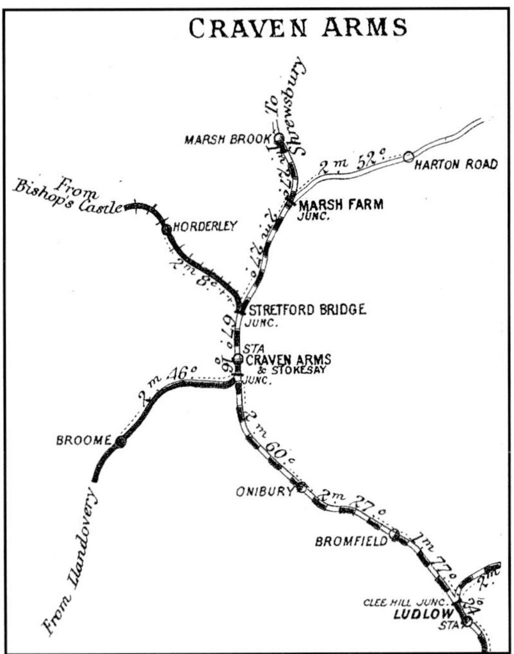

west side was partially protected by an all-over roof but the roof was a casualty of the 'economies' of the mid-1960s. In addition to Shrewsbury-Hereford and Central Wales trains, the station once accommodated trains for the Bishops Castle Railway and the GWR's Buildwas branch. The BCR closed completely on 20 April 1935 and passenger services between Craven Arms and Much Wenlock were withdrawn on 31 December 1951, but Craven Arms retained the air of a not-insignificant railway community until the 1960s.

The Central Wales line proper commences a few hundred yards to the south of Craven Arms station at the appropriately-named Central Wales Junction. On diverging from the Shrewsbury-Hereford line, the Central Wales line curves 90° to the west, the curve being subject to a 10mph speed restriction. Prior to the 1960s the rest of the route as far as Knighton had a 55mph limit — in those days, that was the maximum speed permitted anywhere on the entire Craven Arms–Swansea run.

The 12¾-mile section between the junction and Knighton was doubled in 1871, but was singled again on 12 December 1965. For the first 1¾ miles from Craven Arms the line rises, initially at 1 in 103 but steepening to 1 in 80; it then runs level for a short stretch before falling for just over a mile at 1 in 80. Near the bottom of the descent is Broome station (2½ miles from Craven Arms), which had a small goods yard on the up side.

When the Central Wales line was singled in 1964/65 the master plan was to retain the down line throughout, but the precarious state of the timber-built down platform at Broome resulted in a realignment through the station so that the original up platform could be retained instead. It might seem that BR was taking no chances with the timber platform, but another factor influencing the decision was that the main station buildings (which were considered to be in good condition) were on the up platform.

After leaving Broome the line rises again for two miles, the gradients varying between 1 in 110 and 1 in 200. The next station is **Hopton Heath** (5½ miles), which had a goods yard on the down side of the line. Due to the position of the track leading into the goods yard, the down platform was staggered to the north of the up platform. The original signalbox at Hopton Heath was at the south end of the up platform, but it was replaced in 1945 by a new box on the bank between the down line and the goods yard.

The goods sidings at Hopton Heath were taken out of use on 6 April 1958 and removed on 31 May 1964. That somewhat reflected the contemporary attitude to the Central Wales line, as public goods facilities were not officially withdrawn from Hopton Heath until 1 March 1965.

From Hopton Heath the line drops at 1 in 80 then rises at 1 in 150 before entering **Bucknell station** (8½ miles), which had a goods yard on the down side of the line. The station was noted for its impressively-gabled wooden buildings. Shortly after leaving Bucknell the line enters the valley of the River Teme, which forms the boundary between England and Wales. The route through the valley rises at 1 in 101 then falls at 1 in 183 before embarking on a steady ascent for some 10 miles.

Knighton station (12¾ miles) is on the rising gradient (1 in 250 through the station). The rear corner of the Swansea end of the down platform is actually on the English/Welsh border, the rest of the station being in England while the town of Knighton itself is firmly on the Welsh side. Befitting Knighton's status as an important market town, the station used to have a modest goods yard, situated just beyond the western end of the up platform. On the down side, there was a lay-by siding for 45 wagons. Knighton station marked the end of the double-track section from Craven Arms, but although the Craven Arms-Knighton section was singled in 1965 a crossing loop was reinstated at Knighton in June 1990.

A little to the west of Knighton station the line enters Wales. The railway then meanders between the hills — some of which are over 1,000ft high — and at milepost 14 the gradient steepens to 1 in 60. The speed limit for up freight trains on this section was 20mph.

The first stopping place on the Welsh side of the border is **Knucklas station** (15½ miles). The original station was only a temporary one, but its permanent replacement — a simple platform with LNWR-style timber buildings and a small goods yard at the up end — were hardly elaborate. The station buildings and the goods yard have now gone. Knucklas lost its public goods facilities in October 1957, some years before most of the other stations on the line but, like the facilities at Hopton Heath, those at Knucklas were dispensed with *before* the official cessation of goods traffic.

Some 300yd beyond the station the line is carried across the Heyope Valley by Knucklas Viaduct, a 13-arch stone-built structure with attractively castellated embellishments. The viaduct is 190yd long and stands 75ft above ground level. Some of the stone is reputed to have been acquired from a ruined medieval castle nearby.

About 2¾ miles after the viaduct, the line burrows under Beacon Hill (the top of which is 1,732ft above sea level) by means of the curving 637yd-long Llangunllo Tunnel and reaches its summit of 980ft just beyond the tunnel's southern portal. Author Tom Clift has told of a local legend in which a ghost is reputed to appear in the early hours of misty mornings to haunt heavy trains ascending the bank from Knighton. The ghost is said to be the spirit of a former banking engine driver from Knighton who, seemingly, enjoyed the sight of his earthly colleagues struggling to overcome slipping near the damp tunnel mouth.

Left: Standard '4MT' 2-6-4T No 80069 pulls into Knighton station with a Swansea-bound train in September 1963. *Andrew Muckley*

Above: A taste of typical Central Wales line scenery — Knucklas station in the foreground and the viaduct beyond. The year is 1929 — long before building development between the station and the viaduct interrupted the view. *Real Photographs*

After clearing the summit the line falls at 1 in 100 towards **Llangunllo station** (19¼ miles), which is a couple of miles from the village after which it is named. The station was a passing place with two platforms — the second platform having only a wooden shelter to provide creature comforts — and had a small goods yard and a lay-by siding for 45 wagons. Watering facilities were available at Llangunllo, but the pipes had a propensity for freezing up during hard winters and so, when appropriate, a warning message for drivers would be chalked on the water crane at Knighton. Fill up or else...?

At one time, Llangunllo looked set to become a junction as, in July 1865, the Lugg Valley Railway was incorporated to construct a 10¾ mile-long line between Llangunllo and Presteigne. The Lugg Valley Railway was, however, dissolved in 1874 without having undertaken any work on its proposed line. Presteigne nevertheless became rail-connected in September 1875 when the Leominster & Kington Railway (which was worked by the GWR) opened its extension from Titley.

From Llangunllo the line continues its descent to Treodrhiewfedwin Crossing, then climbs for ½-mile at 1 in 80 before commencing a seven mile-long descent. **Llanbister Road station** (22¼ miles) is at the start of the descent. The village of Llanbister is some four miles from the station — and that is for crows. The station was, if anything, used more by the residents of Llangunllo (despite the fact that they had their own station) than the folks of Llanbister.

Llanbister Road station used to have two platforms, the buildings on the down platform being built of brick and those on the up platform being of timber. It also had a small goods yard, but the now-familiar tale was repeated in that its sidings were taken out of use *before* the official withdrawal of public goods facilities in September 1964. Llanbister Road was never the most intensively-used of stations; indeed, it became partially unstaffed as early as 21 May 1956.

This was the starting point of the next double-track section, which extended for some six miles along the valley of the Cwm Aran to Penybont Tunnel. The doubling was completed in May 1871, and the work was duly inspected by Capt Tyler for the Board of Trade:

Left: On 5 June 1964, Standard '5MT' No 73090 approaches Knucklas from the south with the 12.10 Swansea (Victoria)–Shrewsbury train.
B. J. Ashworth

Below: The line between Llanbister Road and Penybont Junction was singled in 1964 and, although Llanbister Road station is now a simple one-platform affair, it is a rather attractive stopping place. The '4MT' 2-6-4Ts were active on the Central Wales line in 1963/64, but preserved examples returned to the line in 1993. On 9 October that year, No 80080 piloted classmate No 80079 with a special working.
B. J. Ashworth

'The permanent way consists of double-headed steel rails, weighing 84 lbs to the lineal yard, in cast-iron chairs weighing 39¾ lbs each, secured to the sleepers by means of two oak trenails and one wrought-iron spike for each chair.

'The sleepers are of creosoted Memel timber (a very popular engineering timber), *measuring 9 feet long, by 10 by 5 inches, and laid three feet apart. The ballast, of broken stones from the cuttings, is said to be 2 feet thick and 16 inches deep under the sleepers.*

'There are six bridges and one culvert under the second line of rails, the greatest span, crossed by cast-iron girders, being 29 feet. The bridges over the line remain as they were originally constructed.

'The points and signals, and gates at a public road level-crossing, are worked on the locking principle. I found it desirable to recommend that an alteration should be made in the interlocking at Dolau between the gate apparatus and the signal and point levers, namely that the gate-stop lever should be interlocked with the signal-levers and the cross-over road point levers, in place of the mere interlocking of the gate-lever with the signal levers.

'At Llanbister Road, I have recommended the cutting down of a tree which interferes with the view of the Distant signal north of the station — at this station the siding will be connected with the new line and the existing connection with the single line will be taken out'.

Above: Travelling from the south, the line passes through Penybont Tunnel, emerges into a deep rock cutting and, prior to 1964, became double track just beyond the cutting. A home signal was located in the cutting and, to provide drivers with a clearer view of the signal, a large white board was fixed to the top corner of the signalbox. On 6 June 1964, the driver of '5MT' 4-6-0 No 73025 slows at the end of the single line section to exchange the token before continuing with the 12.10pm Swansea–Shrewsbury service. *B. J. Ashworth*

The Llanbister Road–Penybont Tunnel section was reduced to single-track status on 21 June 1964. After Llanbister Road the next stopping place is **Dolau station** (25¾ miles) which, prior to the singling work, had two platforms. Despite the singling of the line through Dolau (which left only the up platform) and the abandonment of the small goods yard at the station, the signalbox at the north end of the up platform was retained to control the level crossing. However, the installation of an unmanned automatic level crossing in 1975 finally resulted in the box's demise.

The double-track section ended at Penybont Junction, where the tracks converged to pass through the 402yd-long Penybont Tunnel. Double-track status was resumed a little beyond the south end of the tunnel, although the up line was removed on 11/12 December 1965. To the south of the tunnel is **Penybont station** (28¾ miles), which used to have two platforms, a goods yard on the down side, and a lay-by for 33 wagons on the up side. The station buildings, which were frequently described as 'impressive', were on the down platform. Impressive or not, they were demolished in 1969. The up platform only ever had a small wooden shelter.

Although the Knighton-Llandrindod line was not completed throughout until October 1865, the railway actually reached Penybont in October 1864. Until the permanent passenger station was opened in 1865, a temporary goods terminus known as Cross Gates was provided.

The doubling of the section from Penybont to the newly-finished No 2 Box at Llandrindod Wells was completed in May 1876, but that section is, of course, now single again. The line leaves Penybont station on a 1 in 74 downhill gradient, then negotiates an undulating stretch of some 1½ miles and crosses the River Ithon which it follows on a rising gradient of 1 in 110 for one mile to **Llandrindod Wells station** (32¼ miles). The station was initially known as 'Llandrindod', the title of 'Llandrindod Wells (LNW)' being applied by 1876. The 'LNW' suffix was dropped in April 1892.

Llandrindod Wells is known to locals (and many not-so-locals) as 'Llandod'. The town grew and prospered after the coming of the railway and the station eventually reflected the importance of the community it served. The station had two platforms, both of which had substantial brick buildings, but the up platform was taken out of use on 11 December 1955 when the line through the station (as far as No 2 box) was singled.

The disused platform was subsequently used for the storage of materials for the proposed Centralised Traffic Control Scheme, but that scheme was never implemented and the equipment lay rusting at Llandrindod Wells for two years before being taken

Right: Dolau station was an unpretentious affair, even in its double-track days before 1964. This view looks south, and was taken on 2 September 1963. *Andrew Muckley*

Centre right: Between 1955 and 1986, only the down platform at Llandrindod Wells station was in use. Arguably, 'Jubilee' class 4-6-0s were not normally used to half-abandoned stations, but, in the last few years of steam, many types of locomotives trod new ground as they were displaced by internal-combustion engined motive power. The 'Jubilees' first ventured on to the Central Wales line in April 1963 and, on 5 June 1964, No 45577 *Bengal* was photographed bringing the 7.25am Swansea (Victoria)–Shrewsbury train into Llandrindod Wells. *B. J. Ashworth*

Below: Although this picture of Builth Road (High Level) is undated, the LNWR logo on the notice board on the left-hand platform provides a bit of a clue. The goods shed can be seen behind the moving train in the distance. *Welsh Industrial & Maritime Museum*

away. The platform was later put to use as the headquarters of the Central Wales line's permanent way department, but was reinstated for passenger use in April 1986.

At Llandrindod Wells, there was a sizeable goods yard on the down side of the line between the station and the level crossing, and there was also a lay-by siding which could accommodate 60 wagons. It is believed that at one time a narrow gauge tramway from a nearby quarry brought wagons alongside the goods yard, the wagons ending their journey on a wooden 'viaduct' from where they were discharged into standard gauge wagons beneath. That operation was allegedly brought to an end when the viaduct burned down.

South of No 2 box at Llandrindod Wells the line reverted to a single track once again. After leaving Llandrindod Wells station, the line has a mile-long climb of 1 in 100, followed by a descent of a similar distance at 1 in 74. There is then a short climb of 1 in 80 before the site of the former crossing place at Howey, the loop having been installed in June 1911 and taken out in November 1962. Given that Howey and the neighbouring village of Crossway had, between them, a not-insignificant population, it could be deemed unfortunate that proposals to provide a station or halt there never came to fruition.

From Howey, the line descends for some three miles at 1 in 74 towards the Wye Valley, just before which is **Builth Road station** (38 miles). Builth Road was the point where the Central Wales line crossed the Mid Wales (Brecon-Moat Lane) line, which the GWR inherited in 1922 from the Cambrian Railways. The stations on each line were almost adjacent, and were connected by a path and luggage lift.

At Builth Road, the Mid Wales station was originally entitled 'Llechryd' and the Central Wales line station was known as 'Builth Junction', although some early Board of Trade reports referred to the latter as 'Cwmbach'. On 1 May 1889, both stations were officially renamed 'Builth Road' and that is how it remained until January 1950 when the Central Wales premises were suffixed 'High Level' and the Mid Wales 'Low Level'. Although the Low Level station closed on 31 December 1962, the High Level station retained its suffix until 5 May 1969.

The Central Wales line station at Builth Road had two platforms connected by a subway. There was a bay for local trains on the up side, but it was taken out of use in May 1964. Just to the south of the station — on the other side of the bridge which crossed the Mid Wales line — were an engine shed, a turntable, a permanent way depot, exchange sidings, and a spur which connected with the Mid Wales line.

The spur at Builth Road was laid in (if not before) November 1866, but appears not to have formed a complete connection between the two lines until some time afterwards. The spur, which remained under the ownership of the Mid Wales Railway until being transferred to the LNWR in July 1870, was only rarely traversed by through trains. Despite the running-down of the Central Wales line in the mid-1960s, the spur was not fully lifted until April 1969.

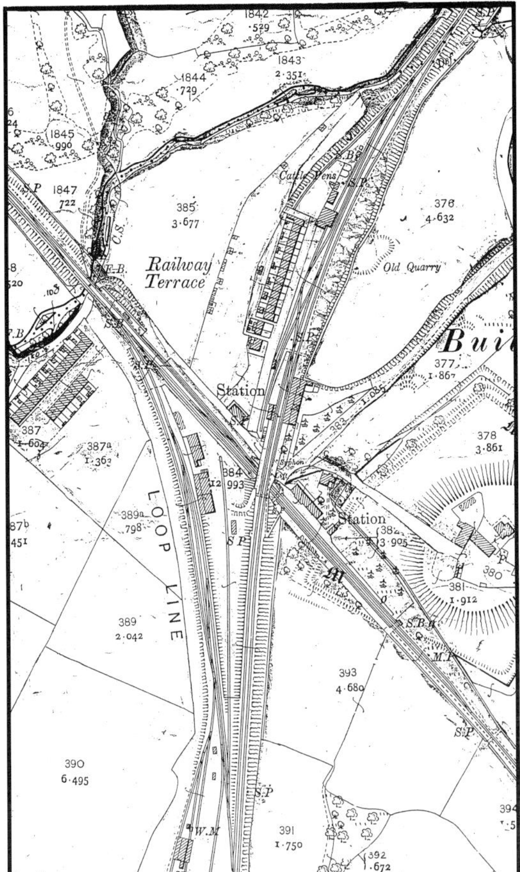

Builth Road station, Second Edition 25in OS map of 1902, the Central Wales line runs from top right to bottom. *Crown Copyright*

In pre-Grouping days the only known instance of a passenger train using the loop was on 2 July 1904 when the Royal Train, comprising six vehicles and hauled by a pair of 2-4-2Ts, travelled from Swansea (Victoria) to Rhayader for the ceremonial opening of the Elan Valley reservoir. Between the wars, a summer Saturdays Barry–Llandrindod Wells service was routed via the spur, while during World War 2 a goods working from Crewe to Swansea and return was routed via Shrewsbury, Welshpool and Moat Lane, and then used the spur to pick up the Swansea line. That goods working was GWR-hauled on the Builth Road-Moat Lane–Shrewsbury section, LMSR motive power being used on the Builth Road–Swansea section.

Above: A Swansea (Victoria)–Shrewsbury train approaches Builth Road on 10 June 1964. The High Level station on the Central Wales line is just to the left of the bridge, the old Mid Wales Low Level station — which closed to passengers at the end of 1962 — being under and beyond the bridge. The last remnants of the connecting spur (on the right) were not completely removed until April 1969. Once again, an interesting mixture of signal types is evident — LMSR on the high level, GWR on the low level and Cambrian on the spur. *B. J. Ashworth*

South of Builth Road, the Central Wales line crosses the River Wye and climbs for 1¾ miles, mostly at 1 in 80. It passes through Builth Road Tunnel (64yd long) and Cefn-y-bedd Tunnel (115yd) before reaching **Cilmery halt** (40 miles) which, until July 1868, was listed in the timetables as 'Cefn-y-Bedd'. The station offered little more than a wooden shelter in the way of facilities, and was downgraded to the status of an unstaffed halt as early as 31 August 1936. Nevertheless, its small goods yard remained open (nominally, at least) until 1959 — the official closure date to goods traffic was 3 August, but the yard was actually taken out of use on 4 January.

The next stopping place is **Garth station** (43¼ miles). It used to be a passing place and, consequently, had two platforms, the up platform having brick buildings but the down platform having only a wooden shelter which, in its later years, might well have been rejected as a garden hut. Garth had a small goods yard on the up side and a private siding to Garth Brickworks; it is believed that the private siding was removed *circa* 1934.

The goods yard at Garth was retained after the station's loss of permanent staff on 30 December 1957. The original signalbox at Garth was not replaced until September 1933, the LMSR's bill of £1,023 for the new box being partly justified by the old one being deemed to 'require immediate renewal'.

Llangammarch Wells station (45 miles), despite its imposing name and sturdy red-brick buildings, has only ever had a single platform. The platform and the station's small goods yard were on the up side of the line. Before World War 2, a regular consignment from Llangammarch Wells was bottled spa water which, because of its barium content, had a longer 'potency span' than other spa waters. The station was originally named, simply, 'Llangammarch', the more-familiar title being applied on 25 June 1883. The original name has, however, recently been reinstated.

In common with Llangunllo, Llangammarch Wells nearly became a junction station. In July 1864, the Neath & Brecon Railway obtained powers to construct a branch from Devynock to Llangammarch

Left: Looking at Cilmery halt as it was on 3 September 1963, it is hard to believe that, even before 1936, it actually required staffing. *Andrew Muckley*

Lower left: Garth was one of the archetypically rural stations on the Central Wales line. In July 1963, '4MT' 2-6-4T No 80099 pulls away with a Swansea-bound train. *Hugh Davies Collection*

Below: Llangammarch Wells station pictured on a damp day in August 1959. Small but smart. *H. C. Casserley*

Above right: A northbound engineer's train, hauled by what appears to be '8F' No 48307, passes through Llanwrtyd Wells station in the summer of 1964. *Hugh Davies Collection*

(as it then was), but only a few miles of the earthworks for the branch were completed before the contractors were declared bankrupt and the work was abandoned. The idea of a branch between Devynock and Llangammarch was later revived by the LNWR but, although powers were obtained in 1883, that scheme also fell by the wayside.

From Llangammarch Wells, the line continues to follow the wide valley of the River Irfon, rising on gradients of between 1 in 80 and 1 in 100, before reaching **Llanwrtyd Wells station** (48 miles). Originally named 'Llanwrtyd', the title of 'Llanwrtyd Wells (LNW)' started to appear in the timetables in January 1876 — the 'LNW' suffix was dropped in 1883 and, nowadays, the word 'Wells' has also disappeared from the title. Despite the economies of the 1960s Llanwrtyd Wells was retained as a passing place.

Shortly after leaving the station, the line crosses the River Irfon for the last time and climbs for three miles at 1 in 80 to Sugar Loaf Summit, 820ft above sea level. There was a passing loop at Sugar Loaf Summit and two small platforms were provided for use by the ganger and two signalmen (and their families) who lived in the now-demolished railway houses adjacent to the line. One platform was erected in 1899, the other being provided when the loop was added in 1909.

The original platforms were built of timber, but were eventually replaced by concrete platforms; the up platform was resited a few yards to the south in LMSR days. It is thought that the unadvertised use of Sugar Loaf platforms ceased *circa* 1951, although a report on the line made in 1960 inferred that they were still in use. They are, however, certainly in public use today, albeit only as a summer Sunday request stop.

After the summit the line falls at 1 in 70. The slog up the gradient to the summit was the stuff of legend and locals reckoned that if early morning trains climbing the gradient could be heard more than a mile away, it was going to be a fine day. No comments are offered here about the comparative reliability of today's state-of-the-art forecasting methods!

Continuing southwards, the line passes through the 1,001yd-long Sugar Loaf Tunnel, the old border between Brecknockshire and Carmarthenshire being midway through the tunnel. The tunnel had to be closed abruptly on 17 November 1949 following the discovery that some of the keystones had become loose and it was not reopened to traffic until 10 January the following year. While the tunnel was closed, a bus service was laid on between Llanwrtyd Wells and Llandovery.

At the southern end of the tunnel the downhill gradient steepens to 1 in 60. The line is carried across

The first of the platforms at Sugar Loaf Summit was provided in 1899 for use by the railway staff who lived in the nearby houses (on the left of the [lower] picture). As is evident, not only were the original timber platforms replaced during their lives, but the platform on the up side was resited a few yards to the south and provided with a hut. Another difference between the two pictures is the siting of the signalbox nameboard. In LNWR days the names were applied to the front (ie track-side) of boxes, while in LMSR days the names were at the ends of the boxes. The picture on the right is believed to have been taken *circa* 1910, the loop having been brought into use on 9 June 1909, while the lower picture, which shows an '8F' dropping away from the rear of a Shrewsbury-bound train after assisting up the ferocious bank, was taken on 26 May 1962. *(Right) Paul Gilson Collection; (Below) R. O. Tuck*

the Bran Valley by means of Cynghordy Viaduct, a splendid structure built of sandstone with 18 brick-lined arches. The viaduct, which is 283yd long and carries the line at a maximum height of 102ft above the valley on a 26-chain curve, is now a listed structure.

The next stopping place is **Cynghordy station** (55¼ miles) which, despite having a passing loop installed in 1929, remained a single-platform affair, the platform being on the down side. The cost of installing the loop was £5,561, but the LMSR estimated that annual savings of £664 in working expenses would subsequently be made and, furthermore, that some traffic from the Swansea Vale line could be diverted via the Central Wales line.

Continuing southwards from Cynghordy, the line falls on gradients of between 1 in 80 and 1 in 200 for some four miles before reaching **Llandovery station** (60 miles). Llandovery was the point where the old Central Wales Extension Railway finished and the

Above: The well-documented closure of Sugar Loaf Tunnel in 1949/50 was not the first time it had required serious attention. This picture of a 'DX' 0-6-0 with an engineer's train is believed to have been taken in 1926, a land-slip at the tunnel entrance clearly needing remedial work. *G. Davies Collection*

Left: Returning to the realms of the better-known, Sugar Loaf Tunnel was closed from November 1949 to January 1950 for essential repairs, some of the keystones having worked loose. Not the most comfortable of working environments, methinks! *Welsh Industrial & Maritime Museum*

joint LNWR/GWR Vale of Towy section started, although the LNWR (and, later, the LMSR) had the responsibility for maintaining the first five miles of the joint line as far as (but excluding) Llangadock. Llandovery station is still a passing place and, consequently, retains both its platforms, albeit with only simple shelters on the up side. The once-sizeable goods yard (on the down side) and siding accommodation (on the up side) have now disappeared.

The cattle dock siding at Llandovery was rather close to the running lines and, on 4 February 1929, that was brought home to engine driver Arthur Seabury in a most uncomfortable manner. Seabury was driving LMSR 2-6-4T No 2316, which was hauling a Swansea-Shrewsbury train due at Llandovery at 8.12pm. In the dark, he did not notice that the door of a cattle wagon standing in the dock had been left open at 90° and while he was looking out from the footplate the door struck his head. Fortunately, he was not badly hurt.

From Llandovery, the line was always single-track. It follows the course of the River Towy on gently falling gradients to **Llanwrda station** (63½ miles), which used to be a passing place with staggered platforms — the up platform was to the south of the level crossing and the down platform to the north. Both platforms had LNWR-style timber station buildings, but these have now vanished and the accommodation on the one remaining platform (the old up platform) now consists of a small wooden shelter. The goods yard used to be on the up side of the line. It once had a small turntable to enable vans which had doors only on one side to be turned before entering the shed.

Above: The supremely elegant Cynghordy Viaduct carries the Central Wales line at a maximum height of 102ft above the Bran Valley. Although 'carriage window' photographs have a certain appeal (this one being taken from a northbound DMU in September 1966), it should always be remembered that there are dangers in leaning out of windows — the resulting mess is no fun to clear up. *Andrew Muckley*

To the south of Llanwrda the line crosses from the west to the east bank of the River Towy before

Right: Cynghordy station had a passing loop installed in 1929, but was not provided with a second platform. It was a simple but very attractive station nestling amid superb scenery, this picture being taken on 6 July 1958. One of the very few clues as to the approximate date of the picture is provided by the signals — the starter on the right is a LNWR lower quadrant (on a wooden post), the platform signal is an LMSR upper quadrant, while the starter on the left is a GWR/WR lower quadrant. The chimney in the distance is that of Cynghordy Brick Works, from where some of the bricks for the nearby viaduct are said to have originated. *H. C. Casserley*

Below: Llandovery station, Second Edition 25in OS map, c1903 *Crown Copyright*

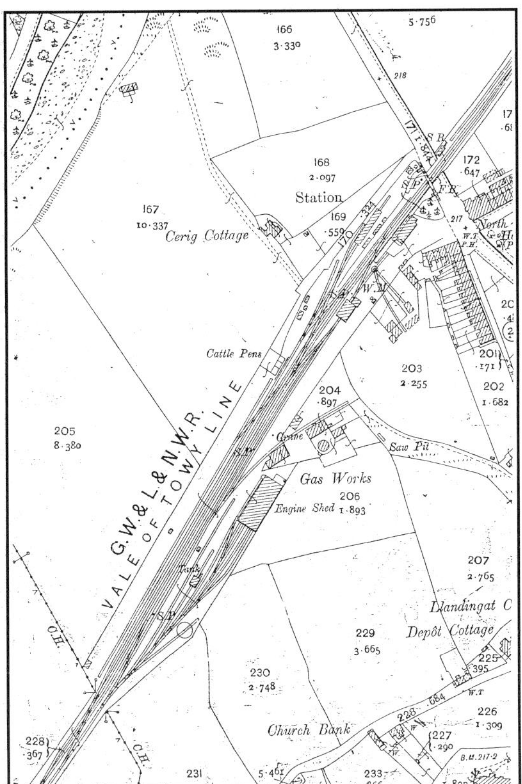

reaching **Llangadock station** (65½ miles). On 15 May 1958 the spelling of the station name was changed to 'Llangadog'. A passing loop — the second of only two on the Vale of Towy section between Llandovery and Llandilo — was laid at Llangadock in 1878, a platform being provided on the loop. The station buildings, with their unmistakeable GWR origins, were on the up platform and there were sidings on both sides of the line. In 1954 a new siding was laid to serve the CWS creamery, which was then nearing completion, but the siding was taken out of use in October 1966.

The line continues to follow the course of the Towy, the valley widening out south of Llangadock, and crosses the river to approach the site of **Glanrhyd halt** (67 miles) on the west bank. Glanrhyd had enjoyed the status of a 'proper' station until 20 July 1931, when it was closed to everything but milk traffic. It was reopened as a halt on 21 December 1938 and was served mainly by local trains (GWR trains only until 1939). It struggled on until 7 March 1955 when it was closed again — this time for good. Public goods facilities had been withdrawn from the single-platform station as early as July 1880.

A little to the south, **Talley Road station** (69 miles) allegedly served a community some seven miles away but, perhaps inevitably, the station was a fairly early casualty. It was closed on 4 April 1955, having been unstaffed since June 1941, and all that remains now is the old station house. The goods sidings were not, however, removed until 1965, public goods facilities (principally for coal traffic) having remained until 2 November 1964. In common with Glanrhyd halt, Talley Road was served only by GWR trains until 1939.

Llandilo station (71 miles), which is still a passing place, used to be the point where Carmarthen branch trains started and ended their journeys. At one time, it seemed that Llandilo might also become the starting point for trains to Lampeter, the appropriately-named Llandilo & Lampeter Light Railway being authorised in August 1908 to construct a 23 mile-long standard gauge line between the two communities. The line was, however, never constructed.

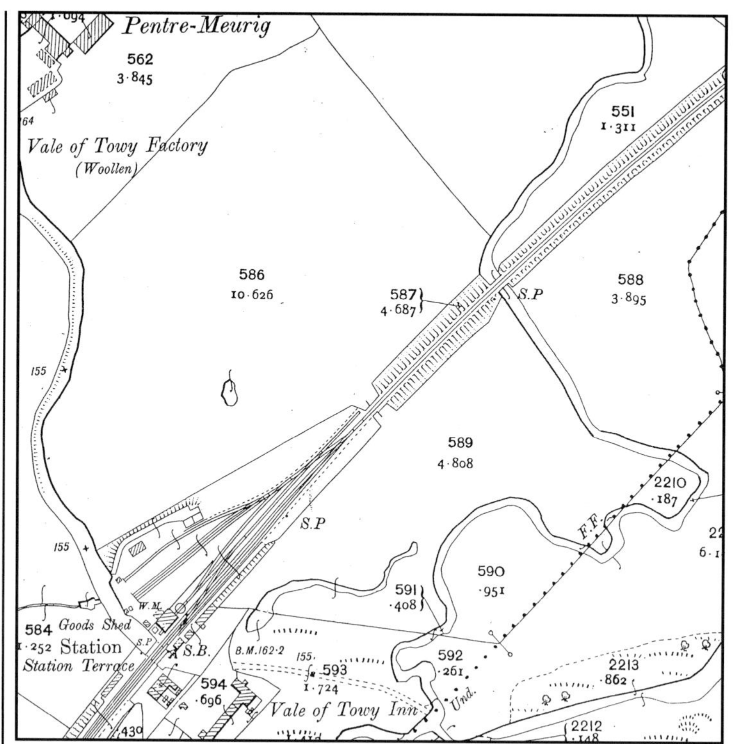

Above: Llanwrda station, Second Edition 25in OS map of 1905/06 — this was one of only two crossing places on the Vale of Towy section. The up platform is to the south of the level crossing, the down platform to the north. *Crown Copyright*

Below: Our intrepid photographer braved the rain to take this picture of Llandovery station. The station was the point where the Central Wales Extension Railway and the Vale of Towy Railway met end-on, and the town became a railway community of no little significance. This view looks south. *Andrew Muckley*

Right: In September 1963 a southbound goods train, hauled by an unidentified '8F' 2-8-0, trundles past the disused platform of Glanrhyd halt, which closed in March 1955. *Andrew Muckley*

Below right: A curious feature of Llandilo station was its 'dual-level' up platform. Not long after the Shrewsbury–Swansea route had opened throughout, the original platform was lengthened, the extension being higher than the existing platform. To the best of the author's knowledge, the higher platforms became possible when foot-boards ceased to be attached to passenger carriages. If that is an incorrect assumption, polite enlightenment would be welcome! This classic study is believed to date to around 1910. *Welsh Industrial & Maritime Museum*

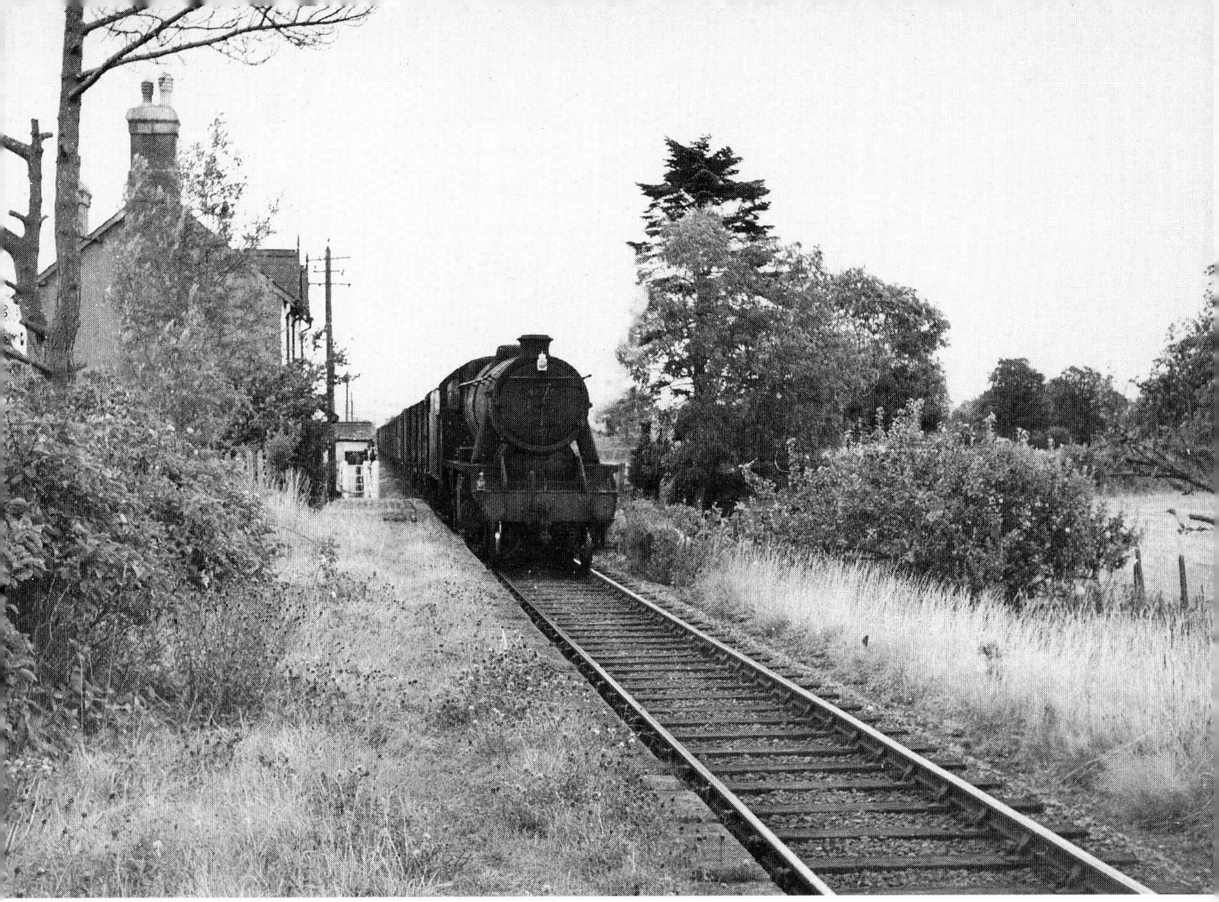

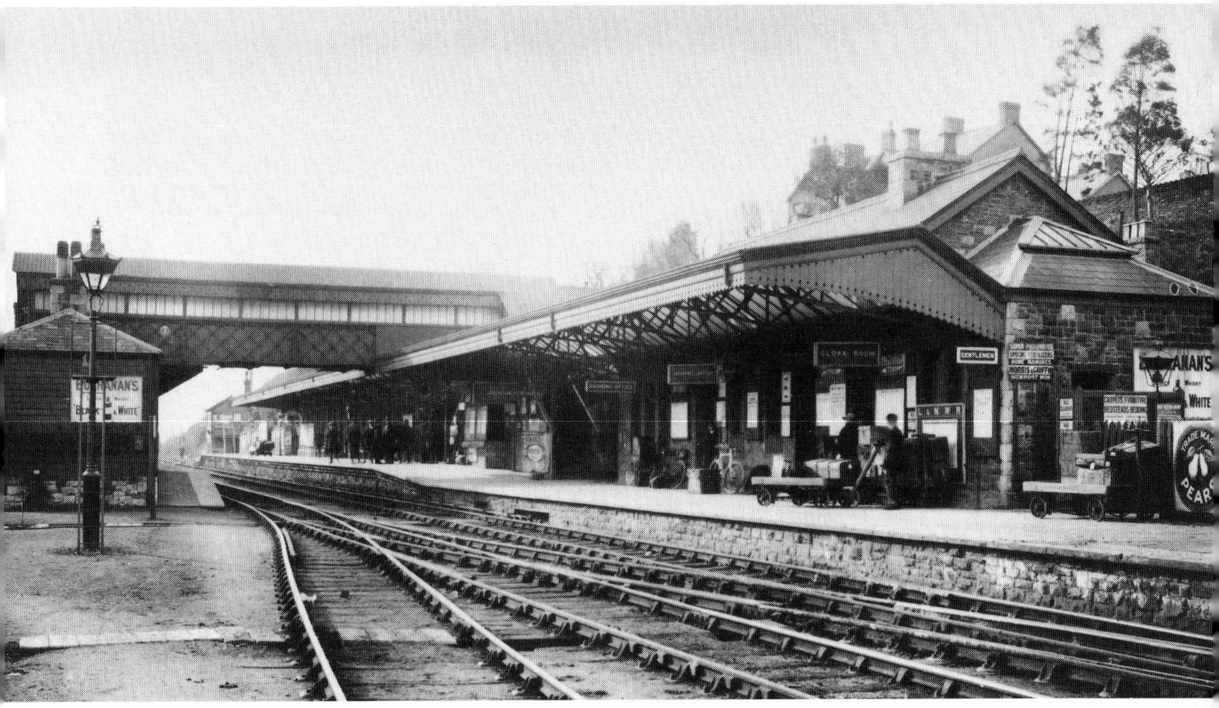
CLOAK ROOM
GENTLEMEN
BLACK & WHITE
WHITE
PEARS

Above: The Pontardulais–Llandovery section of the Central Wales line accommodated LNWR/LMSR and GWR trains. Despite the Western Region getting hold of the entire Swansea–Shrewsbury line after Nationalisation, and some of the local workings towards the southern end of the route gradually being taken over by ex-GWR motive power, the Llanelly–Llandilo locals had invariably been worked by the GWR/WR since 1873. Here, 0-6-0PT No 8749 waits at Llandilo on 25 July 1962, having brought in the 7.35am from Llanelly. *Leslie Sandler*

Below: Llandilo station, 25in OS maps (First Edition *c*1887, Second Edition *c*1903) — apart from a siding serving the saw mill (top of frame) and the sidings at the southeast side of the station, the railway layout at Llandilo changed little between the 1880s and the early 1900s. It is, however, evident that the community grew significantly between those dates. *Crown Copyright*

Right: Ffairfach station, First Edition 25in OS map, c1887 — another of the many rural stations on the Central Wales line. However, Ffairfach was on the GWR-owned section south of Llandilo. *Crown Copyright*

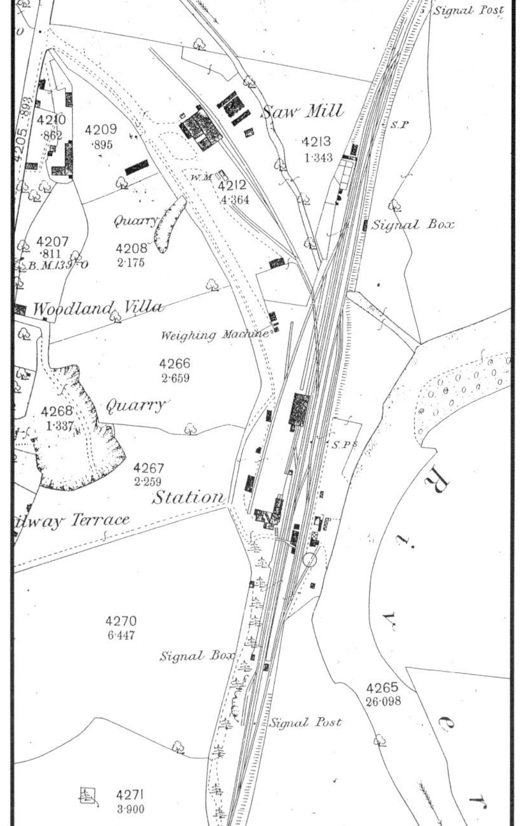

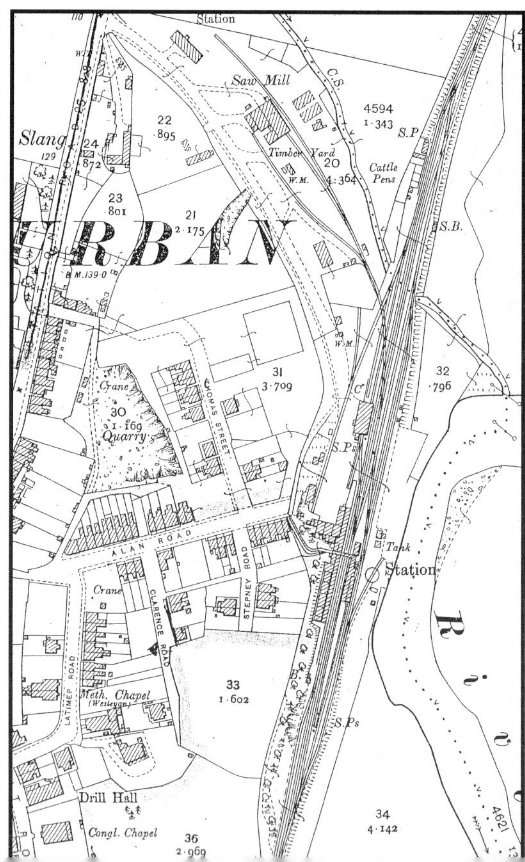

Llandilo station still has two platforms, although the bay at the rear of the down platform (which was used by Carmarthen branch trains) was dispensed with in December 1963 after the closure of the Carmarthen branch. The platforms at Llandilo were originally staggered, but the station was extensively rebuilt by the GWR in its own distinctive style. In pre-Grouping days (at least), Llandilo kept a stock of footwarmers for the benefit of passengers — train heating was not a feature of that period! Llandilo used to have a turntable on the down side of the line and had sidings on both sides of the line, including those serving a sawmill at the north end of the station on the up side.

In March 1955 a new brick-built signalbox was opened (on the down side of the line at the north end of the station) to replace, not only the two old boxes at the station, but also a third at Carmarthen Valley Junction, where the Carmarthen branch diverged. The new box, with 42 working levers and 12 spare, impressed the Government inspector, Lt-Col Wilson:

'..*the detailed workmanship of the mechanical and electrical equipment in the signal box above and below the working floor and of the wiring in the small relay room appeared to be of a very high standard. This new installation is a good example of modern mechanical signalling practice, supplemented by thorough electrical safeguards*'.

The heyday of the new box was, however, shortlived. After the closure of the Carmarthen branch in 1963 the frame in the box was relocked to work a significantly smaller layout, with just 10 levers. The box closed in September 1986.

The Carmarthen branch trains left Llandilo on the main line, which crosses the River Towy for the last time a quarter of a mile south of the station. The branch, which closed on 9 September 1963, veered westwards at Carmarthen Valley Junction, ½-mile from Llandilo station. Southwards from Llandilo — as far as Pontardulais — the line clearly displayed its one-time allegiance with the GWR, which was in marked contrast to the distinctive LNWR-style found on the section north of Llandovery.

The main line continues, now in a more southerly direction, to **Ffairfach station** (71¾ miles), the platform of which is on the down side of the single line. A loop siding serving a new CWS milk loading depot just to the north of Ffairfach station was provided in 1935 and extended in 1936. In September 1935 the station was partially resignalled and a 'new' signalbox was opened, the top of the 'box coming from Margam East. The works were inspected by Lt-Col Mount for the Ministry of Transport on 16 July 1936:

'*The facing connections at each end of the loop are laid with 95lb R.B.S. material...full facing point equipment with 50ft bars has been provided...new running signals have been added...a new box has been built on the south-east side of the level-crossing...the crossing gates (4) are worked by wheel and are interlocked with the signals...the frame contains 17 working, 2 wicket, and 13 spare lever*'.

The milk depot siding was retained after Ffairfach station was closed to public goods traffic in May 1961.

It has often been said that Ffairfach's most conspicuous feature was the 'new' signalbox. One of the signalmen's duties was the control of the level crossing at the south end of the station, but the crossing was automated in 1985.

From Ffairfach the line rises for some two miles at 1 in 105, following the delightful wooded valley of

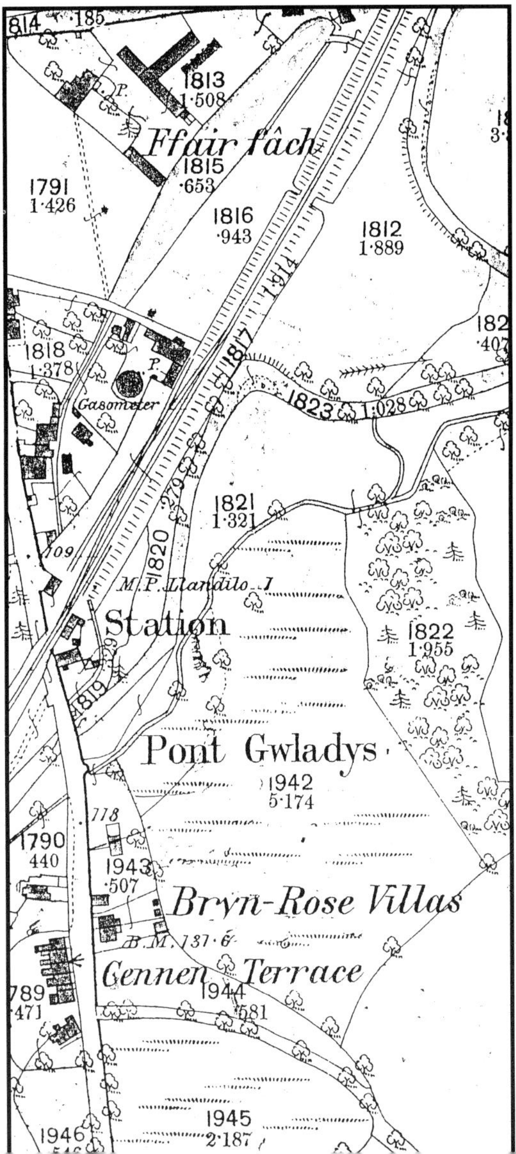

Above: For much of their lives, the majority of the stations on the Central Wales line were very well maintained, but the economies of the 1960s seem to have included a reduction in Ffairfach station's supply of weed-killer. On 25 July 1962, the 7.35am Llanelly-Llandilo waits at Ffairfach's herbaceous platform in the charge of Llanelly shed's 0-6-0PT No 8749. *Leslie Sandler*

the River Cennen, before reaching the site of **Derwydd Road station** (73¼ miles). The station was a passing place, with a platform on each track, but was closed to passengers on 3 May 1954 and to public goods traffic on 14 March 1966. Its signalbox remained until March 1966, although the passing loop had been taken out the previous year.

Another passing place was provided less than a mile to the south at Cilrrychen Crossing. There was no station at that site, but there was once a branch to the limestone quarries on the hills to the west. Trains also used to cross at **Llandebie station** (75¾ miles), but there was only one platform — on the up side. There were a couple of sidings on the down side, but public goods were not handled after 3 May 1965. Despite having been relegated to the status of an unstaffed halt on 17 September 1956, the station retained all of its platform buildings. One of Llandebie's claims to fame is that, in 1960, it boasted its own terminating service — the 5.35pm commuter train from Swansea.

After two miles of 1 in 106 (falling) through the Marlais Valley the line enters **Ammanford station** (77½ miles), a single-platform affair with slate-roofed timber buildings. The station has had a varied life. It was named 'Duffryn' until 1 July 1889, then 'Ammanford', retitled 'Ammanford & Tirydail' on 13 June 1960, became 'Ammanford & Tirydail *halt*' on 6 September 1965 after becoming unstaffed, lost the 'halt' suffix on 5 May 1969, and reverted to plain old 'Ammanford' on 7 May 1973. Phew!

Throughout all that, the goods section of the station officially retained the name of 'Tirydail' until the cessation of public goods traffic on 2 November 1964. The renaming of 1960, incidentally, followed the closure on 18 August 1958 of Ammanford station, half a mile away on the Pantyffynnon –Brynamman branch.

Ammanford was the point at which the character of the Central Wales line changed and, although there is still a change of identity, it is now rather less distinct. Ammanford effectively marked the start of the South Wales mining area, and southwards from there numerous collieries and tips — and other paraphernalia of industrialisation — bordered the railway on both sides.

South of Ammanford, the next stopping place was **Parcyrhun halt** (78 miles), which was opened by the

Below: Llandebie station, Second Edition 25in OS map of 1903. *Crown Copyright*

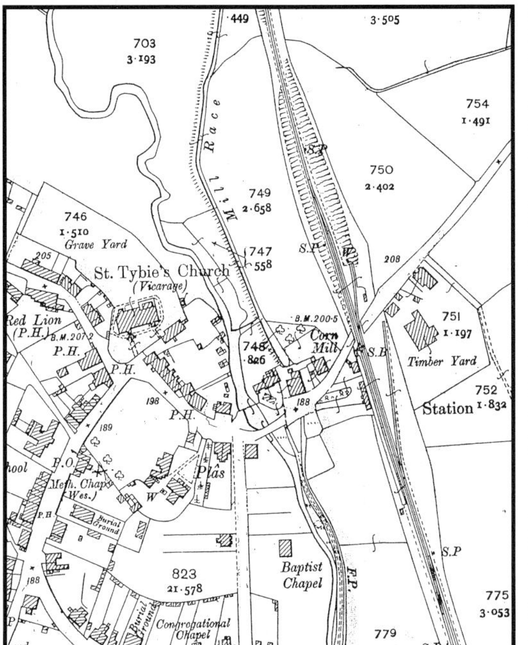

Below: Ammanford station, Second Edition OS map, c1903. *Crown Copyright*

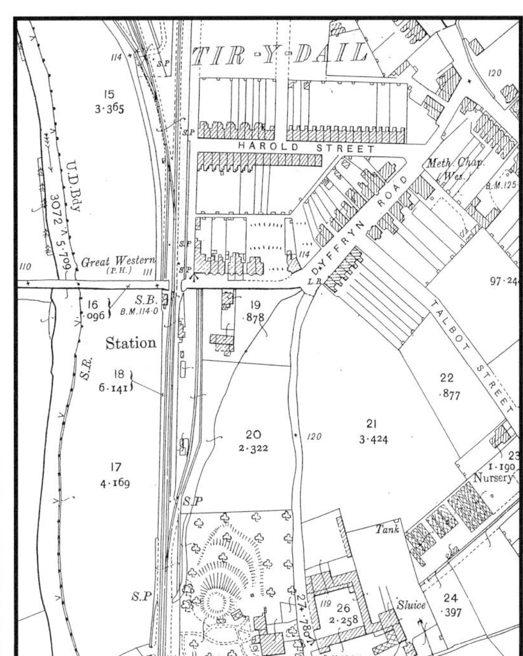

Above: Llandebie station was a simple affair but, even despite being relegated to the status of an unstaffed halt in 1956, was usually very well maintained. The signalbox proved to be very resilient, having been built in (or before) 1884 and lasting until June 1985, albeit with the benefit of a new frame in 1906. This picture was taken on 26 September 1971 — a few years after the passing loop had been taken out. *Andrew Muckley*

Above: Ammanford & Tirydail station, on the former Llanelly Railway section, was never the most luxurious of stopping places. The Mountain branch to Tumble diverged from the line just to the north of the station — the junction is discernible behind the rear carriage of the southbound train. The date is 4 September 1963, and it is clear that ex-LMSR six-wheeled coaching stock is far from extinct.
Andrew Muckley

Below: At Pantyffynnon, the ex-Llanelly Railway branch to Gwaun-cae-Gurwen (GCG) diverged to the east. The Central Wales line platforms are seen here on the left, and the GCG line and platform on the right.
Lens of Sutton

Above: The original route of the Central Wales line diverged from the Llanelly line at Pontardulais. Here, ex-LMSR Fowler 2-6-4T No 42385 brings a Swansea-bound train into Pontardulais in the mid-1950s.
Denzil Penberthy Collection

GWR on 4 May 1936 and closed by BR on 13 June 1955. The halt was inspected by Lt-Col Mount for the Ministry of Transport on 17 July 1936:

'A high level halt platform, 75ft long and 7ft 6in wide, has been provided on the south side of the bridge carrying the Ammanford-Llanelly Road over the line.

'The platform is built with sleeper face walls and filling behind, and is surfaced with ashes. It is lighted by electricity and is adequately fenced with post and wire fencing. There is a shelter 15ft by 8ft with booking office attached, and the halt is approached by a footpath which has been provided from the public road. There is no tendency to cross the line, and trespass notices have been erected at each end of the platform.

'Passengers joining trains at the halt are booked by the guards of the trains, except on Saturdays when a porter is employed at the halt to book trains at certain times. Trains calling at the halt usually consist of one engine and two 8-wheel coaches (twin set), the length of the coaches being 120ft.

'The halt is served by 6 trains (rear coaches) in each direction daily, and it is used by some 700 passengers per month'.

A short distance beyond the site of Parcyrhun halt is **Pantyffynnon station** (78¾ miles), which used to have a passing loop and two platforms. Although the up platform was abandoned on 31 December 1967 when the Pantyffynnon South-Pontardulais section was singled, the old up line was retained to act as a headshunt for the sidings to Wernos Washery. The Brynamman branch joined the Central Wales line at the south of Pantyffynnon station, the rear of the down platform being used by branch passenger trains. At Pantyffynnon North, the railway was realigned for about ¼-mile in April 1872 in order to reduce the number of facing points. The old alignment was subsequently used as a siding.

The doubling of the Pantyffynnon–Pontardulais section was completed on 15 December 1907, and it appears that the work had been desperately needed. In 1905 — only two years before doubling was undertaken — a loop was necessarily installed at Tynycerig (about half way between Pantyffynnon and Pontardulais) for goods trains. When inspecting the works for the Board of Trade, Lt-Col Yorke opined that: *'The arrangements are suitable for enabling a passenger train on the main line to pass a goods train in the loop, but not for the purpose of enabling two passenger trains to pass one another'.*

The line between Pantyffynnon and Pontardulais was singled in December 1967. As a consequence of the major signalling alterations undertaken on the Central Wales line in 1986, Pantyffynnon signalbox now controls the entire section between there and Craven Arms — more of which in Chapter Six.

After leaving Pantyffynnon the line veers slightly to the southwest, and then follows the River Loughor on a fairly straight but undulating course to **Pontardulais station** (83½ miles), which became joint LNWR/GWR property on 1 September 1886. Pontardulais used to be the point where the Central Wales line to Swansea and the Llanelly Railway/GWR line to Llanelly diverged but, as mentioned in greater detail later in this book, the Pontardulais-Swansea section closed to passenger traffic in 1964 and

Pantyffynnon station, First Edition 25in OS map, c1887
Crown Copyright

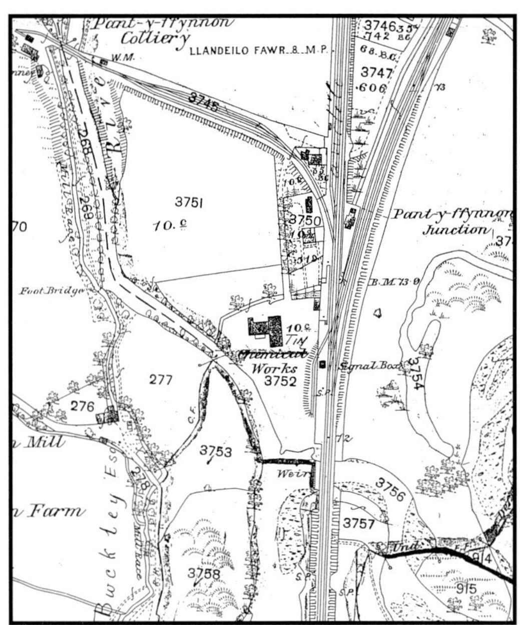

Below: A Swansea (Victoria)–Brynamman train, hauled by 0-6-0PT No 7718, leaves Gorseinon station on 11 July 1958. The industrialisation of the area is very evident.
H. C. Casserley

Swansea trains were subsequently re-routed via Llanelly. Pontardulais station was reduced to the status of an unstaffed halt on 6 September 1965, facilities for public goods traffic having by then been withdrawn.

Pontardulais station used to have four platform faces, the middle pair of which were the two sides of an island. The two platform faces on the east side of the station served the Llanelly line, the western pair served the Swansea line, and all were connected by a distinctive footbridge. Today, however, only the former down track through the Llanelly platform remains. In the station's heyday the Swansea platforms had signboards appended with 'Change here for GW trains to Llanelly', the signs on the Llanelly platforms advising passengers about the corresponding change for Swansea. To the north of the station there were once extensive sidings on both sides of the line, but that is very much a thing of the past.

Despite the changes inflicted on the Central Wales line in the 1960s, an element of traditionalism lingered on in the Pontardulais area for a little longer. Until the mid-1970s, steam traction ruled at the nearby Graig Merthyr Colliery.

The 83¼-miles from Craven Arms to Pontardulais are still in use today but the old Central Wales route southwards from Pontardulais has now gone, the last passenger services having operated on 13 June 1964. The now-deceased section, which was doubled throughout by February 1894, was subjected to a

20mph limit in both directions during its final years in order to reduce maintenance costs.

After leaving Pontardulais, the line veered to the southeast and passed under the GWR's Morlais Junction-Court Sart line. On 22 September 1974 a spur was opened between Grovesend Colliery Loop on the GWR line and Gorseinon, allowing the Pontardulais-Grovesend section of the old Central Wales line to be closed. The diversion via the new spur was necessary because construction of the M4 motorway severed the line immediately south of Pontardulais, thereby denying access to the coalyards at Gorseinon.

Brynlliw Colliery, which was also served by Grovesend Colliery Loop, is, like virtually all its counterparts elsewhere in South Wales, now defunct. Winding ceased on 21 July 1983, the last train from the colliery left on 19 October 1989, and the colliery line was lifted in September 1993.

Having passed under the GWR line south of Pontardulais, the Central Wales line started a one-mile climb of 1 in 83 to Grovesend Colliery Siding

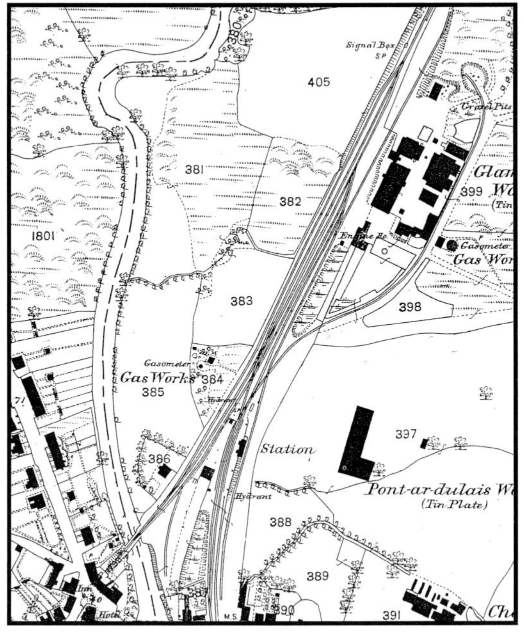

Above: Pontardulais station, 25in OS map of 1879 — more open countryside! The station (lower part of map) was the point where the Swansea and Llanelly lines diverged, the former veering to the southeast and the latter continuing to the southwest. *Crown Copyright; courtesy West Glamorgan County Library*

Below: Gorseinon station and surrounds, 25in OS maps of 1879 and 1935 — from rural outpost to centre of industry in much less than a lifetime; there must have been many who actually witnessed the astounding transformation. The 1879 map clearly shows the single-track status of the Central Wales line. *Crown Copyright; courtesy West Glamorgan County Library*

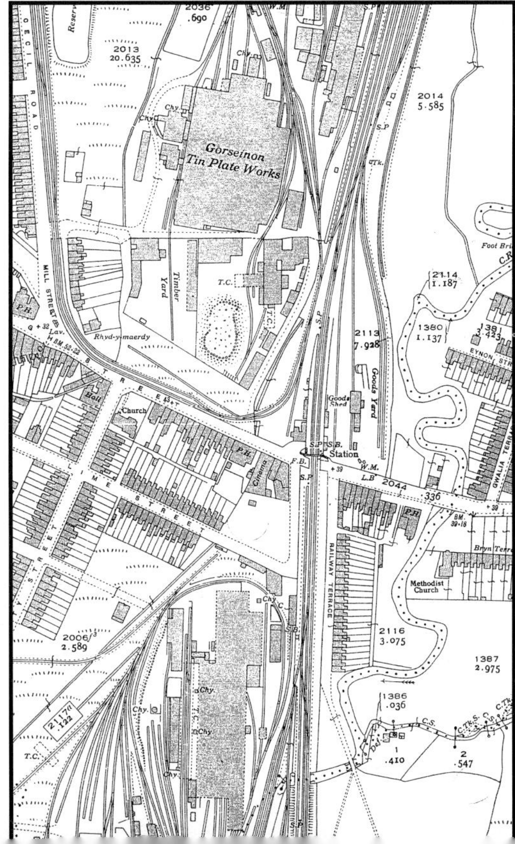

and then reached **Grovesend station** (85½ miles), which was not provided until 1 January 1910. It is assumed that the station was intended primarily for miners working at the nearby colliery, as the fortunes of the station and colliery were somewhat intertwined. The colliery ceased working in the early 1930s and the station closed on 6 June 1932, but whereas the colliery was later revived, the station was not.

From Grovesend, the line turned almost due south and descended at 1 in 116 for around one mile, passing on its way the spoil tips of the local collieries, before entering **Gorseinon station** (87 miles). An early Board of Trade report refers to Gorseinon station as 'Loughor Common', but there seems to be no evidence of that name being used when the line was operational. Gorseinon was a substantial twin-platform station with wooden buildings on the down platform and stone buildings on the up side, and its siding accommodation reflected the heavy industry which once dominated the area.

Southwards from Gorseinon the line traversed comparatively level ground for some 1½ miles, and crossed the GWR's Swansea–Fishguard line just before **Gowerton South station** (88½ miles) which was equipped with LNWR-style wooden buildings on both platforms. That station started life as 'Gower Road', was renamed 'Gowerton' on 1 July 1886, and became 'Gowerton South' in January 1950, when the adjacent GWR station became 'Gowerton North'. At the northern end of Gowerton (South), the branch to Llanmorlais diverged from the Central Wales line. The branch closed to passengers in 1931 and to freight in 1957.

At the turn of the century, the LNWR line at Gowerton was also used temporarily by GWR trains. The collapse of Cockett Tunnel on the GWR's main line to the west of Swansea in June 1899 resulted in trains being diverted via the North Dock lines at Swansea and then the LNWR line to Llanelly. (The alternative GWR route — the Swansea District Line via Felin Fran — was not then built.) The GWR's embarrassment at having to use the lines of its rival was partially eased in July 1899 when a new connection was laid on an old alignment at Gowerton, permitting GWR trains to regain their 'correct' route beyond the Elba steelworks. The embarrassment was not finally overcome until 1 March 1903, when the GWR's own line reopened.

Leaving Gowerton and climbing for a mile at 1 in 70, the Central Wales line reached **Dunvant station** (90 miles), which had wooden buildings on the down platform and a small waiting room, also built of wood, on the up side. It appears that Dunvant was a later addition to the line, as it was conspicuously absent from the Board of Trade inspection report which preceded the line's opening.

From the very early days, various sidings and spurs emanated from the line near Dunvant to serve

Below: The platform buildings at Dunvant station were of a similar style to others on the Pontardulais–Swansea section of the Central Wales line. This view, which was taken on 6 September 1963, looks towards Pontardulais and shows (beyond the right-hand platform) the remains of Dunvant Colliery, which closed in the 1930s. *Andrew Muckley*

S.W.D.—No.

LONDON AND NORTH WESTERN RAILWAY.

Working of Single Line

BETWEEN

GORSEINON AND PONTARDULAIS

BY

NEW ELECTRIC STAFF APPARATUS.

Instructions to Station Masters, Engine Drivers, Guards, & Breaksmen.

On and after Sunday, October , the present Single Line Train Staff and Tickets between the above-mentioned places, will be dispensed with, and the Line will be worked with the new Electrical Apparatus and Staffs, one Staff for each Section constituting the SOLE AUTHORITY for Engine Drivers to travel over the Single Line. The Staff Stations are as under:—

GORSEINON and PONTARDULAIS.

The points at Birch Rock Siding will be locked by means of a key, which will be fixed upon the Train Staff.

Each staff has engraved upon the metal end of it, the section of the single line over which it constitutes the authority for travelling, and drivers must be very careful to see that they receive the proper staff for the section of line, over which they are about to travel.

The staffs between Gorseinon and Pontardulais will be lettered " and ," and coloured

Under this system of working, every train engine driver, or driver of a light engine, or the driver of the last engine, in the case of two or more light engines coupled together, must carry a train staff. If a train is assisted by a bank engine in the rear, the staff must be carried by the driver of that engine, who must show it to the driver of the engine attached to the front of the train before starting.

No train must be allowed to shunt on the single line outside the home signal unless in possession of the staff for the section so occupied.

The station masters at Gorseinon and Pontardulais will be held responsible for regulating the trains and arranging, when a train is ready to start from both ends of the section, whether the up or down train shall take precedence, bearing in mind, that, as a rule, the up train with a main line connection to maintain, should be despatched first.

In cases where two engines are attached to a train, and where, by Rule 369, a train staff ticket would be given to the driver of the first engine, and the train staff to the driver of the second, or train engine, under this new system of working, the **train staff ticket** will be **altogether dispensed with** and one staff only will be in use, which will be carried by the driver of the train engine, when there is more than one engine in front of the train, and by the bank engine driver when there is a bank engine in rear of the train. The driver who carries the staff must show it to the driver or drivers of the other engine or engines when there is more than one engine on the train.

In the event of an engine becoming disabled between two Staff Stations, the Fireman must take the Staff to the nearest Staff Station, and if that is the Station from which assistance can be obtained, must personally hand over the Staff to the Driver of the engine rendering assistance, and accompany him to the place where he left his own disabled engine. If assistance has to be obtained from the Station at the other end of the Section, the Signalman at that end must be informed of what has taken place, and the Staff may then be replaced in the pillar so that a Staff can be released at the Station from which assistance will be sent. The Driver of this assisting engine, after removing the disabled engine, or engine and train, to the most convenient end of the Section, will then hand over the train Staff to the Signalman to be at once replaced in the train Staff pillar. It will be the duty of the Fireman when going with the Staff to the nearest Station to protect the standing train by placing detonators on the line in accordance with Rule 213. The Guard or Breaksman must protect the train in the opposite direction. In the case of light engines, it will be the duty of the Firemen before going with the Staff to the nearest Station, to place detonators on the rails in the opposite direction to that to which he is taking the Staff, in the manner described in Rule 213, he must also protect the train in the direction in which he is proceeding with the Staff, in accordance with Rule 213.

Should the breakdown be of such a nature as to prevent the train or engine being removed, and it is likely that the traffic may be stopped for any considerable time, special arrangements must be made for working trains to and from the point of obstruction on each side. The electric staff apparatus must be used to work trains or light engines between the point of obstruction and the station or signal box from which the staff was issued, the necessary forms (No. 1960) being first filled up and signed by all concerned; and on the other side the traffic must be conducted by a pilotman after the forms for such working (No. 1960) have been filled up and signed by all concerned.

When a train or portion of a train is left upon the main line from accident or inability of the engine to take the whole forward, or from any other cause, and it becomes necessary for the engine to return to the train or rear portion of the train from the signal box in advance, the engine driver must retain possession of the staff, until the whole of the train is removed from the Section.

Should the rear engine of any train which is being banked fail, or should the engines be unable to take forward the whole of the train, the driver of the leading engine must send his fireman to the driver of the bank engine, and obtain from him an order in writing stating that the driver of the rear engine is in possession of the staff, and authorising him to return from the box in advance, for the remainder of his train. The leading engine must then proceed to the signal box in advance, and after the driver has delivered up the order to the signalman, he must return and remove the rear portion of his train and the disabled engine.

Under no circumstances (except in the case of a disabled Train or Engine as named above) must a train staff be transferred from one train to another without being passed through the instrument in the signal cabin and dealt with in accordance with the Block Telegraph Regulations

Should the apparatus fail, the telegraph lineman must be at once sent for, and immediate steps, in the meantime, taken to work the line by pilotman, in accordance with Rules 375—379, the special forms provided for working traffic during the failure of the electric staff (No. 1959) being filled up and signed by all concerned before the working by pilotman is put into operation. Ten minutes margin must be left between each train in the case of two or more trains requiring to follow in the same direction.

Should a failure of the apparatus occur rendering it necessary to run trains in charge of a pilotman, the Single line working must be arranged by **the Station Master** at for **up and down trains** between Gorseinon and Pontardulais.

F. SMITH,
Assistant District Traffic Superintendent, Swansea.

J. BISHOP,
District Traffic Superintendent, Abergavenny.

October, 1891.

collieries, quarries and a brickworks. The line then crossed the River Clyne and descended on gradients of up to 1 in 70 to **Killay station** (91 miles), the spacious platforms of which rather belied its usual sparsity of traffic. Killay's general lack of use was emphasised when it was downgraded to an unstaffed halt on 31 December 1956, Dunvant station becoming partially unstaffed at the same time.

At Killay, the sidings behind the down platform were once controlled by a signalbox sited at the south end of the station (on the down side of the line), but the box was replaced by a ground frame in April 1939. A little to the south of Killay a siding served Rhydydefed Colliery (on the north of the line), but it seems that the colliery had a relatively short life as the connection to it opened in 1876 and was closed by 1911. However, by 1925 the Clyne Valley Brick & Tile Works were established near the 'main line' end of the colliery siding. The section of the Central Wales line between Gower Road (Gowerton) and Killay was doubled as early as February 1876, but doubling south of Killay was not completed until 29 May 1892.

From Killay the line continued its descent. It snaked through Clyne Woods and then had a short climb of 1 in 90 to **Mumbles Road station** (92¾ miles), which opened in January 1868. The down platform at Mumbles Road was built of timber. The line then ran parallel to the Swansea & Mumbles Railway along the shore towards Swansea, passing through **Swansea Bay station** (94¾ miles). The first Swansea Bay station was opened on 1 January 1878, but was replaced by a new station some 400yd to the west on 2 June 1892.

The line climbed away from Swansea Bay station at 1 in 90 — sharpening briefly to 1 in 80 — then turned inland and passed Beach Sidings (on the up side) which had a capacity of 350 wagons. It then entered **Swansea (Victoria)** (95¾ miles from Craven Arms), which was the end of the journey for passengers.

Victoria was originally a through station and was connected to the Swansea & Mumbles Railway, but only goods traffic used the lines beyond the station. The report of a Board of Trade inspection in 1890 noted that: '*...the goods lines have been placed at the back of the station, instead of running through the passenger station as heretofore*'. That report, incidentally, also mentioned two of the signalboxes — No 3, with 23 levers and one spare, and No 2, with 24 levers and one spare. The three boxes at Swansea were originally numbered 1, 2 and 3 from south to north, but that was later changed so that the numbers ran from north to south.

The approach to Victoria was via a sharp curve on a 1 in 45 downhill gradient and this was obviously treated with due respect by crews setting out from the terminus. Sometimes, though, assistance was on hand for hill starts in damp conditions — the line from Mumbles Road ran along the shore and liberal helpings of sand were often blown right along to Victoria. On the rest of the seashore line, however, the sand was not viewed so charitably as it often required special engineers' trips to clear it away. This writer can certainly confirm that Swansea Bay is not exactly the most sheltered spot in the universe.

In Llanelly Railway days the station was referred to as the 'Low Level station', but the first locally-printed public timetable referred to it as 'Victoria-Street' station and a version of that name stuck. As already related, the station was still in an unfinished state when the LNWR took over in 1873. It was not completed until 1882. A report on the facilities at 'Victoria' in July 1872 noted that:

Below: Gowerton stations, 25in OS map 1879 — the LNWR station on the Central Wales line is towards the left of the frame, the station slightly to the north being that on the GWR's South Wales main line. The line diverging to the west from the LNWR line is the Penclawdd (Llanmorlais) branch. *Crown Copyright; courtesy West Glamorgan County Library*

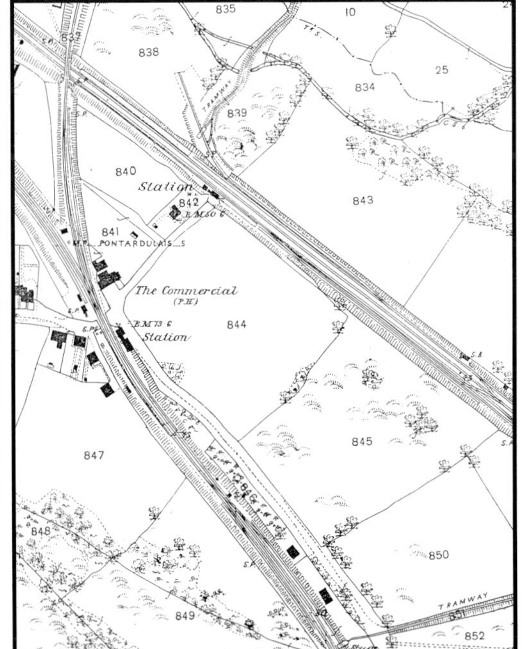

Above: The 9.50pm York-Swansea (Victoria) overnight train, hauled by 'Black Five' No 45143, pulls into Swansea Bay station on the morning of 11 June 1960. *Hugh Ballantyne*

Right: Ex-LNWR 'Coal Tank' 0-6-2T No 7807 pulls out of Swansea (Victoria) with the 8.20pm to Pontardulais on 27 June 1938. The station roof displays its full prewar set of glazing. *H. C. Casserley*

'*...there is only a single platform at the terminal station at Swansea. Two railway companies, i.e. the London and North Western Railway and the Llanelly Railway, work passenger traffic into this station. The station-master and the foreman porter are in the service of the London and North Western Company, but the other servants at the station are provided by the Swansea & Carmarthen Company*'. (The S&C had been specially formed in 1871 to administer the LR's Swansea and Carmarthen lines).

When completed by the LNWR, Victoria station had two curving platforms, and a single run-round line was later provided between the platforms. Various alterations were made to the station and its

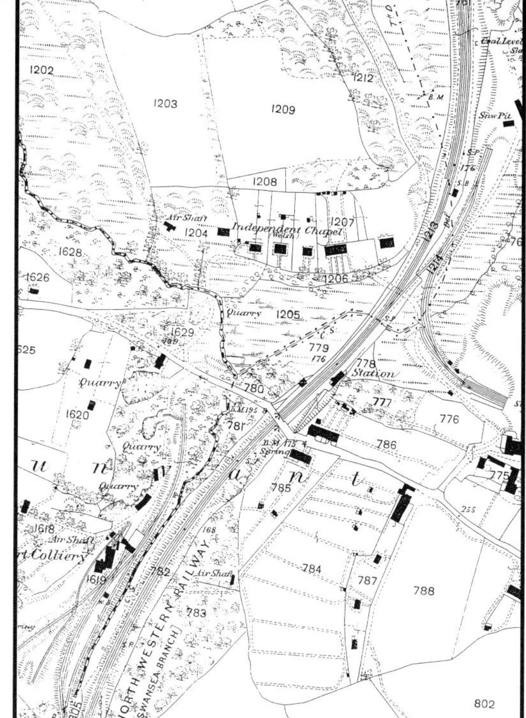

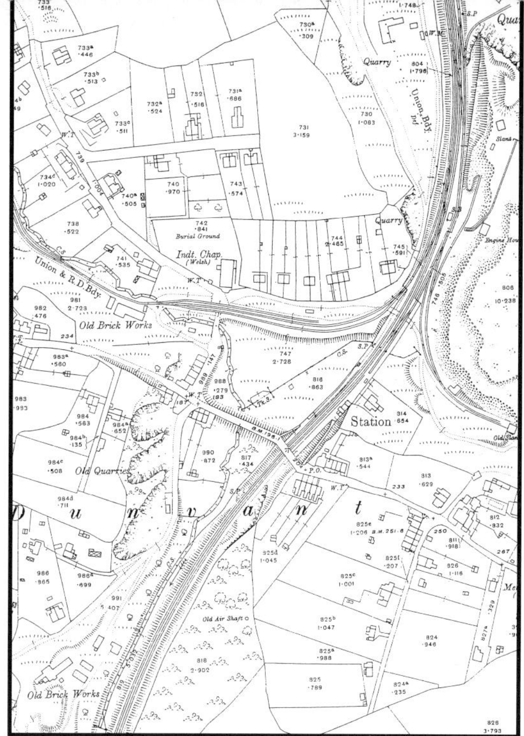

Above: Dunvant station, 25in OS maps 1879 and 1916 — perhaps surprisingly, the area around Dunvant station didn't change too much between the dates of these surveys. In railway terms, the most conspicuous changes shown in the 1916 map are the 'new' siding to the brick works and beyond (left of frame), and the disappearance of the quarry and the sidings serving Voilert Colliery (which had closed by 1896) in the lower part of the map. *Crown Copyright; courtesy West Glamorgan County Library*

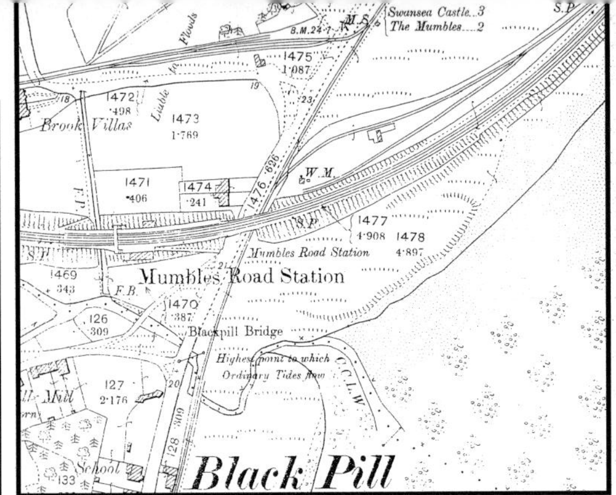

Above: Mumbles Road station, 25in OS map 1899 — the LNWR line goes from west to northeast, the other railways shown on the map being the famous Swansea & Mumbles Tramway (north to south) and the Clyne Valley Tramway (which joins the S&M and continues off left). *Crown Copyright; courtesy West Glamorgan County Library*

connecting lines over the years, but apart from the conversion of the station in 1890 to a terminus, most of the changes were relatively minor.

In its later years the terminus was painfully neglected. Its overall roof suffered air-raid damage during World War 2, but instead of being repaired after the war, further sections were gradually removed as a safety precaution. The dismantling of the roof might have made the station a little less dark and gloomy, but it did precious little for cosmetic appearances.

It has often been suggested that, as the station was a little removed from the centre of Swansea, the authorities felt scant need to repair the war damage. An alternative — and popular — opinion is that, after the Western Region took over, the new management preferred to channel their resources into their 'own' main line facilities, rather than into a station they had inherited.

As mentioned elsewhere in this book the GWR and LMSR had, shortly after the war, explored the possibility of re-routing Central Wales trains into High Street station at Swansea, and although that did not materialise it could hardly have elevated Victoria to the WR's list of investment priorities. Despite being closed to passenger traffic in June 1964, Victoria officially remained open to freight until 4 October 1965. The site was later cleared for redevelopment and is now occupied by the Swansea Leisure Centre.

Victoria station was only a stone's throw from South Dock. As could be expected there was not only a substantial goods shed and yard near the station, but also connections to the lines of the GWR and, via a gateway, the Swansea Harbour Trust lines. The main connecting line to the GWR was carried on a series of arches above and alongside the southeast side of the station, although the connection came under GWR jurisdiction at the very beginning of the line (alongside South Dock). The LNWR had a half-mile long spur to its own goods station on the south side of South Dock.

Private sidings at selected stations — August 1960

Llangadog*:	CWS Milk Factory
Llandilo:	Llandilo Builders Supply Co; Ben Hughes Coal Merchant
Ffairfach:	CWS Milk Factory (closed 1/10/59); Wales Gas Board (no traffic now passing)
Llandebie:	Cilyrychen Lime Works
Tirydail:	British Anthracite Co Carriage & Wagon Works; Llandebie Lime Works; Llandebie Colliery (NCB) (closed); Wales Gas Board
Pantyffynnon:	Dynevor Works; NCB Collieries
Glynhir Siding:	Glynhir Tinplate Co
Pontardulais:	Lewis Bros Saw Mills; Glamorgan Tin Works; Duffryn Saw Mills Ltd; Thomas Bros; Evans & Williams Wagon Repairers; Toddington Aircraft Controls Ltd; Webb Shakespeare & Williams; South Wales Electricity Board (Dulais Siding)
Gorseinon:	R. Thomas & Baldwin; Steel Co of Wales; Bryngwyn Sheet Works; Mountain Colliery (NCB); Grovesend Colliery (NCB); Bevans Saw Mills; Cross Foundry & Engineering Co
Gowerton South:	R. Thomas & Baldwin (Elba Works); Fairwood Tinplate Works; Western Light Casting Foundries Ltd; Garngoch Colliery (NCB)

* Spelling changed from Llangadock in 1958

Goods facilities at selected stations — August 1960

Station	No of sidings	Wagon capacity	Cattle pens	Crane	Warehouse	Wharfage
Broome	3	50	3	-	95sq yd[1]	Radnorshire Co
Hopton Heath	2	18	-	5ton	676sq yd	Radnorshire Co
Llangunllo	1[2]	10	-	-	14sq yd[3]	C. H. Hammond
Llanbister Road	1	23	1	-		Radnorshire Co
Dolau	2	30	1	-	-	-
Penybont	4¶	120¶	4	5ton	[6]	Radnorshire Co; C. D. Venables; West Brecon Farmers; A. Davies
Garth	2[2]	32	2	-	50sq yd	-
Llangammarch Wells	1	14	-	-	20sq yd	-
Cynghordy	1	11	-	-	-	-
Llanwrda	4	40	1	30cwt	-	Pumpsaint & District CWS
Llangadog *	3	57	[4]	30cwt	-	Llangadog & District ACS
Ffairfach	1	18	-	-	-	-
Llandebie	3	40	-	30cwt	-[5]	J. John (coal merchant)
Tirydail	1	8	-[6]	-		-
Gorseinon	2	45		-	108sq yd	C. Harris; H. Lewis; I. Lewis; L. Hughes; Dummer & Fage; A. Hart; Pontardulais CWS
Gowerton South	1	15	-	-	-[6]	D. Howells; L. Howells
Dunvant	3	123	-	-	[6]	-
Killay	2	11	-	-		J. W. Jenkins (coal)
Mumbles Road	2	30	-	-	-	Ferguson & Son; D. J. Morgan; Morgan Bros; Bresnan Bros; K. Parker
Swansea Bay	3	41	-	-	-	B. W. Plumb; Godbeer & Son; W. Brown; Anderson; S. Silvey; Shapland; G. Hopkins; Gabriel; Ellis Partridge; G. Shapland

* Spelling changed from Llangadock in 1958

¶ Includes up refuge siding for 33 wagons

1 Warehouse not used
2 Plus refuge sidings at Llangunllo and Garth
3 Small warehouse on platform
4 Previously removed
5 Described as 'small galvanised shed'
6 Yes, but size/number not known

The Carmarthen branch

Although not really a part of the Central Wales line itself, the branch between Llandilo and Carmarthen was an important feeder route for the main line. To recap briefly on the branch's history, it was opened by the Llanelly Railway to goods traffic in 1864 and to passenger traffic in 1865, the LNWR having running powers from the outset. In 1871 it was hived off to become part of the Swansea & Carmarthen Railway and was formally purchased by the LNWR in 1891.

The branch actually started at Carmarthen Valley Junction, a ½-mile to the south of Llandilo station. It was single track and followed the course of the River Towy — in later years parts of the line's foundations were almost continuously eroded by the river, and the branch therefore proved costly to maintain.

The branch stations were **Llandilo Bridge** (¾-mile from Llandilo), **Golden Grove** (3¼ miles), **Drysllwyn** (5¾ miles), **Llanarthney halt** (7 miles), **Nantgaredig** (9¾ miles) and **Abergwili** (13 miles). Trains could pass at Golden Grove, Llanarthney and Nantgaredig, which each had a platform on its loop, although the second platform at Llanarthney lasted only until February 1938 when the loop there was taken out of use.

For a time, Golden Grove station saw a burst of activity each year as it accommodated traffic for the Royal Welsh Agricultural Show which was held nearby. At Llandilo Bridge, a new shunting neck was provided in January 1927 to facilitate the movement of cattle wagons, such movements having previously occupied the single-track line. The LMSR calculated that the £448 bill for the shunting neck would be offset by an annual saving of £40 on GWR engine power.

The only significant engineering feature on the branch was the 76yd-long tunnel between Nantgaredig and Abergwili stations. Half-a-mile beyond Abergwili station, at the appropriately-named Abergwili Junction, the branch joined the Carmarthen-Pencader line of the Carmarthen & Cardigan Railway and, as the C&CR was originally laid with broad gauge rails, the Llanelly Railway had to provide a third rail between Abergwili Junction and Carmarthen Town.

Below and Below right: Swansea (Victoria) station, 25in OS maps 1876 and 1899 — although only 23 years separate the two surveys, many changes are evident. The most conspicuous are the conversion of the station into a terminus and the new goods and carriage sheds on the north of the running lines. *Crown Copyright; courtesy West Glamorgan County Library*

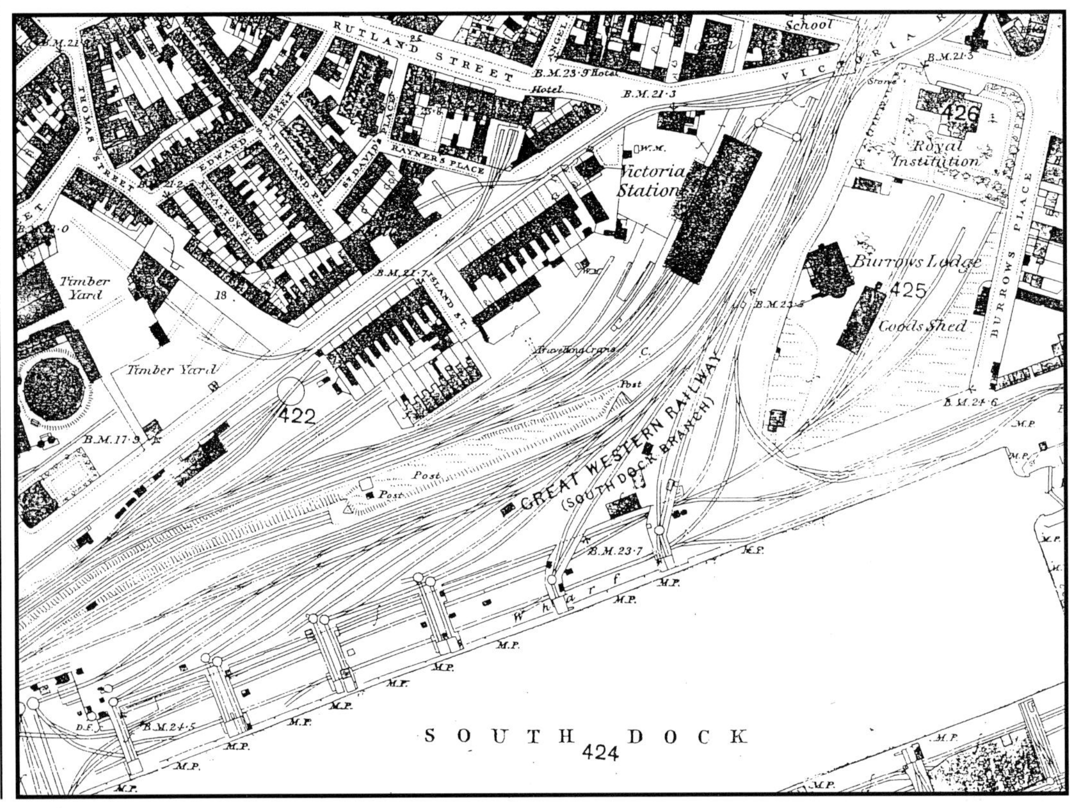

Above: By the start of the 1960s, most local and shunting duties at Swansea (Victoria) were handled by ex-GWR 0-6-0PTs. On 7 June 1960, No 9677 shunts the empty stock of an arrival from Shrewsbury. The signalbox — Swansea No 3 — opened in February 1889 to replace the former Swansea No 1 box a few yards further from the platform.
Hugh Ballantyne

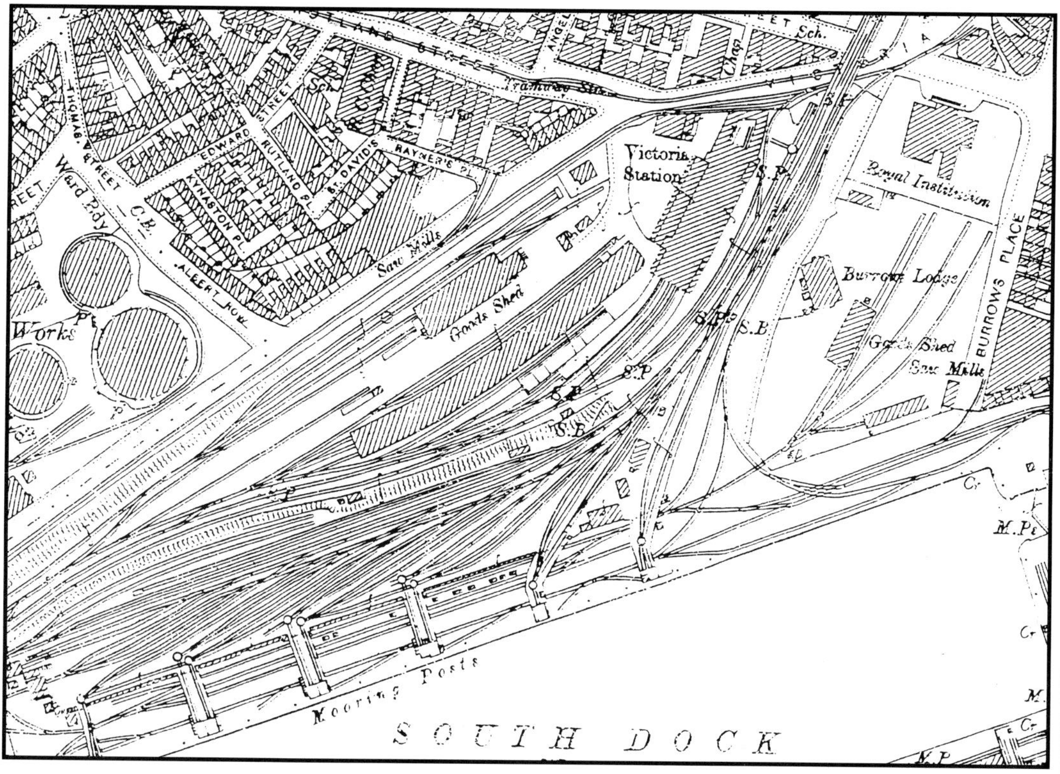

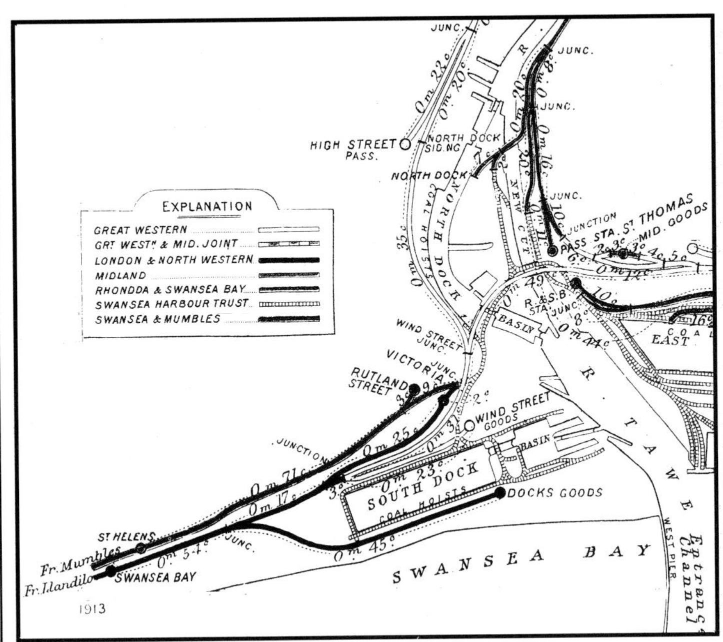

Left: Swansea hosted several different railway companies — a fact that is clearly evident in this RCH Junction Diagram of 1913. *Courtesy: I. C. Coleford*

Below: The Llandilo–Carmarthen branch boasted simple but attractive stations. In this early 1960s picture, a Carmarthen-bound train pulls away from Nantgaredig. *Andrew Muckley*

Right: In May 1958, 0-6-0PT No 7425 waits in the bay platform at Carmarthen station with a branch train for Llandilo. *Hugh Davies Collection*

Before the branch was built, it had been proposed to circumvent the gauge problem by building an independent alignment into Carmarthen with a terminus near the Market Place. That plan was, however, shortlived, and the use of a mixed gauge line between Abergwili Junction and Carmarthen proved adequate for the needs of the LR and LNWR. The broad gauge rails were dispensed with in 1872, and the following year the LNWR gained running powers over the South Wales Railway between Carmarthen Town station and Carmarthen Junction, albeit only for coaching traffic. Carmarthen Junction station, incidentally, closed to passenger traffic on 27 September 1926.

The Llanmorlais branch

The branch between Gower Road (later renamed Gowerton South) and Llanmorlais was built by the Llanelly Railway, and opened as far as **Penclawdd** (3 miles) on 14 December 1867 — the same day as the Pontardulais-Swansea main line opened to passenger traffic. The extension from Penclawdd to **Llanmorlais** (4¾ miles from Gower Road) was opened to goods traffic in 1877, and to passenger traffic on 1 March 1884. By then, the branch was LNWR property.

The original section of the branch was built partly on the route of a defunct canal, which had opened in 1814. The branch's primary purpose was to serve local collieries and, later, the Elba Steel Works (which became part of the Guest, Keen & Nettlefold [GKN] empire and was eventually connected to the GWR's main line as well), but one of the regular sources of traffic from Penclawdd is betrayed by the the branch's nickname of the 'Cockle Line'.

During the 1920s the passenger services on the single-track branch usually comprised six or seven trains each way on weekdays, one or two of the up trains continuing to Swansea. The trains were, however, sparsely patronised, and passenger services were withdrawn on 5 January 1931. The branch nevertheless remained open for freight, much of the traffic being generated by a small cluster of collieries.

After the cessation of passenger traffic, the signalling of the branch between Gowerton No 1 (Elba) box and Llanmorlais was altered to permit working on the 'one engine in steam' principle instead of the electric train-staff system. That alteration produced a saving in operational costs of £69 per annum. Freight traffic continued sporadically until the end of August 1957, the branch closing completely on 2 September that year.

GOWERTON AND LLANMORLAIS BRANCH.—Passenger Trains 3rd Class only.

Distance from Gowerton. M's	DOWN TRAINS. Week Days.	1 Emp. Coach SO	2 Empt Minrl C	3 Pas	4	5 Empt. Min'rl S	6 Pas SO	7 Empt Min'rl SO	8 Mixed G'ds & Pas S	9 Pas SO	10 Eng. and Van. SO	11 Empt Minrl SO	12 Local Goods S	13 Pas SO	14 Pas S	15 Eng. & Van for Minr'l Train. S	16 Pas SO
		a.m.	a.m	a.m.		a m	a.m.	a.m.	p.m.	p.m.	p.m.	p.m	p.m.	p m	p.m.	p.m	p.m.
...	GOWERTON ...† dep	6 15	7 40	8 5	...	1015	10 30	11 55	2 27	2 37	...	...	3 10	5 55	6 20	7 10	8 38
0¼	ELBA STEEL WORKS SIDING † arr	...	...	...	...	...	...	12 0	...	...	...	...	...	...	...	...	...
	dep	6 17	...	8 7	...	10 17	10 32	...	2 29	2 39	2 47	...	3 12	5 57	6 2	7 12	8 40
...	Elba Colliery	...	...	...	...	...	...	...	...	...	For Empty Mineral.	...	...	...	...	...	...
...	Cefn Stylle Siding	...	...	...	...	10 C20 10 25	...	12 18 12 20	...	...		...	...	...	...	...	...
...	Berthllwydd Siding	...	...	...	...	10 30 10 50	...	12 30 12 40	...	...		...	3 20	...	...	7 20	...
...	New Penlan Siding	...	...	...	...	...	...	...	...	...		...	3 40	...	...	...	...
3	PENCLAWDD †...arr	...	7 50	8 13	...	1055	...	12 45	...	...	2 57	...	3 45	6 5	...	...	8 46
...	„ ...dep	...	—	8 15	...	1125	10 40	—	2 35	2 45	—	3 20	4 15	6 10	6 30	...	—
...	Lynch Siding.........	...	...	...	...	...	...	...	...	...	...	...	...	...	...	...	...
4¼	LLANMORLAIS † arr	6 30	...	8 20	...	1135	10 45	...	2 39	2 50	...	3 40	4 25	6 15	6 35	...	...

Distance from Llanmorlais. M's	UP TRAINS. Week Days.	1 Pas SO	2 Pas	3 Minr'l C	4	5 Minr'l S	6 Pas SO	7 Minr'l SO	8 Mixed Goods and Pas S	9 Pas SO	10 Min'rl SO	11 Min'rl S	12 Pas SO	13 Pas S	14 Min'rl S	15 Pas SO
		a.m.	a.m.	a.m.		p.m.	a.m.	p.m.	p.m.	p m	p.m.	p.m.	p.m.	p.m.	p.m.	p.m
...	LLANMORLAIS † ...dep	6 40	8 35	...	...	12 35	11 40	...	2 45	3 5	4 10	4 45	6 30	6 45	...	...
...	Lynch Siding... arr	...	...	...	..	12 37	...	...	...	...	4 15	4 47	...	...	...	...
	dep	...	...	...	...	12 50	...	...	...	...	4 30	5 5	...	...	...	...
1½	PENCLAWDD † arr.	6 44	8 39	...	...	12 55	11 44	...	2 49	3 9	4 40	5 12	6 34	6 49	...	...
	dep.	6 49	8 42	8 55	...	1 30	11 45	1 0	2 50	3 12	5 0	5 17	6 37	6 51	...	8 53
...	New Penlan Siding... arr	...	...	9 0	...	...	...	1 5	...	...	...	...	...	...	...	...
	dep	...	...	9 15	...	...	...	1 20	...	...	...	...	...	...	...	...
...	Berthllwydd Siding... arr.	...	...	9 20	...	1 35	...	...	...	...	5 10	5 25	...	...	...	...
	dep.	...	...	9 35	...	1 45	...	...	...	...	5 20	5 35	...	...	7 35	...
...	Cefn Stylle Siding......	...	...	...	...	...	...	1 15 1 40	...	...	...	...	...	...	X	...
	Elba Colliery	...	...	...	...	...	...	...	...	...	...	...	...	...	...	...
4½	ELBA STEEL WORKS SIDING.† arr	...	...	9 45	..	1 50	...	1 50	...	...	5 25	5 40	...	...	7 50	...
	dep	6 54	8 46	—	...	—	11 52	—	2 54	3 16	6 20	...	6 43	6 57	9 30	8 59
4¾	GOWERTON † ......arr.	6 55	8 50	...	...	...	11 55	—	2 57	3 19	6 25	...	6 45	6 59	9 35	9 1

The LNWR working timetable for the Llanmorlais branch, February 1913 until further notice. *Courtesy: Bryan Wilson*

Above: The Llanmorlais branch closed to passenger traffic in 1931, but remained open to freight until 1957. On 2 August that year — the last month before total closure of the branch — the 11.20am goods from Gowerton South to Llanmorlais is seen at Penclawdd. *Hugh Davies*

Below: In the late 1920s, the LMSR's Fowler 2-6-4Ts started a long association with the Central Wales line. They were still at work on the route in the 1960s, as is evidenced by No 42390 taking on water at Builth Road (High Level) on 7 June 1960 before continuing with the 7.40am Craven Arms-Swansea (Victoria) train. *Hugh Ballantyne*

Chapter 3

Up and Running

By the time the Llanelly Railway opened the Pontardulais-Swansea section to passenger traffic in December 1867 — thereby providing the penultimate section of the Central Wales line — the company was in a poor financial position. It might be considered that the completion of the Swansea section would have marked the start of a new and promising era for the LR, but the immediate outlook was rather gloomy.

Below:
Various changes of administration affected various parts of the Central Wales line, but some scenes were timeless. This is Knighton station, probably not long after the removal of the wagon turntables from the goods yard in 1903. *Lens of Sutton*

An uninspiring start

Mineral traffic had been conveyed over the Swansea section since December 1865, but at about that time the local copper smelting trade had entered a period of decline. Consequently, the need for coal transportation had diminished. Originally, it had been projected that some 300,000 tons of coal would pass over the Swansea line each year, but for the line's first full year of operation (1866) the total was only a little over 20,000 tons.

The LR faced an uphill financial battle — certainly not the first it had known — and resisted official attempts to have the Swansea and Carmarthen lines regarded as part of its total corporate undertakings. (The Carmarthen section, as explained earlier, took the form of a branch from Llandilo to Carmarthen, which opened to passenger traffic in June 1865.) The LR wished to keep the Swansea and Carmarthen lines nominally separate as it didn't fancy having the meagre profits from its long-established operations prop up those lines.

The traffic figures for the Swansea and Carmarthen lines came under close scrutiny. For the 12-month period ending 30 June 1868, they were:

	Passenger train traffic	Goods and mineral traffic
Swansea line:	£1,655 6s 9½d	£7,142 19s 10d
Carmarthen line:	£2,993 8s 8d	£4,073 16s 8d

At a quick glance those figures might seem relatively satisfactory, but they included the charges for through traffic which had originated elsewhere. The matter of apportioning the relevant working expenses between those lines and the original sections was, to say the least, somewhat hazy.

The matter was resolved on 16 June 1871 when the Swansea & Carmarthen Railway was formed to incorporate the Pontardulais–Swansea and Llandilo–Carmarthen lines — although those two lines were separated by 12¾ miles of LR tracks. A revision of 28 July 1873 separated the two lines, the Carmarthen branch becoming the Central Wales & Carmarthen Junction Railway. Throughout all this, the LNWR kept a very close watch on proceedings.

In 1867 the LR had granted the LNWR running powers over all of its lines in return for financial assistance. The LNWR's assistance was, however, far from philanthropic and the company soon abandoned its pretence of 'Mr Nice Guy' and started to attack the LR's jugular. The LNWR knew that the LR could not continue its financial struggle indefinitely and it wanted to have a corporate foot firmly in the door when the LR was ripe for the picking. The 'hiving off' of the LR's Swansea and Carmarthen lines in 1871 suited the LNWR rather well.

Relations between the LR and the LNWR deteriorated. The former tried to terminate the agreement for the joint lease of the Vale of Towy section, but finally lost its case in the House of Lords. The LR hardly had time to consider its plight as, on 1 July 1871, the Swansea & Carmarthen Railway was handed over to be worked by the LNWR. The LR's protests cut no ice.

The battle-scarred LR tried to retaliate against the mighty LNWR. On 13 July 1872 Richard Glascodine, the LR's Secretary, issued a circular to the company's goods customers:

'I regret to say that in consequence of the course of action taken by the LNWR, we are unable to arrange through Bookings to and via their system.

'We have, however, made such arrangements with the GWR as will enable us to forward (via Llanelly) all traffic hitherto sent via Llandovery at the same through rates as usual, and with equal despatch, which will obviate any interruption to the traffic you have hitherto sent by us.

'All traffic loaded in LNWR Wagons, and consigned by their route we shall be compelled to enter and charge only to our junction (Llandovery) at existing Local Rates.

'I shall be glad to supply you with GWR Wagons for the purpose of loading and sending via Llanelly as proposed, and shall be further glad to hear from you that you assent to order your traffic accordingly; failing such assent we shall be reluctantly compelled to require payment of our local charges before forwarding any traffic via Llandovery'.

The LR's attempted obstructiveness was viewed by the LNWR as only a minor irritation. After all, the latter was, by then, close to getting what it really wanted.

New ownership

On 28 July 1873, the LNWR bought outright the Swansea–Pontardulais section (including the branch from Gower Road to Penclawdd). The Carmarthen branch did not become LNWR property until 21 July 1891 and, by then, the Llanelly Railway was no more. On 1 January 1873 its remaining lines had been handed over to the GWR to work and, in 1889, the LR was officially absorbed by the GWR and formally dissolved. The GWR inherited the LR's interest in the Vale of Towy Railway (Llandilo–Llandovery) and that section of the Central Wales line remained 'joint' until

Despite the strong LNWR/LMSR influence on much of the Central Wales line, the GWR held its own between Llandovery and Pontardulais. The Llandovery–Llandilo section remained under joint LMSR/GWR ownership until Nationalisation and so the sight of pannier tanks on that section was certainly not a post-1948 innovation. This picture of a southbound goods trundling through Llangadog (neé Llangadock) station could easily pass for a pre-Nationalisation picture, but it was, in fact, taken on 6 September 1963. *Andrew Muckley*

Following Nationalisation, many locomotives had something of an identity crisis. For example, Fowler 2-6-4T No 42305 clearly displays its new BR number, but it seems reluctant to deny its LMSR pedigree. The engine is leaving Llandovery on 8 September 1951 with the 7.45am service from Swansea. *H. C. Casserley*

Nationalisation. Conversely, the LNWR retained right of passage over the Llandilo–Pontardulais section, which became GWR property, and so the LNWR's access to Swansea was not affected by the upheavals.

When the LNWR acquired the Pontardulais –Swansea section outright in 1873, the line and its accommodation fell somewhat short of the standards normally expected by the folks at Euston. Only five years earlier, the LNWR's Outdoor Superintendent, G. P. Neale, had reported on an inspection of the LR's lines:

'The Llanelly group of lines, all narrow (4ft 8½in) *gauge, was far from being up to date. The stations and platforms were dilapidated, the crossing loops short, the permanent way weak; but the Engineers had introduced one of the simplest forms of interlocking for loop-line facing points that could be schemed. Attached to the point lever was a flat plate, working horizontally, the plate perforated by a single hole. When the lever was in position for allowing a train to pass through the facing points, the hole admitted a perpendicular rod, attached to the signal arm adjoining, to pass down it, and the signal was accordingly lowered to "caution". When the plate was not in this position, the signal could not be so lowered, and remained at "Danger" — a cheap and effective locking so far as it went'.*

Mr Neale might have been mildly impressed by the LR's signalling in 1868, but one of the many aspects of the Pontardulais-Swansea section which still needed desperate attention in 1873 was the station at Swansea. Although the station had opened for business in 1867, it was still in a very incomplete state — meriting the oft-used description of 'an unfinished shack'. The station was not finished until January 1882, by which time it was LNWR property.

The LNWR went to considerable lengths to develop the traffic on the Central Wales line. It had, in fact, taken a close interest in through traffic from the start, the company's renowned Chairman, Richard Moon, having replied on 8 April 1870 to suggestions made by Mr J. Biddulph, the LR's Traffic Superintendent at Swansea:

'The early morning train to which you refer (the 6.30am) *is, I understand, the best train of the day from Swansea during the Summer for through traffic, and also accommodates your chief local stations, and with every year it will become more productive if only it be not disturbed. But our own experience shows that all train arrangements take some time to work out and become known and relied upon. Interfering with them spoils the ultimate profits resulting.*

'As regards the reduction of local fares, besides being an immediate loss as regard the direct payment to your company, it would create great confusion and difficulty to your neighbouring competitors, and no doubt provoke retaliation on their part. I venture therefore to hope that you will pause before taking such a step which we could not agree to extend to the Vale of Towy Joint Line'.

The LNWR also developed local passenger services in the Swansea area — to the north of Swansea the railway attracted more industries, the industries required manpower, and the men and their families needed a means of transport. Mutual benefits of a different kind were seen farther to the north. The 'Three Wells' — the spa towns of Llandrindod, Llangammarch and Llanwrtyd, which were served directly by the Central Wales line — and the not-too-distant Builth Wells all prospered after the coming of the railway. The heyday of the spa towns was, arguably, the 1890s and early 1900s, a slight decline having set in even before the outbreak of World War 1.

The increase in passenger traffic to and from the spa towns indirectly resulted in the introduction of through coaches. Before long, there were through carriages between Swansea and Manchester, Liverpool, York (mainly for mails) Birmingham and Euston. The LNWR's fares between Euston and

Above:
As a result of a pooling agreement between the LMSR and the GWR, the latter's engine shed at Llandovery closed in 1935 and the engines and staff were transferred to the nearby LMSR shed. This picture was taken on 30 May 1936, the then-disused GWR shed being visible behind the up platform. The shed remained *in situ* until August 1954, when it was sold to two railwaymen, albeit with the proviso that they take it away! The coaching stock behind GWR 0-6-0PT No 9766 rather fits the popular description of a mixed rake. It comprises a B set with a gas-lit clerestory coach — ageing clerestories were often added to provide extra accommodation for school parties or workmen. *R. M. Casserley Collection*

Below:
The 'Special DX' 0-6-0 and the train entering Bucknell is clearly a special working but, frustratingly, the writing on the headboard cannot be determined. The leading coach appears to be a 42ft eight-wheeler, the others seeming to be six-wheelers. Judging by the popularity of boaters, the date is probably the mid-1890s. *Lens of Sutton*

Right: The 'Black Fives' were the LMSR's 'go anywhere, do anything' main-line engines. The Central Wales line was one of their strongholds for over a quarter of a century (where wasn't it?) and, here, No 45143 is seen entering Llanwrda with the midday Shrewsbury–Swansea train on 7 July 1958. The engine displays the 84G shedplate of Shrewsbury depot. *H. C. Casserley*

Swansea were identical to those for the GWR's Paddington-Swansea services, despite the somewhat different route-mileage — to the LNWR almost anything that took traffic from the rival was worth the price! The parity of fares between the Euston–Swansea and Paddington–Swansea routes (and also the St Pancras-Swansea route), incidentally, was retained until Nationalisation.

A through carriage was advertised daily between Manchester and Carmarthen (via Llandilo and the Carmarthen branch), while on summer Saturdays a Liverpool–Pembroke Dock through carriage was introduced, primarily for holidaymakers to Tenby. The Pembroke Dock carriage ran on GWR metals between Carmarthen Town and Carmarthen Junction, the LNWR having secured running powers over that section (for coaching traffic only) in 1873. The Pembroke Dock through carriage was suspended during World War 1, but was reinstated in the summer of 1922. During the 1920s the carriage concerned was usually an ex-LNWR slip coach.

The Central Wales line also saw an increase in through goods traffic. At least one of the daily trains worked through to or from Garston, near Liverpool, while an overnight beer train worked through from Burton-on-Trent, the 'empties' (in more sense than one, perhaps) also making their return journey via the Central Wales line. At Swansea, the beer was stored under the arches adjacent to Victoria station.

Llandilo became a marshalling point for northbound fish trains, wagons from Swansea and Milford Haven (via the Carmarthen branch) being joined before starting on the rest of their journey. Another well-documented regular working was that of the cattle trains to Carmarthen on market days — Wednesdays and Saturdays.

Accidents

The Central Wales line had a comparatively good saftey record, but the occasional mishaps were almost inevitable. It is hoped that the more-sensitive among us do not find the following accounts too traumatic.

SWANSEA VICTORIA, 15 July 1872. Collision between train and shunting engine. Accident report by Col Yolland:

'The London & North Western 9.5 am Up passenger train consisted of an engine and tender and five vehicles, including the break-van (sic), *and when all was ready the station-master gave the signal for the train to start. The engine in front of the train had previously brought out one of the carriages and had placed it in front of the other four vehicles in the train, and to do this the facing points had to be set open to the siding while the signals were at danger.*

'When the signal to start was given by the station-master, and repeated by the guard of the passenger train, the engine-driver at once turned on the steam and proceeded, and although he admits that the signal was on he did not look to see whether the points were set right for the Up line, and it was not until he had proceeded some distance, and was travelling, according to his own account, at about eight miles an hour, that he discovered he was running up into the siding, instead of being on the Up line. As soon as he found out his mistake he shut off the steam, reversed the engine, and turned on the steam the reverse way, but he failed to stop his train until the engine had come into contact with the tender of the shunting engine, which was in motion on the siding, and proceeding in the opposite direction'.

Fortunately, a derailment was avoided and, although seven passengers were injured, none of the injuries were serious. The driver of the train engine was held responsible, although the reporting officer, Col Yolland, opined that *'there is no doubt that a loose system of working had crept into the station, as the signalman who attends to the signals at the platform is sometimes away from his post'*. It appears, however, that the LNWR had already apportioned blame, the driver concerned being suspended from 15 July (the day of the accident) until 3 August.

PONTARDULAIS, 19 August 1872. Partial derailment:

'As the 12.15pm London & North Western train, consisting of engine and tender, four coaches, and a break-van, from Swansea to Llandovery, was running into Pontardulais station (where it has to stop) at a speed of 6 or 7 miles an hour, the boy who was standing by the point lever suddenly pushed it over, so as to open the right-hand road, on which the engine of a goods train was standing. The driver called to the boy to let the lever go, but he allowed the engine and tender to pass through the points to the right-hand road, and then let them go, so that the carriages next to the tender took the left-hand or proper road. The engine stopped on coming into collision with the goods engine about 65 yards from the points; the front carriage and two following ones were dragged off the rails'.

Largely because of the low speed involved, there were no casualties. The boy who had changed the points was 13½ years-old and was employed by the Llanelly Railway which provided the station staff at Pontardulais. It was revealed that the boy had been in the company's service for 12 months, during which time he had had charge of gates and points at various stations and had also worked as telegraph boy and parcels deliverer. Somewhat predictably, the official report of the accident soundly condemned the practice of placing such a young lad in charge of facing points and level crossings.

LLANDILO, 22 November 1872. Train engine collided with stationary stock — two passengers slightly hurt:

'It has been customary to place some empty coaches, for attaching to a Carmarthen train, on the second line of rails to the north of the cross-over road. These empty coaches have usually been taken away before the London & North Western train arrived. On the day in question three carriages and a van were taken by the yard shunter with his horse to the north end of the station, to wait till the engine of the Carmarthen train should take them away.

'The shunter should have placed these coaches at the north side, clear of the cross-over road, but he left them where the van was foul of the cross-over road, and the engine of the London & North Western train as it arrived at Llandilo ran into the van and empty carriage next to it at a speed variously estimated at four to eight miles an hour. The engine and tender of the London & North Western train were thrown off the rails'.

The reporting officer, Lt-Col Rich, held the yard shunter responsible.

KNUCKLAS, 16 May 1874. Partial derailment:

'The 12.25pm Up passenger train from Swansea to the Craven Arms station consisted of an engine and tender, one third-class carriage, three composites, one van, one composite, and one van, making seven vehicles altogether. As it was approaching Knucklas station on a curve to the left after passing over a high viaduct, the driver, who was looking back from the left side of the engine on the inside of the curve, observed the left trailing wheels of the third vehicle from the tender (a composite carriage) drop inside the left rail. He immediately reversed the engine, sounded the whistle for the guards' breaks, caused the tender break to be applied, and did all in his power to stop.

'As soon as the train had been stopped, he went back to ascertain the cause of the accident. He could not discover anything wrong on the line, but the whole of the seven vehicles, with the exception of the third-class next to the tender, were off the rails, but all remained coupled together and to the engine'. Three passengers and one railway employee sustained bruising in the accident, but otherwise

The LNWR and, later, the LMSR did much to develop through goods traffic on the Central Wales line. The nature of the route, in particular, required the attentions of the best locomotives and it was the '8F' 2-8-0s which ultimately dominated. In this early 1960s picture, No 48761 enters Llangunllo station with a northbound goods. *Andrew Muckley*

After the upheavals of the 1870s, the LNWR and the GWR reluctantly learned to live with each other on the Llandovery-Pontardulais section of the Central Wales line. However, the relationship between the two companies didn't often extend to joint double-heading, and so the sight of an LNWR 5ft 6in 2-4-2T and a GWR 'Stella' 2-4-0 in tandem at Llandilo was not particularly common. This author was prepared to suggest that the double-header might have been for a special occasion, but in the *Welsh Railways Archive* magazine the late George Hookham propounds that the mixed double-header could have been a regular working, since the 9.45am Swansea-Llandilo had no obvious balanced working. The date, apparently, is 1908, and the 'Stella' is No 3204. *Lens of Sutton*

there were no injuries. The accident report suggested that excessive speed might have been the cause. It was pointed out that, as the composite carriages were all six-wheeled vehicles (each with a wheelbase of about 18ft), they were more likely to derail when travelling around sharp curves of 15ch radius at high speed. The reporting officer, Col Yolland, recommended that the line be doubled at Knucklas and have a second platform and catch points added: *'Knucklas passenger station is constructed on a steep incline of 1 in 60...and in the event of any vehicle breaking away from a Down train, when in the act of starting or otherwise, it might run all the way to Knighton...'* Despite Col Yolland's recommendation, the line through Knucklas station was never doubled.

BUILTH ROAD, 1 May 1877. The 9.15am passenger train from Swansea ran into a goods train which was standing in the siding. The official report necessarily included an outline of signalling procedures:

'Before an Up train is allowed to leave Cilmery station (the previous stopping place) *the signalman stationed there has to receive "line clear" from Builth Road, and "line clear" from Builth Road is not given until the telegraph clerk at Builth Road has communicated by means of gong signals with the signalman on duty at the Mid-Wales Junction* (250yd to the south of Builth Road station), *who acknowledges the gong signals by repeating them.*

'On the day of the accident "line clear" was given to Cilmery (for the Up passenger train), after the usual precautions had been taken at Builth Road, and when the line was actually clear and ready for the passenger train to leave Cilmery.

'After the signalman at the Mid-Wales Junction had replied to Builth Road station that the line was clear for the passenger train to approach, he pulled off his Up distant-signal and his Down home-signal. This mistake in pulling off the down home-signal was observed by one of the porters who was standing on the Builth Road station platform, who called the man's attention to his mistake by ringing the gong. The Down home-signal was put back to danger, and the Up home was lowered for the passenger train.

'The points did not require moving, but it was the junction man's duty to steady these points while the passenger train was passing through them; and he walked towards the points and laid hold of the lever handle with the intention of doing so, but instead of steadying them he pressed the lever down and moved the facing-points, so as to send the passenger train into the siding'.

As soon as the driver of the engine found that he had been routed into a siding he applied the brakes, but realising that the engine was not going to stop before hitting the goods train in the siding, he and his fireman jumped from the engine. The engine's speed prior to impact had been reduced to about 4mph, and that was sufficient to avoid any serious injuries to passengers.

SWANSEA VICTORIA, 1 September 1893. A passenger train from Craven Arms was due at Swansea at 7.45am. The engine was 2-4-2T No 214 and the train consisted of six carriages, all fitted with automatic vacuum brakes. The engine collided with the buffer stops — but it could have been an awful lot worse:

'As the driver (of the train from Craven Arms) *was approaching the Down home-signals of No.3 cabin, which are 399 yards from the stop-block, he saw a man step across from the siding adjacent to the*

goods shed, and stand close to the main line, almost in front of his engine. He says that he at once applied the brake full power, at the same time opening his whistle to warn the man of his danger. The latter appears to have turned round just as the engine reached him, but before he could get out of the way, he was knocked down by the left leading buffer of the engine, and thrown into the 6ft-way between the main line and the siding, and fortunately escaped without any injury. The attention of Driver Harvey (who was in charge of the train from Craven Arms) *was almost unavoidably diverted from his train by his natural anxiety to ascertain whether the man who was knocked down had sustained any serious injury. Instead of watching his train and looking ahead, he looked back, and seeing the man in the 6ft-way clear of the rails, he released his brake, and then looked back again and saw the man get up from the ground.*

'By this time Harvey's engine was entering the station, and he at once applied his brake full power, and finding that the train had gained too much speed he also reversed his engine, but these measures had not sufficient time to take effect, the platform being only 152 yards long, and the engine struck the buffer-stops'.

In his report for the Board of Trade, Maj Yorke sympathised with the driver's dilemma and placed no blame on him. The guard of the train came in for criticism, Maj Yorke opining that had the hand-brake been applied as per the rule-book, the train would have been slowed sufficiently for the collision with the buffer stops to have been averted.

Twentieth century traffic

Returning to the matter of train services on the Central Wales line, a fairly settled routine was eventually established. The Working Timetable for February 1913 (NB a *winter* month), for example, listed the following through passenger services on weekdays:

Dep Shrewsbury:	3.40am	11.30am	2.15pm	5.10pm
Arr Swansea:	7.55am	3.40pm	6.20pm	9.10pm

Dep Swansea:	6am	7.55am	9.45am	12.30pm	3pm	7pm
Arr Shrewsbury:	10.25am	11.28am	[1]	4.35pm	[2]	10.30pm

Notes: [1] Terminate at Craven Arms 1.24pm
[2] Terminate at Craven Arms 6.15pm

There were, of course, various local passenger workings as well. The same WTT showed that down services on the northern section of the line included two from Craven Arms to Builth Road, one to Knighton and one to Llandovery. The Llandovery train (8am ex-Craven Arms) was shown as stopping at Sugar Loaf Summit at 10.1am on Fridays to pick up if required. On Thursdays, a 4.20pm departure from Knighton was advertised to terminate at Llandrindod Wells at 5.10pm, the carriages continuing empty to Builth Road and the engine running light to Llandovery. In the up direction, there were two trains from Knighton to Craven Arms, one from Llandovery to Craven Arms and a Thursdays Only from Llandrindod Wells to Knighton.

Local passenger workings on the southern section included six trains each way between Pontardulais and Swansea (eight on Saturdays), one through from Llanmorlais to Swansea (two on Saturdays), two Saturday specials from Gorseinon to Swansea and a Saturdays Only Swansea–Llandovery train. GWR trains were also accommodated between Llandovery and Pontardulais. These included locals on the Brynamman branch, through workings to Llanelly and a Sundays Only 4.25pm passenger and milk train from Llangadock to Llanelly.

Among the through goods workings were the 11.20pm express mineral from Shrewsbury (arrive Swansea Goods Yard 8.30am), the 4.25am express goods from Shrewsbury (arrive 11.30am — worked by a 'D' class engine and limited to 40 vans plus a brake), the Saturday and Sunday night 10.15pm express goods ex-Crewe (depart 10.15pm, arrive Swansea 6.15am — worked by a 19in engine and restricted to 34 vans plus a brake) and a mineral train leaving Shrewsbury at 6.15am and arriving in Swansea at 5.25pm.

The through goods workings in the up direction were the 10.10am mineral train from Swansea to Shrewsbury (arrive 8.25pm — worked by a 'D' class

The 7.45am departure from Swansea (Victoria) for Shrewsbury had been a feature of the timetables since pre-Nationalisation days. On 7 June 1960 it was hauled by 'Black Five' No 45422, which is seen approaching Builth Road. The spectator on the down line is NOT a suicidal enthusiast — he is the lookout for the permanent way gang (who are standing by the 50mph sign).
Hugh Ballantyne

engine and limited to 34 wagons plus a 20-ton brake), the 6.15pm express goods from Swansea to Shrewsbury (arrive 1.20am), the 8.30pm express mineral (arrive Shrewsbury 4.25am), the 11pm mineral (arrive Shrewsbury 7.30am), and the midnight coal train (arrive Shrewsbury 8.15am). Local goods workings included the 7.20am mineral from Shrewsbury to Llandovery and the 9.30am goods from Craven Arms to Llandrindod Wells. On the southern section the various local GWR goods and mineral workings included those from the Glanamman and Mountain branches to Llanelly.

In the northbound direction, local goods workings included a 3.30am ballast train from Llandovery to Shrewsbury (Tuesdays/Thursdays/Saturdays Only), a 4.25am mineral train from Llandovery to Shrewsbury and a 9.30am from Llandovery to Llandrindod Wells. Cattle trains from Carmarthen arrived at Llandilo at 4.10pm and 7.55pm to be taken on to Shrewsbury and there were fish trains from Swansea (depart 5.10pm) to Llandovery and from Carmarthen via Llandilo to Shrewsbury.

For the record, the first working from Swansea Victoria each day was a train of colliery empties, which left at 4.40am for Birch Rock Siding, north of Gorseinon. The empties were, in fact, bound for Graig Merthyr Colliery which, prior to the laying of a standard gauge siding, *circa* 1900, was connected to Birch Rock by a tramway.

By July 1922 — the last summer before the Grouping — the public timetables advertised six through passenger services each way on weekdays:

Dep Shrewsbury:	3.30am	6.30am	11.45am	12.50pm	2.40pm	5.10pm
Arr Swansea:	8.12am	11.52am	4.28pm	5.15pm	6.58pm	9.30pm

Dep Swansea:	5.40am	8am	10.10am	12.30pm	2.35pm	6.25pm
Arr Shrewsbury:	11.10am	12.15pm	2.7pm	4.38pm	7.3pm	10.30pm

Through carriages were a conspicuous feature of those services. In the down direction, the 12.50pm ex-Shrewsbury had carriages from Liverpool (depart Lime Street 10.35am) and from Manchester (depart London Road 10.40am) to Pembroke Dock. The 2.40pm from Shrewsbury was even more cosmopolitan, as it had carriages from Euston (depart 11am), Liverpool (depart midday) and Manchester (depart 11.50am). On the 5.10pm from Shrewsbury, there were carriages from Liverpool (depart 2.45pm) and Manchester (depart 2.50pm).

In the up direction, the 8am ex-Swansea had through carriages for Liverpool (arrive 2.40pm), while the 10.10am from Swansea had through carriages not only for Liverpool (arrive 4.28pm) and Euston (arrive 6.25pm), but also from Pembroke Dock for Manchester (arrive at London Road at 4.17pm). The 6.25pm ex-Swansea had a through carriage for York. That service, irrespective of its actual timing, was known over the years as the 'York Mail'. At Llandilo, a through parcels van from Carmarthen was attached to the 'York Mail', that practice continuing until the closure of the Carmarthen branch in 1963. The local services advertised in the same 1922 timetable included Shrewsbury–Builth Road, Shrewsbury–Llandovery, Craven Arms–Knighton, Swansea–Pontardulais and Swansea-Gowerton workings, plus GWR trains on the Llandovery-Pontardulais section.

The LMSR era

At the Grouping in 1923, the LNWR became part of the LMSR. So did the Midland Railway, which also operated in and around Swansea. The LMSR effected a number of economies by dispensing with various duplications of staff and facilities, one of which was the combining of the LNWR and MR Traffic Superintendents' offices at Swansea. The anticipated annual saving to the LMSR was calculated at £3,036.

In 1925 it was proposed to concentrate the administration of the goods departments at Victoria station, thereby permitting the ex-Midland offices at Wind Street and Fabian Street to be vacated. Despite the need for increased office accommodation at Victoria at a cost of £3,558, the LMSR anticipated a subsequent annual saving of £1,526.

As for traffic, around 1924 the LMSR introduced a Carmarthen-Euston express, although the term 'express' might seem a little out of place on the timings normally associated with the Central Wales line. The Carmarthen–Llandilo leg was run non-stop, normally with a 2-4-2T in charge of four or five elderly coaches from various absorbed companies and, although the train often started empty from Carmarthen, it usually picked up a worthwhile amount of passenger traffic at the three spa towns along its route. The return working was even less auspicious, the carriages being attached to an ordinary branch working (the 6.10pm) from Llandilo.

Throughout the 25 years of the LMSR's existence, there were usually five trains each way between Craven Arms and Swansea on weekdays. Towards the end of the LMS era, the public timetables for the winter of 1946/47, for example, listed five through trains each way on weekdays:

Dep Shrewsbury:	3.55am	6.30am	12.30pm	2.40pm	5.30pm
Arr Swansea:	8.4am	11.28am	4.53pm	6.57pm	10.9pm

Dep Swansea:	6.15am	7.45am	10.5am	12.30pm	6.30pm
Arr Shrewsbury:	11.4am	11.36am	2.2pm	5.2pm	10.36pm

Of those, the 3.55am ex-Shrewsbury and the 6.30pm ex-Swansea both had through carriages to or from York.

Local workings were not a particularly strong feature of that 1946/47 timetable. Apart from

Above:
It might be thought that another 'pannier tank' picture could be asking for trouble from LNWR and LMSR enthusiasts, but devotees of Crewe engineering might enjoy speculating whether any of this ex-GWR engine's steam actually managed to reach the cylinders. There seems to be a slight loss. The engine is No 9621, the location is Llanwrda and the date is between January 1962 and October 1964, the loop having been taken out on the former date and the engine withdrawn on the latter. *Andrew Muckley*

Below:
While the approach to Sugar Loaf might have given several generations of railway travellers a visual treat, footplate crews didn't view the climb in quite such a kindly light. Again, here is a picture that could have been taken almost any time between 1937 and 1964 — it was, in fact, taken on 26 May 1962 and shows an '8F' 2-8-0 at the head of a northbound goods. *R. O. Tuck*

Above:
Apart from the coaching stock and the locomotive's five-digit number, this scene at Llanwrtyd Wells could have been taken at any time between 1937 and 1964. But it was, of course, taken in BR days, by which time the ex-LMSR '8Fs' had become well established on the Central Wales line. The engine appears to be No 48436. *Hugh Davies Collection*

Below:
A southbound goods train, hauled by '8F' No 48369, emerges from Llangunllo Tunnel on 16 May 1964.
B. J. Ashworth

Left: The Llandilo-Carmarthen section was taken over by ex-GWR motive power very soon after Nationalisation, but that did little to change the delightful nature of the branch. This view of a one-coach Carmarthen-bound train at Dryslwyn was taken on 3 September 1963. *Andrew Muckley*

Left: For many years, Webb's delightful 5ft 6in 2-4-2Ts monopolised the Carmarthen branch passenger workings. No 6619 poses alongside a classmate outside Carmarthen shed on 1 June 1936. The engine was withdrawn in May 1947. *Courtesy: LNWR Society*

Swansea–Pontardulais services there were only the 1.55pm from Craven Arms to Llandovery — leave Llandovery at 6.5pm for Shrewsbury — and the GWR trains between Llandovery and Pontardulais.

The Carmarthen branch

Until the late 1930s services on the Carmarthen branch usually comprised five or six trains each way on weekdays, a regular feature of pre-Grouping working timetables (at least) being that the first and last trains of the day from Llandilo to Carmarthen were mixed goods and passenger. For much of the branch's pre-Nationalisation life it was worked by LNWR 2-4-2Ts. Six-wheeled carriages were the norm until after the Grouping, when two pairs of ex-North Staffordshire bogie coaches became the regular branch sets.

During World War 2 the branch passenger service comprised only three trains each way, but after the war a service of five each way was reinstated. The branch accommodated local and through goods traffic. The locally-generated traffic was mainly agricultural — produce and cattle — while the through traffic included an afternoon fish train from Carmarthen which, on arriving at Llandilo, was joined to a Swansea fish train before continuing northwards.

A glimpse into the future?

Very shortly after World War 2, the GWR proposed

major changes at Swansea. These centred on alterations to its High Street station, part of the plan being modifications to the approach lines to permit LMSR trains on the Central Wales line to be diverted from Victoria station to High Street. The plan also allowed for the diversion of trains from the ex-Midland station at St.Thomas into High Street.

Representatives of the GWR and LMSR attended a meeting at Swansea on 26 March 1946 to discuss the proposals in detail. The minutes noted that:

'There is a small transfer of passengers between High Street and Victoria which increases in the summer...To those who have to change stations — and they would be mainly holiday-makers to and from the area known as "The Wells" — a Central Station would be a great convenience, but there is little or no actual evidence of any demand by travellers for such a facility.

'The creation of a Central Station is a physical feasibility and could be effected by a new junction between the two Companies' lines at Gowerton to accommodate the Central Wales Passenger trains...thus enabling trains which now run to and from Victoria to run to and from High Street where additional accommodation for their reception would be necessary.

'If all the trains now running into and out of Victoria and St.Thomas stations are transferred to High Street, the additional number would be approximately 21 in and 21 out, but some 7 or 8 would cease to run owing to the altered circumstances. Siding accommodation would be required for 42 coaches. It would also be necessary for 13 L.M.S. Passenger Locomotives to be transferred to the G.W. Locomotive Depot at Landore.

'The diversion of the L.M.S. Passenger trains to High Street means, among other things, the withdrawal of a train service between Gowerton L.M.S. and Swansea Victoria, and although a local

If the postwar discussions between the LMSR and the GWR had borne fruit, this scene would have disappeared long before 1964. As related in the text, in 1946 it was proposed to close the Swansea Bay line and re-route traffic into Swansea (High Street). That, however, didn't happen and so the sight of a train passing along the shoreline after leaving Swansea Bay station *en route* for Swansea was retained for another 18 years. An almost permanent feature of the Swansea Bay section was a liberal helping of sand, but the 'mini-beach' seen on the lineside in this picture was nothing when compared to the quantities which sometimes accumulated. *Andrew Muckley*

In its postwar 'rationalisation' proposals (see text), the LMSR referred to the household coal traffic in the Swansea area. The planned economies of 1946 didn't take place — at least, not for several years! — and so the coal traffic remained. This picture of the exterior of Swansea Bay station was taken on 18 August 1959, and clearly shows that coal was still in demand. Among the many items of interest is the track of the Swansea & Mumbles Tramway, the cricket ground and — for those who remember the frustration of air-controlled windscreen wipers — a Ford Thames van in the station forecourt. *Welsh Industrial & Maritime Museum*

service between Gowerton and Mumbles Road could be provided, it is the view of the L.M.S. District Manager that it would not be worth while and he anticipates the closing of the stations at Gowerton, Dunvant, Killay, Mumbles Road, Swansea Bay and Victoria on the Central Wales Line'.

As the minutes of the meeting unfold, it becomes increasingly obvious that considerable homework had been undertaken all round:

'The resulting total loss in passenger revenue on the Central Wales Line is anticipated as £50,446.

'The removal of the railway from the sea front means cutting off the access to the L.M.S. Beach Freight Marshalling Sidings and Locomotive Shed.

'All the Freight Traffic for and out of Swansea L.M.S. is dealt with at the Beach Sidings where approximately 15 outwards trains per day are marshalled and about the same number of inwards trains are received. An alternative method is to reproduce some of the Beach Sidings and Engine Shed at Upper Bank, and transfer the work and the Staff of the Beach Sidings to that point.

'The arrangements would be that L.M.S. Freight trains now starting from Beach Sidings for Central Wales via Mumbles Road and Pontardulais, would start fully formed and marshalled from Upper Bank, travel up the Swansea Vale Line, which would be doubled between Upper Bank and a point near Llansamlet, and by means of a new connection near Llansamlet L.M.S. and Felin Fran G.W., would pass on to the G.W. District Line and run via Llangyfelach and Pont Lliw as far as Graig Merthyr and by means of a new connection pass on to the L.M.S. line near Pontardulais.

'Local L.M.S. Freight trains today convey traffic for Gowerton, Llanmorlais, Pontardulais, Dunvant etc., and under the altered routing of through trains such traffic would have to be picked up and put off at Pontardulais. The Siding room there is very limited and provision of two Up side sidings and some extension of the Down side accommodation would be essential at an estimated cost of £10,500.

'It would also be necessary to stable probably two L.M.S. engines at Llanelly Dock for the purpose of local working in the Pontardulais area.

'There is a considerable household coal mileage traffic dealt with at Mumbles Road, Swansea Bay and Victoria — 236 wagons in November 1945 — also at Killay, 40 wagons, and at Dunvant 7 wagons per month. It is pretty safe to assume that strong opposition will be offered by the Coal Merchants concerned.'

As the history books show, most of those plans were not implemented. The old Midland Railway station at St Thomas was closed to passenger traffic in September 1950, but Victoria station and the Swansea Bay route were left open — at least, for the time being.

The camaraderie displayed by the GWR and LMSR at Swansea in 1946 was admirable, but those two concerns had only a very short time left as British Railways took over lock, stock and barrel on 1 January 1948. Initially, there were relatively few outward signs of change on the Central Wales line, but that state of affairs did not last for long. The 1950s brought various changes but, before looking at how the character of the line was affected, attention must be turned to the locomotives which had worked the line during LNWR and LMSR days — and earlier.

The Locomotives

The Central Wales line is usually associated with LNWR and, later, LMSR forms of motive power. The first section of the route to open — and also later appendages — were, however, nominally worked by a company which was ultimately taken over by the Great Western Railway.

The Llanelly Railway Engines

The first engines to work on the embryonic Central Wales line were those of the Llanelly Railway. The LR's locomotive stock can be charitably described as a motley collection of primitive machines although, in fairness, it should be emphasised that when the company's first engines were delivered in 1839, locomotive engineering was still a fairly new science.

The LR's locomotives of 1839 were 0-6-0s named *Victoria* and *Albert*, built by the famous Timothy Hackworth at Shildon, in County Durham. Little is known about the machines, except that they originally had 4ft-diameter coupled wheels, 14¼in x 16in inside cylinders (at the trailing end), boiler pressures of 80lb, and weighed 14 tons. Each locomotive had its furnace, smokebox and chimney at one end of the boiler and its combustion chamber at the other end; consequently the driver and fireman stood at opposite ends of the engine — some 12ft apart.

Victoria was withdrawn for ballasting work in 1856. It appears that it was altered sometime during its life, as the official report of its boiler explosion at Pantyffynnon in January 1858 referred to an engine weighing 18 tons. The story of *Albert* is even more vague, little being heard about it until it was offered for sale in 1859. Its reserve price of £200 failed to attract buyers and, two months later, a reduction to £80 seems not to have created any greater interest. The engine was finally disposed of in 1861, when it was exchanged for a truck.

Later engines included a new 0-6-0 from Messrs Fossick & Hackworth, which was delivered in 1842 and continued working (albeit erratically) on the LR until 1859 when it was leased to the Mynydd Mawr Co at Cross Hands. Another 0-6-0 was assembled by the LR in premises at Llanelly which had been rented for the purpose, the work commencing late in 1840 and finishing in May 1843. The home-built engine was named *Prince of Wales* and it was constructed to burn anthracite coal — the usual fuel of the period being coke — but the experiment was unsuccessful. Nevertheless, after being extensively modified between 1854 and 1856, a diet of coal proved far more to the machine's liking. It worked on the LR as a coal-burner, apparently giving reasonable satisfaction, until being sold in 1872.

The LR acquired three Bury 0-4-0s from the LNWR between 1847 and 1855, two of them later being rebuilt as 0-4-2s at Llanelly. A pair of comparatively modern-looking Beyer Peacock 0-4-2s arrived in 1857 and two new 0-6-0s were ordered from Fossick & Hackworth in 1858. One of those 0-6-0s was converted to an 0-8-0T in 1871 and later became GWR No 902; in 1877 it was sold by the GWR to the Landore Siemens Steel Co.

The activities of the engines so far described are very sparsely documented. Thus it might be assumed that they performed a fair proportion of their duties on the Llanelly-Garnant line and not only the section which ultimately formed part of the Central Wales line proper. However, one early locomotive which had an unmistakable 'Central Wales' pedigree was *Towy*, a tank engine used by the contractor for the Vale of Towy Railway. The LR purchased *Towy* from the contractor early in 1858 but, less than a year later, offered the engine for sale at a reserve price of £275.

A passenger 0-4-2 and a goods 0-6-0 were delivered by Fossick & Hackworth in 1860, the order for the engines having been placed soon after the opening of the Llandilo-Llandovery (Vale of Towy) section, which the LR nominally worked. In May 1864, the impending completion of the Llandilo–Carmarthen branch prompted the acquisition of additional engines. They included a pair of 2-4-0s, named *Loughor* and *Amman*, which were built by Messrs Hopkins, Gilkes of Middlesbrough. It is believed that those two engines were intended mainly for use on the Carmarthen branch. *Amman* was converted to a tender engine at Llanelly in 1871 and, as GWR No 900, survived until 1884.

Of the LR's subsequent acquisitions, Kitson-built 2-4-0 *Napoleon III* (delivered in May 1868) definitely worked on the Llandovery section, a report of an accident near Glanrhyd on 31 October 1868 noting that the engine had derailed and overturned after a wheel tyre had broken. That was by no means the only mishap to befall the engine as, during its early life, it achieved notoriety by setting fire to the countryside with disconcerting regularity.

The LR's final acquisitions — six Beyer Peacock 0-6-0s delivered in 1868/70 — were also used on the Llandovery section. Twenty-one of the LR's locomotives were active in 1873 when the GWR took over what was left of the old LR network. They became GWR Nos 894-914, but several were retired within a few years, and all but one of the others were dispensed with by 1886. The tenuous one was *Napoleon III* which, as GWR No 894, soldiered on until the end of 1906 when it was withdrawn from Chester.

Although reference has been made to the locomotives of the Llanelly Railway, a degree of qualification is in order. From February 1850, the LR was worked and maintained under contract by Messrs Ianson, Fossick & Hackworth, but the seven-year contract was terminated prematurely in August 1853. A working arrangement was later agreed with Joseph Hepburn, who had been the contractor's Locomotive Superintendent.

The motive power for the LR's new lines — the Pontardulais–Swansea section and the Carmarthen branch — was to have been supplied by Messrs Watson & Overend, the contractors who had been engaged to construct those lines, but in 1866 they were declared insolvent. It appears that Joseph Hepburn subsequently assumed responsibility for all the LR's motive power requirements, that state of affairs lasting until 1868. Hepburn's operating costs were 7½d (3p) per train mile for goods and 5¾d (2½p) for passenger work — about a tenth of what it costs to run an ordinary saloon car these days!

After the GWR took over part of the LR system in 1873, the replacements for the ex-LR engines included '517' class 0-4-2Ts, the ubiquitous 'Metro' class 2-4-0Ts, various standard 0-6-0STs, and 'Dean Goods' 0-6-0s. From the 1890s 'Stella' class 2-4-0s started to appear on the line after the transfer of many of the class from their old haunts in Cornwall.

There are reports of ex-Manchester & Milford and Port Talbot Railway 2-4-2Ts being used on the GWR-owned sections of the Central Wales line after those two companies had been taken over by the GWR in 1906 and 1908 respectively. The ex-M&M engines were GWR Nos 1304 *Plynlimmon* and 1306 *Cader Idris*, which are thought to have worked in from the Carmarthen direction; the ex-PTR locomotive retained its original number (36) until the Grouping, when it became GWR No 1326. It is also thought that, in 1908, Llanelly's steam railmotor had its usual workmens' turns on the Gwaun-cae-Gurwen branch interrupted in the afternoons by a school service from Llandilo to Ammanford.

The GWR engines were, of course, usually restricted to the Llandilo–Pontardulais section and the jointly-owned Vale of Towy section between Llandovery and Llandilo. The motive power for the rest of the line was provided by the LNWR which, as we have seen, was the other joint owner of the Vale of Towy section and also enjoyed running powers over GWR metals between Llandilo and Pontardulais.

As has already become very evident, GWR-style motive power was a common feature on much of the southern section of the Central Wales line. On 13 July 1956, the 8.20am Llanelly–Llandovery service was hauled by 0-6-0PT No 3761 — it is seen at Llangadock station, on what used to be the joint GWR/LMSR Vale of Towy section. *H. C. Casserley*

And even more pannier tanks — the token is changed as the 7.35am ex-Llanelly, hauled by No 8749, crosses the 8.25am ex-Llandovery, in the charge of No 9621. It seems that the location is the disused Derwydd Road station, which closed to passenger traffic in 1954. *Leslie Sandler*

The LNWR engines

The Craven Arms–Llandovery section of the Central Wales line was worked from the outset by the LNWR which, of course, ultimately operated right through to Swansea. That said, one of the local companies which made up the LNWR section, the Knighton Railway, actually had a locomotive of its own. This was a Beyer Peacock 0-4-2ST of 1861 named, appropriately, *Knighton*. It was taken into LNWR stock in July 1864 (as LNWR No 1328), but was transferred to the duplicate list in November 1865 (as No 1115) and sold to Messrs Partridge & Jones of Pontypool in May 1869.

The LNWR initially used various types of 2-2-2s and 2-4-0s for passenger services on the Central Wales line. From 1866, freight services were usually entrusted to Ramsbottom's 'DX' class 0-6-0s — one of the most numerous types ever to appear in Britain. The successors of the 'DXs' were Francis Webb's famous 'Cauliflower' 0-6-0s, introduced in 1880. Officially designated '18in Goods' (on account of their cylinder diameter), the better-known nickname was derived from the company crest being carried on their splashers. Throughout the LNWR network, the 'Cauliflowers' were frequently used on passenger workings as well as goods turns, and they performed their fair share of passenger work on the Central Wales line.

Webb's 'Precedent' class 2-4-0s (also known as 'Jumbos') later took over most of the Central Wales

Classic LNWR — a fine portrait of a 'Cauliflower' 0-6-0. Although officially designated '18in Goods', the better-known nickname was derived from the company crest on the splashers, a more dignified nickname for the class being 'Crested Goods'. They were designed by Francis Webb and 310 were built between 1880 and 1902. No less than 75 were still active at the time of Nationalisation and the last three were retired in December 1955. They were constructed at Crewe. The 'Cauliflowers' were all-purpose engines and were familiar sights on the Central Wales line for decades. This well-scrubbed example, No 930, was built in February 1890, later had its cylinder diameter reduced to 17in and was withdrawn in August 1927. *Ian Allan Library*

Above: In what is probably a posed shot, an immaculate but sadly unidentified LNWR 'Special DX' 0-6-0 waits at Broome *circa* 1890 with an impressive assortment of rolling stock (headed by a horse box). The 'Special DXs' and 'Cauliflowers' were not dissimilar, but the footplate arrangement of each type provides a ready means of differentiating between the two. The signalbox on the left, incidentally, was replaced in 1901 by a new box at the Knighton end of the up platform. *Lens of Sutton*

Below: Like the 'Cauliflowers' Webb's 5ft 6in 2-4-2Ts had a long association with the Central Wales line, and a pair of the 2-4-2Ts was still resident at Swansea (Paxton Street) shed at Nationalisation. At the other end of the line, No 46727 was photographed at Craven Arms on 10 September 1949, the position of the lamp on the engine's front bufferbeam indicating that it was performing station pilot duties. *H. C. Casserley*

This excellent study shows 5ft 6in 2-4-2T No 6740 at Carmarthen station on 17 June 1939. The engine was built in April 1891 and was withdrawn in May 1948. Had it been reliveried by British Railways, it would have worn No 46740. *Courtesy: LNWR Society*

Several of the LNWR's '19in Goods' 4-6-0s were used on the Central Wales line over a period of several years, but it cannot be confirmed whether this example — LMSR No 8834 — was one of those which worked the line. A fine picture of a type which had strong 'Central Wales' links, nevertheless. *Ian Allan Library*

'G2A' Class 7F No 49035 bore witness to the complex family tree of the LNWR 0-8-0s. Built in 1898 as an 'A' class compound, it was rebuilt in 1908 as a 'D' class simple, upgraded in 1929 to 'G1' specifications and in 1949 was modified as a 'G2A'. It was photographed at Swansea (Paxton Street) shed, on 17 April 1955, and was retired in January 1957. *R. E. Vincent*

An extract from the LNWR working timetable for February 1913. *Courtesy: Bryan Wilson*

Shunting and Banking Engines Central Wales and Swansea District.

No. of Engines employed	Station.	Description of Engine.	Description of Work.	Commence Work.	Finish Work.	Meal Hours	Time. Mins.
1	Swansea	Shunting	Goods Yard and Coach Shunting. Remanned 2.30 p.m. daily and 11.45 p.m. Saturdays excepted.	Mon. a.m. 4 0	Sat. midnig't 12 0	...	...
1	Swansea	Shunting	Beach Sidings Remanned 2.30 p.m.	a.m. 5 30	p.m. 11 30	...	...
1	Swansea	Special Shunting	South Dock Shipping.	As required		...	...
1	Gorseinon.	Engine from Swansea attached to 6.15 a.m. from Swansea.	Yard Shunting	a.m. 7 30	p.m. 11 0	Sats. excepted	...
			Remanned 2.30 p.m. daily.	a.m. 7 30	p.m. 9 0	Sats. only	...
1	Pontardulais	Shunting	Joint Yard Shunting (extra Engine)	a.m. 6 45	p.m. 3 0	...	...
1	Llandovery.	Banking.	Banking Regular Trains as per Diagram. Special Banking arranged by Loco. Dept.	...	...	...	...
1	Builth Road.	Banking	Banking Regular Trains as per Diagram. Special Banking arranged by Loco. Dept.	...	...	...	...
1	Knighton	Banking	Banking Regular Trains as per Diagram. Special Banking arranged by Loco. Dept.	...	...	...	...

Shunting and Banking Performed by Train Engines.

Station.	Time.	By Engine of
Swansea	7.55 p.m. to 8.30 p.m., Midland Traffic.	7.0 p.m. from Pontardulais.
	9.30 a.m. to 12.30 p.m. (S.O.) Carriage shunting.	8.50 a.m. from Pontardulais.
	3.40 p.m. to 5.15 p.m. (S.O.) Carriage shunting.	3.5 p.m. from Llanmorlais.
	5.45 p.m. to 7.45 p.m. (S.O.) Carriage shunting.	4.55 p.m. from Pontardulais.
	10.45 p.m. to 12.0 night (S.O.) Carriage shunting.	10.10 p.m. E.C. from Pontardulais
	10.0 p.m. to 11.30 p.m. (S.O.) Carriage shunting.	9.15 p.m. from Pontardulais.
Dunvant	9.30 a.m. to 11.0 a.m.	4.40 a.m. Assistant Engine from Swansea.
	11.35 a.m. to 12.40 p.m.	9.30 a.m. from Pontardulais.
Gowerton	9.0 a.m. to 10.15 a.m. (S.O.)	8.35 a.m. from Llanmorlais (SO).
	1.15 p.m. to 3.15 p.m. (S.)	12.30 p.m. from Pontardulais (S).
	7.0 p.m. to 8.30 p.m. (S O).	6.30 p.m. from Llanmorlais (SO).
	8.0 p.m. to 9.20 p.m. (S).	2.15 p.m. from Swansea (S).
Llanmorlais	11.0 a.m. to 11.30 a.m. (SO).	10.30 a.m. from Gowerton (SO).
	11.40 a.m. to 12.30 p.m. (S).	10.15 a.m. from Gowerton (S).
Gorseinon	12.45 noon to 2.30 p.m., (Sats. exc.)	11.35 a.m. from Swansea (S).
	12.35 p.m. to 2.15 p.m. (S.O.)	11.15 a.m. from Swansea (S O)
	5.15 p.m. to 7.15 p.m. (S).	4.15 p.m. from Swansea (S).
Llanelly	5.50 a.m. to 11.0 a.m.	5.30 a.m. from Swansea
	4.5 p.m. to 6.45 p.m. (S.)	11.0 a.m. from Swansea (S)
Carmarthen	3.0 p.m. to 4.0 p.m. (S).	12.40 p.m. from Llandilo (S)
	9.0 a.m. to 9.45 a.m. (S O).	7.45 a.m. from Llandilo (SO).
Llandrindod Wells	12.15 p.m. to 2.20 p.m.	9.30 a.m. from Craven Arms.

line passenger services, while 'Newton' class 2-4-0s, which had been introduced by Ramsbottom in 1866 and perpetuated by Webb, were, despite their 6ft 7½in driving wheels, occasionally used on through goods workings. Shunting duties and local goods turns were usually handled by 0-4-0STs or 'Special Tank' 0-6-0STs, the latter type (a tank version of the 'DXs') being, once again, a Ramsbottom design perpetuated by Webb.

By the turn of the century Webb's 5ft 6in 2-4-2Ts monopolised the through passenger workings, but although those engines were very well respected (several actually survived until the 1950s) their 1,347gall tank capacities were not altogether ideal for duties on the Central Wales line. From about 1911, Charles Bowen-Cooke's new '2665' class 4-6-2Ts, which had 1,700gall tanks, started to replace the 2-4-2Ts on through workings. The 2-4-2Ts were then largely relegated to local duties, which they shared with Webb's famous 'Coal Tank' 0-6-2Ts.

It is widely believed that at least one of George Whale's 'Experiment' 4-6-0s worked a Shrewsbury–Swansea passenger train just before the Grouping. This writer is unable to offer confirmation, but it is just possible that there might be a degree of confusion over that suggestion. The '19in Goods' 4-6-0s, which were often referred to as 'Experiment Goods', were certainly working between Shrewsbury and Swansea by 1913, if not before. Indeed, the Working Timetables for 1913 show that an 'express goods' — which left Crewe at 10.15pm on Saturday and Sunday nights and was scheduled to arrive at Swansea Goods Yard at 6.15am — was rostered to a '19in engine'. Could it be feasible that the reported appearance of an 'Experiment' was, in fact, the unusual sight of an 'Experiment Goods' on a Central Wales passenger train?

The continuing increase in goods and mineral traffic on the Central Wales line eventually required something a little more modern and powerful than the ageing 'DX' 0-6-0s. Bowen-Cooke's 'G1' class two-cylinder superheated 0-8-0s provided the solution soon after their introduction in 1912. The LNWR's first 0-8-0s had been built to a Webb design in 1892 and eventually spawned several different types. In later years the rebuilding, upgrading, and reclassification of numerous engines of various types resulted in one of the most complex family trees of any British locomotive design.

The tank version of Bowen-Cooke's earlier 'G' class 0-8-0s — the '1185' class 0-8-2Ts which were introduced in 1911 — eventually appeared on the Central Wales line. So did the '380' class 0-8-4Ts, which were designed by Bowen-Cooke's successor, Maj Hewitt Pearson Montague Beames, in LNWR days but not delivered until after the Grouping. Beames's 0-8-4Ts were based on Bowen-Cooke's 0-8-0s and, although initially intended for the Merthyr, Tredegar & Abergavenny section, they were to have a lengthy association with the Central Wales line. Another Beames design, the 'G2' 0-8-0s of 1921/22 which were based on Bowen-Cooke's 0-8-0s but had higher boiler pressures, first appeared on the Central Wales line in 1923, and by 1925 they were in regular use.

LMSR days

At the Grouping in 1923, the LNWR came under the control of the LMSR. The ex-LNWR faction soon felt somewhat aggrieved by the LMSR's seemingly blatant Midland bias — after all, the LNWR had positively revelled in its nickname of 'The Premier Line'. The Midland influence was soon seen throughout much of the LMSR empire, but the Central Wales line managed to maintain a respectable proportion of its LNWR pedigree. That said, the line was certainly not immune to changes.

The domination of Bowen-Cooke's 4-6-2Ts on the Central Wales line lasted only until the late 1920s,

Above: The LNWR's '1185' class 0-8-2Ts were tank versions of the 'G' class 0-8-0s and some were used on the Central Wales line. Only four of the class survived long enough to carry their allotted BR numbers, No 47884 being one of them. It must be emphasised that this picture was NOT taken at a Central Wales line engine shed, the 0-8-2Ts having departed from the route by the BR era. A clue as to the location of this picture can, however, be found! *Ian Allan Library*

Below: The first of Beames's 0-8-4Ts to be delivered was No 380, which entered traffic in February 1923. The class was intended primarily for duties in South Wales, but several were allocated elsewhere from new and, later, Edge Hill shed at Liverpool had around 10 of the class. This official portrait shows the engine's LNWR number, but the logo on the tanks confirms that it did not enter traffic until after the Grouping. *Ian Allan Library*

Above: The LMSR's Fowler 2-6-4Ts first appeared on the Central Wales line in 1928. No 42305 (ex-LMSR No 2305) was one of the later arrivals, being transferred to Swansea (Paxton Street) shed from Wigan in June 1948. It is seen bringing the 7.45am Swansea-Shrewsbury train into Craven Arms on 10 September 1949. *H. C. Casserley*

Below: Beames 0-8-4T No 7956 entered traffic in November 1923 and was withdrawn in November 1948. It did not carry its allotted BR number of 47956. It spent the last years of its life at Paxton Street shed in Swansea, having been transferred there in November 1944 — this picture of the engine at Swansea is believed to have been taken in 1946. *C. R. L. Coles*

Fowler 2-6-4Ts at Swansea (Paxton Street) shed

It has often been stated that the Fowler tanks had a long and unbroken association with Swansea (Paxton Street) shed. However, information collated by Mr Bryan Wilson from lists supplied by Steam Archive Services proves otherwise. As can be gleaned from the following table, there was a time when the shed had *no* Fowler tanks.

Loco	Date in	From	Date out	To
2305	12.6.48	Wigan L&Y	29.8.59	Landore
2307	3.10.42	Shrewsbury	16.10.43	Shrewsbury
2307	3.8.46	Shrewsbury	16.7.55	Neyland
2307	5.11.55	Neyland	29.8.59	Landore
2315	28.7.28	Stafford	31.10.28	Shrewsbury
2316	28.7.28	Longsight	31.10.28	Shrewsbury
2317	28.7.28	Longsight	11.11.33	Carnforth
2318	28.7.28	Longsight	11.11.33	Tebay
2319	7.7.28	Lancaster	11.11.33	Longsight
2320	31.10.28	Stafford	23.5.36	Stafford
2321	7.7.28	Crewe Nth.	25.11.39	Stafford
2322	7.7.28	Shrewsbury	15.6.35	Plaistow
2323	11.3.50	Stoke	13.5.50	Stoke
2354	14.5.30	Stoke	1.1.38	Kentish Tn.
2360	11.7.42	Shrewsbury	15.3.47	Stoke
2362	18.5.32	Lancaster	1.6.32	Carnforth
2362	3.8.46	Shrewsbury	20.12.47	Wigan L&Y
2381	30.5.42	Longsight	20.12.47	Wigan L&Y
2385	30.5.42	Longsight	29.8.59	Landore
2387	27.7.46	Shrewsbury	29.8.59	Landore
2388	30.5.42	Longsight	16.7.55	Neyland
2388	10.9.55	Neyland	19.8.59	Landore
2390	30.5.42	Crewe Nth.	29.8.59	Landore
2392	30.5.42	Crewe Nth.	31.10.42	Crewe Nth.
2394	30.5.42	Crewe Nth.	29.8.59	Landore
2402	11.11.33	Carnforth	25.4.36	Edge Hill
2403	11.11.33	Tebay	22.6.35	Kentish Tn.
2404	11.11.33	Longsight	8.2.36	Shrewsbury
2404	26.9.42	Shrewsbury	16.10.43	Shrewsbury

when they were replaced by Henry Fowler's new LMSR 2-6-4Ts. Swansea shed received no less than eight of the 2-6-4Ts in July 1928, although two of those were transferred to Shrewsbury four months later. The allocation lists for Craven Arms shed for 3 July 1929, incidentally, included two of the Fowler tanks, Nos 2349/50.

The last 4-6-2T to leave the Central Wales line was No 6988 which, by September 1929, had been transferred to Warwick for working the Nuneaton–Coventry–Leamington route. Another post-Grouping change was that ex-Midland '1F' 0-6-0Ts and, from about 1924, new LMSR '3F' 0-6-0Ts ('Jinties') started to replace some of the older LNWR shunting engines.

In the 1930s, significant comings and goings included the transfer of '19in Goods' Nos 8721/22 and 0-8-0s Nos 8951 and 9051 to Swansea in June 1930, where the latter joined four of their classmates. In July 1933 two of Swansea's last three 'Special Tanks', Nos 7342/62, were transferred to Shrewsbury and Holyhead respectively. Also in July 1933, '19in Goods' 4-6-0s Nos 8708/21 were transferred *from* Swansea while 0-8-0s Nos 8893, 8930, 9058 and 9367 were moved *to* Swansea. Two of Swansea's three 'Cauliflower' 0-6-0s, Nos 8621/24, were withdrawn in 1933 — the third, No 8622, was to survive until 1955 (as BR No 58430) although, by then, it had left Swansea. In November 1933 three of Swansea's resident Fowler 2-6-4Ts, Nos 2317-19 (which had been allocated there in July 1928), were exchanged for Nos 2402-04, which had side-window cabs.

Two of the LMSR's Horwich-built 'Crab' 2-6-0s, Nos 13086/88, were allocated to Swansea in May 1934, although the former stayed only for three

Above: Ex-Midland '1F' 0-6-0T No 1676 spent several years at Swansea and, although still there at the time of Nationalisation, was withdrawn in February 1949 without carrying its designated BR number of 41676. It was photographed on empty stock duties at Victoria station on 27 June 1938 — note the station's intact roof.
H. C. Casserley

Below: Fowler 2-6-4T No 2390 (later BR No 42390) was transferred to Swansea (Paxton Street) shed from Crewe North in May 1942 and remained on Paxton Street's books until the shed closed in August 1959. It was photographed on 27 August 1948.
H. C. Casserley

Name of Signal-Box.		Closed: Weekdays From	Closed: Weekdays To	Closed: Week-ends From	Closed: Week-ends To
SWANSEA (VICTORIA) TO PONTARDULAIS JUNCTION (G.W.R.).					
Swansea (Victoria)	No. 3	10.45 p.m.	5.30 a.m.	10.45 p.m. Sat.	5.30 a.m. Mon.
,,	No. 2	1. 0 a.m.	4. 0 a.m.	2. 0 a.m. Sun.	5.30 a.m. Mon.
,,	No. 1	—	—	Last train Sun. Morning	5.30 a.m. Mon.
Swansea Bay	No. 2	—	—	Last train Sun. Morning	5.30 a.m. Mon.
,,	No. 1	Open as required.			
Mumbles Road	Station	9.50 p.m.	6. 0 a.m.	9.50 p.m. Sat.	6. 0 a.m. Mon.
		9.10 a.m.	10. 0 a.m.		
Killay	Station	Open as required.			
Dunvant	Station	12.10 a.m.	6.20 a.m.	10.30 p.m. Sat.	6.20 a.m. Mon.
Gowerton	No. 2	—	—	Last train Sun. Morning.	5.0 a.m. Mon.
,,	Glassbrook's Colliery	Open as required			
,,	No. 1 Elba Steel Works	5. 0 p.m.	8.30 a.m	Last train Sat.	8.30 a.m. Mon.
Gorseinon	No. 2	—	—	Last train Sun. Morning	5.0 a.m. Mon.
,,	No. 1	10.40 p.m.	7. 0 a.m.	10.40 p.m. Sat.	7. 0 a.m. Mon.
,,	Grovesend Colliery Siding	10.10 p.m.	7.30 a.m.	10.10 p.m. Sat.	7.30 a.m. Mon.
,,	Birch Rock Siding	Open as required.			
,,	Pontardulais Crossing	—	—	Last train Sun. Morning	5. 0 a.m. Mon.
LLANDILO NORTH (G.W.R.) TO CRAVEN ARMS (CENTRAL WALES JUNCTION).					
L M S & G.W. Jt. Llangadock	Station	—	—	Last train Sun. Morning	3.30 a.m. Mon.
L M S & G.W. Jt. Llanwrda	Station	—	—	Last train Sun. Morning	3.20 a.m. Mon.
L M S & G.W. Jt. Llandovery	No. 2	—	—	Last train Sun. Morning	1.50 a.m. Mon.
L M S & G.W. Jt. ,,	No. 1	—	—	Last train Sun. Morning	1.50 a.m. Mon.
Cynghordy	Station	—	—	Last train Sun. Morning	1.45 a.m. Mon.
Llanwrtyd Wells	Sugar Loaf Summit	—	—	Last train Sun. Morning	1.30 a.m. Mon.
,,	Station	—	—	Last train Sun. Morning	1.15 a.m. Mon.
Garth	Station	—	—	Last train Sun. Morning	12.55 a.m. Mon.
Builth Road	No. 2	—	—	Last train Sun. Morning	12.40 a.m. Mon.
,,	No. 1	—	—	Last train Sun. Morning	12.40 a.m. Mon.
,,	Howey	—	—	Last train Sun. Morning	12.30 a.m. Mon.
Llandrindod Wells	No. 2	—	—	Last train Sun. Morning	12.25 a.m. Mon.
,,	No. 1	—	—	Last train Sun. Morning	12.25 a.m. Mon.
Penybont	Station	—	—	Last train Sun. Morning	12.20 a.m. Mon.
,,	Junction	—	—	Last train Sun. Morning	12.10 a.m. Mon.
Dolau	Station	5. 0 p.m.	9. 0 a.m.	5. 0 p.m. Sat.	9. 0 a.m. Mon.
Llanbister Road	Station	—	—	Last train Sun. Morning	12. 5 a.m. Mon.
Llangunllo	Station	—	—	Last train Sun. Morning	11.35 p.m. Sun.
Knighton	No. 2	—	—	Last train Sun. Morning	11. 0 p.m. Sun.
,,	No. 1	Open as required.			
Bucknell	Station	—	—	Last train Sun. Morning	10.40 p.m. Sun.
Hopton Heath	Station	6. 0 p.m. Open alternate Mondays (Craven Arms Auction Day) 9. 0 a.m.	10. 0 a.m. 5. 0 p.m.	6 0 p.m. Sat.	10. 0 a.m. Mon.
Broome	Station	3.30 p.m.	7.30 a.m.	3.30 p.m. Sat.	7.30 a.m. Mon.
PONTARDULAIS TO LLANDILO.					
Pontardulais	South	—	—	Last train Sun. morning.	3.30 a.m Mon.
,,	North	—	—	4. 0 a.m. Sun.	6. 0 a.m. Mon.
Pantyffynnon	Glynhir	Open as required weekdays only.		—	—
,,	South	—	—	Last train Sun.	3.30 a.m. Mon.
,,	North	—	—	Last train Sun.	4.40 a.m. Mon.
Tirydail	Station	—	—	Last train Sun.	4.30 a.m. Mon.
Llandebie	Station	—	—	Last train Sun.	4.25 a.m. Mon.
Derwydd Road	Cilyrychen Crossing	—	—	Last train Sun.	4.15 a.m. Mon.
,,	Station	9.35 p.m. MO 10.0 p.m. TWThF	6.0 a.m. Tues. 6.0 a.m. WThFS	10. 0 p.m. Sat.	5.35 a.m. Mon.
Ffairfach	Station	—	—	Last train Sun.	4.15 a.m. Mon.
Llandilo	Carmarthen Valley Jn.	—	—	Last train Sun.	4.15 a.m. Mon.
,,	South	—	—	Last train Sun.	3.45 a.m. Mon.
,,	North	—	—	Last train Sun.	3.10 a.m. Mon.
CARMARTHEN JUNCTION TO ABERGWILI JUNCTION.					
Carmarthen	Myrtle Hill Junction	—	—	8. 5 a.m. Sun. V 3.30 p.m. Sun. F 8.15 p.m. Sun. D	2.20 p.m. Sun. 6.30 p.m. Sun. 4.30 a.m. Mon.
,,	Station	—	—	8.10 a.m. Sun. 2.35 p.m. Sun. 9.45 p.m. Sun. E	11.30 a.m. Sun. 5.15 p.m. Sun. 4.30 a.m. Mon.
,,	Crossing	10.15 p.m. or after clearance of last train to or from Goods Yard	3.55 a.m.	9.40 p.m. or after clearance of last train to or from Goods Yard Sat. 7.45 a.m. Sun. V 8.15 p.m. Sun.	5.15 a.m. Sun. 6.15 p.m. Sun. 5.15 a.m. Mon.
,,	Goods Yard	9.45 p.m. after day's service completed	5.25 a.m.	9.45 p.m. after day's service completed, Sat.	5.25 a.m. Mon.
,,	Abergwili Junction	9.45 p.m. after day's service completed	5.25 a.m.	9.45 p.m. after day's service completed, Sat.	5.25 a.m. Mon.
,,	Bridge Junction	—	—	7.40 a.m. Sun. V 3.20 p.m. Sun. F 8. 5 p.m. Sun. D	1.30 p.m. Sun. 6. 0 p.m. Sun. 4.50 a.m. Mon.
ABERGWILI JUNCTION (G.W.R.) TO LLANDILO (CARMARTHEN VALLEY JUNCTION) G.W.R.					
Nantgaredig	Station	Last train	6.30 a.m.	Last train Sat.	6.30 a.m. Mon.
Llanarthney	Station	Last train	6.30 a.m.	Last train Sat.	6.30 a.m. Mon.
Golden Grove	Station	Last train	6.45 a.m.	Last train Sat.	6.45 a.m. Mon.
Llandilo Bridge	Station	Last train	6.45 a.m.	Last train Sat.	6.45 a.m. Mon.

D—Fishguard Harbour to advise boxes concerned when required to open beyond times shewn.
E—Or after clearing of 5.50 p.m. Bristol.
F—Or after clearing of 1.25 p.m. Fishguard Harbour.
V—Or after clearing of 6.5 a.m. Fishguard Harbour.

The hours of duty at signalboxes from the LMSR working timetable of 28 September 1936 until further notice. *Courtesy: Bryan Wilson*

months. Four 'Jinty' 0-6-0Ts also went to Swansea around the same time. Departures from Swansea in 1934/35 included two 2-4-2Ts, No 6756 being transferred and No 6737 withdrawn, and Swansea's last 'Special Tank' 0-6-0ST, by then No 27309.

By the start of 1936 the ubiquitous 'Black Five' 4-6-0s had started to work passenger trains on the Central Wales line, but the 2-6-4Ts and 2-6-0s were not completely ousted. At that time, the 0-8-0s and assorted 0-6-0s were in charge of most of the through freight workings, with the 'Coal Tank' 0-6-2Ts usually looking after the Swansea-Pontardulais locals.

During 1936 2-6-0 No 2777 had a brief stay at Swansea, classmate No 2778 arriving in July the following year for a slightly longer residency. Swansea shed received its first brand new 'Black Five', No 5292, in January 1937, classmates Nos 5190/91 being sent there in October. Stanier 2-6-4T No 2581 arrived at Swansea in March 1937 and remained there until January 1938 — the following year the shed had an allocation of three of the type (and also one Fowler 2-6-4T).

The LMSR '8F' 2-8-0s made their debut on the Central Wales line in 1937. Other noteworthy visitors to the line during that year — albeit only temporarily — were Aston shed's 2-6-4T No 2441, which worked an eight-coach excursion from Birmingham to Llandovery and return on 13 June, and Plodder Lane's 'Coal Tank' No 27602, which was loaned to Swansea between August and September. The following year, at least one Midland Compound is known to have worked a scheduled train between Shrewsbury and Swansea.

During the latter half of the war Fowler 2-6-4Ts were used regularly on through passenger workings between Shrewsbury and Swansea, the Stanier 2-6-4Ts performing less frequently. At the start of the war the only Fowler representative at Swansea had been No 2321, but in 1942 no less than seven were transferred there, four of those wartime incomers remaining at Swansea until the 1950s.

Between May and July 1943 a total of 15 WD 'Austerity' 2-8-0s were allocated to Shrewsbury to replace 12 of the depot's 0-8-0s. The 'WDs' promptly took up regular duties on the Central Wales line, and four of Shrewsbury's contingent, Nos 7050-53, were soon transferred to Swansea, also ousting 0-8-0s. In December 1944 and January 1945 most of the 'WDs' at Swansea and Shrewsbury were returned to the War Department and replaced by LMSR '8F' 2-8-0s.

Even before then, the '8Fs' had played a significant part in moving traffic on the Central Wales line. No 8310 had been transferred from Shrewsbury to Swansea late in 1943, and 11 brand-new '8Fs' (plus another transfer from Shrewsbury) had arrived there early in 1944. Before long, their

During LMSR days, Paxton Street shed at Swansea was home to anything between 30 and 50 locomotives. On 27 June 1938, the interesting line-up included 0-8-0 No 8954, 'Black Five' No 5191, and an unidentified 'Cauliflower' 0-6-0. The much-needed repairs to the shed roof were not undertaken until 1942. *H. C. Casserley*

duties regularly took them to Stafford, while on August Bank Holiday 1944 No 8307 was noted working local passenger services between Swansea and Pontardulais. A correspondent to one of the railway magazines, who visited Swansea one Sunday in March 1944, reported seeing six '8Fs', three 'WDs', two 'Black Fives' and three 0-8-0s on shed, and commented that the '8Fs' and 'WDs' appeared to have largely replaced the 0-8-0s on the Swansea-Shrewsbury trains.

In April 1944 two WD 2-10-0s were dispatched to Shrewsbury for use on the Central Wales line, but were returned to Crewe after a week or so. They were replaced by American 'S160' class 2-8-0s, which had been shipped to Britain to assist with the war effort. The 'S160s' had already struck up an acquaintance with Wales, a total of 358 having been dealt with after their arrival by the 756th Railway Shop Battalion at Ebbw Junction, in Newport. Nevertheless, the 'S160s' proved unsuitable for use on the Central Wales line, due to the difficulty of changing the train-staff on the single track sections, although No 2153 was noted at Swansea in August 1944. In 1947, new Class 2 2-6-0s Nos 6414/15 underwent successful trials on the Central Wales line and the two engines were subsequently allocated to Swansea, albeit only until 1948.

The engine sheds

The locomotives for the through workings on the Central Wales line were provided by Swansea and Shrewsbury sheds. The latter depot, of course, provided motive power for a wide range of other turns as well and, therefore, it cannot really be considered solely as a 'Central Wales line' shed.

The biggest depot with a Central Wales line pedigree was at **Swansea**. When the LNWR started working through to Swansea in June 1868, the company rented engine shed space from the GWR for about a month until its own shed next to Victoria station was ready. As traffic on the Central Wales line increased over subsequent years the shed at Victoria was enlarged, but when the LNWR undertook the much-needed reconstruction of Victoria station in 1881/82 a new site had to be found for the engine shed.

The site chosen was alongside Paxton Street, near the junction of the dock line west of Victoria station. As an unashamed slice of nostalgia, how many of us remember these directions: *'Turn left outside Swansea Victoria Station along Victoria Road, changing to Oystermouth Road, and turn left into Paxton Street. The shed entrance is on the right hand side just past the railway over-bridge. Walking time 10 minutes'.*

Paxton Street shed was single-ended and had six roads, each 195ft long. It originally had a 42ft turntable, but a 60ft 'table was installed in 1920. Apart from the new turntable, the only real modernisation undertaken at Paxton Street throughout its life was the the provision in 1942 of a new ash pit, alterations to the inspection pits, and repairs to the roof.

Over the years the depot's allocation varied between some 30 and 50 engines, although several locomotives were outstationed at Carmarthen and Llandovery at any one time. In LNWR days Paxton Street shed was coded No 33, and after the Grouping it became W33 as part of the LMSR's Western 'A' Division. In 1930 the ex-Midland sheds at Upper

Bank and Gurnos effectively became sub-sheds of Paxton Street, but under the LMSR's new coding system of 1935 Paxton Street became 4B and Upper Bank regained its own identity, this time as 4C and with Gurnos as its sub-shed.

Of Paxton Street's two regular sub-sheds, that at **Carmarthen** had a relatively short life. The original shed at Carmarthen was built *circa* 1873 by the Central Wales & Carmarthen Junction Railway, which had been formed to administer the Llandilo-Carmarthen branch. The shed was just beyond the northern end of Carmarthen Town station, and by 1890 was reported as being virtually derelict. It was replaced in the mid-1890s by a modern-looking twin-road timber building, the old building later being destroyed by a gale.

Swansea (Paxton Street) shed — allocation January 1933: 50 engines

Midland '1F' 0-6-0T:	1676
LMSR '4P' 2-6-4T:	2317, 2318, 2319, 2320, 2321, 2322, 2354
MR '2F/'3F' 0-6-0:	3389, 3657
LNWR '1P' 2-4-2T:	6737, 6740, 6756, 6757
LNWR '1F' 0-6-0ST:	7309, 7342, 7362
LNWR '1F' 0-6-0PT:	7477
LNWR '2F' 0-6-2T:	7603, 7781, 7782, 7783, 7787
LNWR '4F' 0-8-2T:	7870, 7871
LNWR '6F' 0-8-4T:	7947, 7948,
LNWR '2F' 0-6-0:	8543, 8621*, 8622, 8624*
LNWR '4F' 4-6-0:	8708, 8720, 8721, 8722, 8723, 8786
LNWR/LMSR '6F'/'7F' 0-8-0:	8944, 8945, 8948, 8950, 8951, 8952, 8953, 8954, 9133, 9304, 9305

* Officially withdrawn in 1932.

Note: Some of the engines noted would have been outstationed at Carmarthen and Llandovery.

Ivatt 2-6-0 No 6414 underwent trials on the Central Wales line in November and December 1947, and was officially transferred to Paxton Street shed from Bank Hall at the end of December. It was photographed inside Paxton Street shed on 27 August 1948. The engine spent only 12 months at Swansea and was returned to Bank Hall at the end of 1948. *H. C. Casserley*

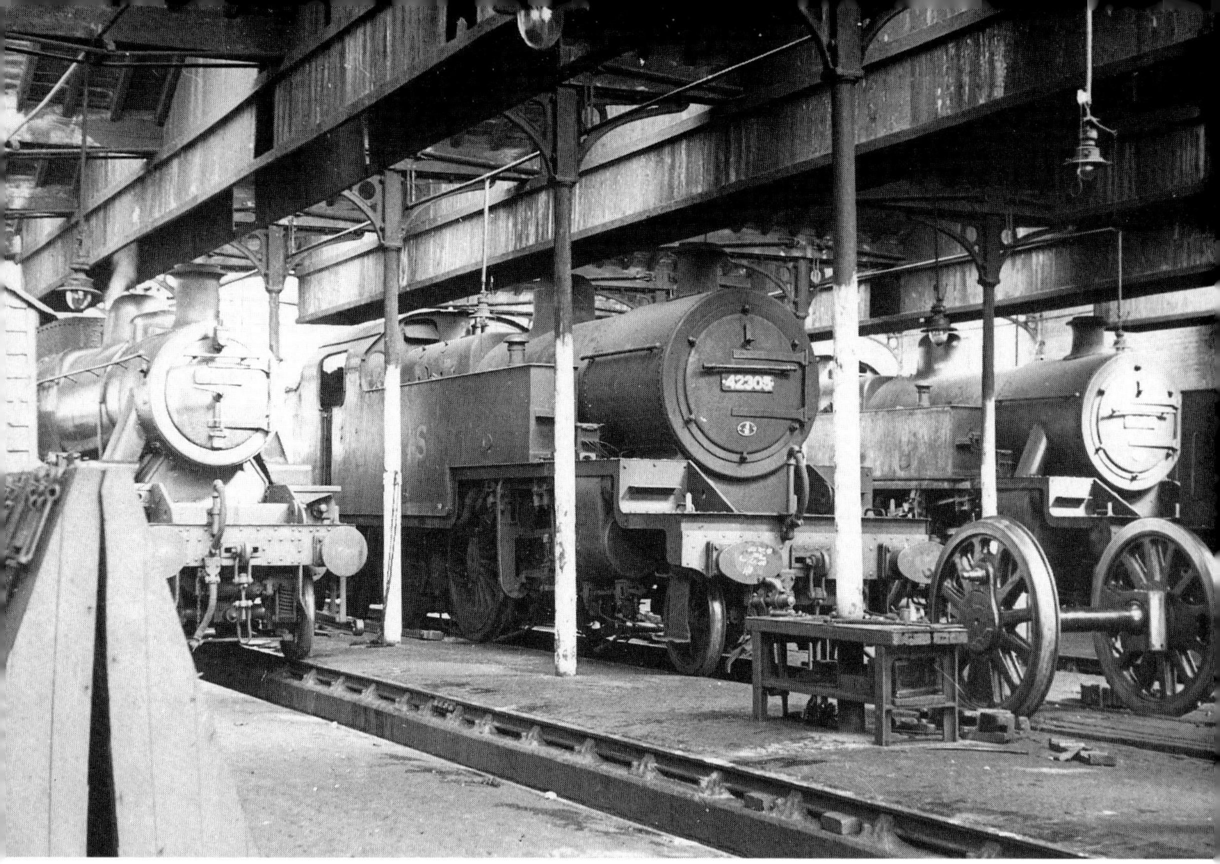

Above: The line-up inside Paxton Street shed on 27 August 1948 included an Ivatt 2-6-0 (No 6414) and a pair of Fowler 2-6-4Ts, of which recently-renumbered 42305 is clearly undergoing repairs. *H. C. Casserley*

Below: A trio of Stanier-designed engines — two '8Fs' and a 'Black Five' — stand outside Paxton Street on 27 August 1948. The arches on the left of the picture carried the line to South Dock. *H. C. Casserley*

Swansea (Paxton Street) shed — allocation 10 November 1945: 38 engines

Midland '1F' 0-6-0T:	1676
LMSR '4P' 2-6-4T:	2320, 2360, 2381, 2385, 2388, 2390, 2394
LNWR '1P' 2-4-2T:	6620, 6757
LNWR '2F' 0-6-2T:	7715, 7741, 7807, 27261
LNWR '6F' 0-8-4T:	7931, 7941, 7948, 7956
LMSR '8F' 2-8-0:	8175, 8325, 8335, 8343, 8344, 8345, 8366, 8367, 8664, 8665, 8673, 8689, 8691
LNWR/LMSR '6F'/'7F' 0-8-0:	8893, 8948, 9033, 9260, 9358
LNWR '2F' 0-6-0:	28543, 28622

Note: Some of the engines noted would have been outstationed at Carmarthen and Llandovery.

The shed was closed as early as July 1938, LMSR engines engaged on Llandilo-Carmarthen duties subsequently being housed at the spacious six-road GWR shed (which had opened in 1907) alongside Carmarthen Town station. The engines concerned were usually 2-4-2Ts, and immediately prior to Nationalisation Nos 6620 and 6740 were noted at Carmarthen (GWR) shed.

Paxton Street's other long-term sub-shed was at **Llandovery**. The first shed there was a timber-built three-road structure, which was provided when the CWER's line from Llandrindod was opened throughout in 1868. Somewhat embarrassingly for the LNWR part of the building stood on land which was jointly owned by the GWR, but that was rectified in 1901 when a much-needed replacement shed was erected wholly on LNWR land.

The replacement shed at Llandovery was a substantial four-road building, although one of the roads was abandoned and the pit filled in during the late 1930s. The building is thought to have incorporated part of the roof from the remains of Longsight shed in Manchester, which had suffered severe fire damage in 1901. Llandovery shed was on the down side of the line just to the south of the station, and was equipped with a 42ft turntable.

Llandovery shed played an important role on the Central Wales line, as it was the usual practice for engine crews to be changed there. Furthermore, the shed provided the banking engines for the climb to Sugar Loaf, the common practice being for the banker to return to Llandovery as pilot to the next

The second LNWR shed at Carmarthen was built in the mid-1890s and was closed in 1938, the engines subsequently being transferred to the town's GWR shed. The principal duty of the LNWR shed was to service the Carmarthen–Llandilo branch, which for many years was worked by Webb 2-4-2Ts. On 1 June 1936, 2-4-2Ts Nos 6619 and 6695 stand outside the shed.
R. M. Casserley Collection

The ex-LNWR depot at Llandovery was a sub-shed of Swansea (Paxton Street), but was a more substantial affair than some parent sheds elsewhere in Britain. The shed inherited the engines from the nearby GWR premises, which closed in 1935. This photograph was taken on 8 September 1951.
H. C Casserley

down train, thereby reducing light-engine mileage and also giving extra braking power to the descending train. Llandovery's importance was reflected by its roll-call of staff, which for many years usually included around 25 sets of men.

The banking duties handled by Llandovery shed — and also the Llandovery–Llandrindod Wells local goods — were normally entrusted to 0-8-4Ts, the usual practice being for two of the regular trio to be based at Llandovery with the other 'spare' at Llandovery or Swansea. However, it seems that the normal practice was not observed between 1935 and 1937 as, according to reports, one of the three, No 7948, was in store at Llandovery for much of that period. No 7948 went to Crewe for a general overhaul in June 1937, and the departure of No 7941 to Shrewsbury for repairs that same month necessitated the substitution of 0-8-0 No 9155 on banking duties.

As the LMSR did not usually maintain separate allocation lists for sub-sheds (parent sheds sending engines on an 'as required' basis), it is not possible to provide a definitive post-Grouping list for Llandovery. In pre-Grouping days, however, the LNWR was a little more obliging, and a list for an unspecified date in 1917 reveals that the shed housed two 2-4-2Ts (Nos 1145 and 1758), two 'Cauliflower' 0-6-0s (Nos 128 and 676), and two 'Coal Engine' 0-6-0s (Nos 1085 and 3117).

Delving briefly into the obscure, it is known that the first LNWR shed at Llandovery replaced a shed and coaling stage which had been provided at **Llandrindod**, when the latter point was the temporary terminus of the line from Craven Arms. No records of the shed at Llandrindod seem to have survived, but the theory that the structure was moved to Llandovery for re-erection can almost certainly be ruled out — the temporary nature of Llandrindod's facilities would hardly have warranted a three-road building.

Returning to Llandovery, it was not only the LNWR which had an engine shed there. The Vale of Towy Railway also had a shed at **Llandovery**, a single-road timber building being provided when the line from Llandilo opened in April 1858. The shed was behind the up platform of the station.

The VoT shed eventually became GWR property and in the 1920s and 1930s 'Dean Goods' 0-6-0s were the shed's usual residents. Selected allocation lists show that No 2354 was at Llandovery in the first week of January 1921, Nos 2364, 2486, and 2540/60 in January 1926, and No 2558 in January 1934. Other engines allocated to Llandovery (GWR) during that period included 'Stella' class 2-4-0 No 3203 (in 1921/22) and '5800' class 0-4-2T No 5819, which was sent there from new in August 1933. The GWR closed its shed at Llandovery in February 1935 and the locomotives were transferred to the LNWR shed.

Farther to the north on the Central Wales line the LNWR had three other engine sheds, all of which were sub-sheds of Shrewsbury (coded 30 in LNWR days and recoded 4A under LMSR auspices in 1935). The northernmost of those three sub-sheds was at **Craven Arms**, but in common with its parent depot at Shrewsbury its duties included far more than just the Central Wales line.

It is believed that the Shrewsbury & Hereford Railway provided a small single-road shed at Craven Arms in 1856, but the better-known LNWR shed was erected in 1869. The building, which was constructed of stone and had a slate roof, originally had four roads, but in 1937 the road on the west side was dispensed with and the pit filled in. Around that time, the shed's allocation usually comprised one '4F' 0-6-0, one 2-6-4T, one '18in Goods' and one 'Coal Tank'. Craven Arms's turntable, which had once been the subject of so much discussion, was alongside the shed.

The shed was at the north end of the station on the up side of the Shrewsbury-Hereford line. It was an important little shed, as evinced by its separate coding of 30C in the early 1930s, but as most of the trains on the Central Wales line started or terminated at Shrewsbury its relevance to this story is not particularly great.

To the south, another of Shrewsbury's sub-sheds was the stone-built single-road shed at **Knighton**, which was opened by the LNWR in 1870. One of Knighton shed's purposes was to house the banking engines for the climb to Llangunllo. In LNWR days these were usually 'Special DX' 0-6-0s while, in LMSR days, 0-8-4Ts were normally used. Until the 1940s two more engines (usually 0-6-0s) were outstationed at Knighton for working local stopping trains. The shed was devoid of a turntable until 1945, when the 42ft turntable from Harborne was transferred and installed.

Craven Arms shed was effectively reduced from a four- to a three-road shed in April 1937 when the westernmost road was taken out of use and the pit filled in. However, this picture was taken in May 1939 and it appears that the disused road remained at least partly *in situ*. The locomotives simmering outside the shed are Stanier 2-6-4T No 2612 and '4F' 0-6-0 No 4309. *Rail Archive Stephenson*

Ex-Midland '2F' 0-6-0 No 58213, a veteran of 1882, rests inside Craven Arms shed on 11 September 1952. Throughout much of the 1950s, one of Shrewsbury's '2Fs' was often out-stationed at Craven Arms for station pilot duties. Several of the class survived until the early 1960s, but No 58213 didn't quite make it. It was withdrawn in August 1959. *H. C. Casserley*

Shrewsbury's third sub-shed on the Central Wales line was at **Builth Road**. It was a small wooden structure, sited alongside the loop leading to the Mid Wales line, and was equipped with a 42ft turntable. The shed opened in 1869 and could house two engines, but in 1941 it was shortened to single-engine length. The usual resident(s) were 'Cauliflower' 0-6-0s or 'Coal Tank' 0-6-2Ts, which undertook transfer trips to and from the GWR at Builth Road and also station pilot duties along the line at Llandrindod Wells.

For the sake of completeness, two other engine sheds need to be mentioned — both were near the southern end of the Central Wales line. The first was at **Pantyffynnon**. The shed, which was a four-road structure built by the GWR with the aid of 'Loans Act' finance, opened in March 1931 as a sub-shed of Llanelly depot. It maintained an allocation of some 15-20 engines principally for hauling the coal trains from various collieries around the Pantyffynnon area to Llanelly or Swansea Docks. The shed's involvement with the Central Wales line was minimal.

The other shed warranting a brief mention is the old Llanelly Railway premises at **Llanelly Dock**. The stone-built twin-road shed opened *circa* 1839/40, and housed the engines which worked the Llanelly-Llandilo section in the early days. The shed was replaced in March 1925 by the GWR's new twin-roundhouse depot, built on an adjacent site.

In 1948 Britain's railways were Nationalised and the administration of the Central Wales line passed, not to the London Midland Region of British Railways, but to the Western Region. In many quarters that was viewed as a prelude to major changes in the essential character of the line, but the worst nightmares proved to be largely unfounded.

Swansea (Paxton Street) shed — allocation 31 December 1947: 42 engines.

Midland '1F' 0-6-0T:	1676
LMSR '4P' 2-6-4T:	2307, 2385, 2387, 2388, 2390, 2394
LMSR '2F' 2-6-0:	6414, 6415
LNWR '1P' 2-4-2T:	6620, 6740
LNWR '2F' 0-6-2T:	7700, 7715, 7741, 27621, 27625
LNWR '6F' 0-8-4T:	7931, 7932, 7948
LMSR '8F' 2-8-0:	8175, 8325, 8335, 8343, 8344, 8366, 8427, 8473, 8551, 8664, 8665, 8673, 8691, 8717
LNWR/LMSR '6F'/'7F' 0-8-0:	8893, 9033, 9035, 9260, 9358, 9407, 9418
LNWR '2F' 0-6-0:	28543, 28622

Note: Some of the engines noted would have been outstationed at Carmarthen and Llandovery.

After Nationalisation, most of the above engines took their numbers in the 40000 series. Those numbered out of sequence were:

'Coal Tank' 0-6-2Ts

LMSR No	BR No
7741	58910
27621	58891
27625	58892

'Cauliflower' 0-6-0s

LMSR No	BR No
28543	58406
28622	58430

'Coal Tanks' Nos 7700/15 (of Swansea) were withdrawn early in 1948 without being allotted BR numbers.

The small timber-built shed at Builth Road paid allegiance to Shrewsbury. The parent shed's ex-Midland '2F' No 58213 saunters past the permanent way office on 12 July 1956. The turntable — perhaps a smidgin underused — is behind the wagon on the right. *H. C. Casserley*

Craven Arms shed was in use until the mid-1960s. On 2 June 1964, '8F' No 48400 sits partly inside the shed while an unidentified 0-6-0PT has just taken on water. *B. J. Ashworth*

7439

SUGAR LOAF SUMMIT

Chapter 5
A New Administration

When the Central Wales line passed to Western Region control shortly after Nationalisation, traditionalists were understandably apprehensive. Changes were indeed implemented, but the evidence of the line's predominantly LNWR/LMSR pedigree did not suddenly disappear.

One of the earliest changes involved the motive power on the Llandilo–Carmarthen branch, the ex-LNWR 2-4-2Ts (including Swansea's last representative, which became BR No 46620) and 'Coal Tank' 0-6-2Ts quickly being replaced by GWR 0-6-0PTs and veteran 'Dean Goods' 0-6-0s. Paxton Street's 'Coal Tanks' were certainly not rendered redundant, as they handled most of the Swansea–Pontardulais locals in the late 1940s and early 1950s, while their stable mates, the 0-8-0s, usually looked after shunting duties at Gorseinon. The LNWR/LMSR pedigree of the Central Wales line was to remain very evident until 1964.

The WR nevertheless had an early stab at dispensing with one aspect of the main line's customary motive power. Soon after taking control it transferred 'WD' 2-8-0s to Swansea primarily to dispense with the LMSR '8F' 2-8-0s, but the plan backfired. The 'WD' engines were not permitted to work passenger trains (except as pilots), whereas the '8Fs', although intended for freight duties, were quite at home on passenger workings. That said, the '8Fs' outings on passenger turns were normally confined to the summer months as they were not fitted with train-heating apparatus.

As early as the summer of 1950 '8Fs' showed their versatility by appearing on passenger workings from Shrewsbury to Swansea, and by mid-December of that year 12 of the class had been officially transferred to Swansea. During the 1950s, Swansea-based '8Fs' worked as far afield as Burton-on-Trent, those trips being with the Bass 'empties'.

A relatively minor WR incursion was the transfer in 1950 of an ex-GWR 0-6-0PT (what could be more GWR than a Swindon-built 'matchbox'?) to Swansea shed which, by then, was coded 87K and was officially referred to by the WR as Swansea (Victoria). The 0-6-0PT was, however, the only ex-GWR locomotive among the shed's allocation of 31 (in June 1950), the remainder comprising eight LNWR/LMSR 0-8-0s, seven Fowler 2-6-4Ts, two Webb 'Coal Tanks', one Webb 2-4-2T, and 13 'WD' 2-8-0s. The depot nominally had nine veteran Midland '1F' and seven LMSR 'Jinty' 0-6-0Ts on its books as well, but those were all outstationed at Upper Bank or Gurnos.

Allocation list for Swansea (Paxton Street) shed — 17 June 1950

GWR '7400' class 0-6-0PT:	7439
LMSR '4MT' 2-6-4T:	42305, 42307, 42385, 42387, 42388, 42390, 42394
LNWR '1P' 2-4-2T:	46620
LNWR/LMSR '7F'/ '8F' 0-8-0:	48893, 49033, 49035, 49148, 49177, 49260, 49358, 49376
LNWR '2F' 0-6-2T:	58892, 58910
WD 'Austerity' 2-8-0:	90102, 90173, 90186, 90188, 90205, 90225, 90297, 90307, 90359, 90546, 90568, 90579, 90712

Total: 32 plus 16 0-6-0Ts sub-shedded at Upper Bank

Above left: One of the first indications of the new WR administration was the use of 0-6-0PTs on the Llandilo–Carmarthen branch, the 'matchboxes' retaining a domination until the branch's closure in September 1963. On the rather wet morning of 24 July 1962, No 7439 waits at Abergwili with the 10.20am Carmarthen–Llandilo service.
Leslie Sandler

Left: The LMSR 'Black Fives' were synonymous with the Central Wales line until 1964. No 45298 (with a self-weighing tender) waits at Sugar Loaf platform on 30 October 1961.
B. J. Ashworth

Like the 'Black Fives', the '8Fs' played an important role on the Central Wales line until 1964. Here, No 48665 hauls a Swansea-bound goods train through Craven Arms station on 10 September 1949. *H. C. Casserley*

The news of the day

The comings and goings on the Central Wales line during the 1950s were dutifully reported in the railway press. Arguably the most reliable reports were those in the *Railway Observer* and *Trains Illustrated* magazines, and it is the 'Motive Power Miscellany' section of the latter which has been selected to provide a (hopefully) nostalgic look at events.

In 1952, *Trains Illustrated*'s trusty band of correspondents noted that:

'On 2/1/52 0-8-0 No 49177 was pressed into service on the 7.55am Swansea Victoria-Shrewsbury when 2-6-4T No 42387 failed at Llandovery; the 0-8-0 was relieved by 4-6-0 No 75004 (commandeered from a northbound freight) *at Llandrindod. The train reached Shrewsbury 80 mins late...The principal reason for the dispatch of LM 2-6-2Ts to South Wales is that the local footplate staff had refused to work the Webb 0-6-2Ts any longer* (March issue)...*Ex-GW pannier and 0-6-2 tanks are to be seen more frequently on the Central Wales line* (by June 1952 0-6-0PT No 7439 was in regular use as Swansea Victoria's station pilot), *and ex-GW sets have displaced some of the ex-LMS rolling stock. Western pattern signals have been noted at Swansea and Llandrindod Wells* (May issue)...*An 0-8-0 again headed a Central Wales passenger train on 8/5/52, when No 49083 took the place of a defaulting "5MT" 4-6-0, No 45283, on the 6.30pm Swansea-York at Llandovery; the 0-8-0 itself failed at Llanwyrtyd Wells, and was replaced by "4MT" No 75002* (It is believed that the first working of a Standard '4MT' on the Central Wales line had been on 12 September 1951 — the engine had been No 75002)...*A WR "56XX" class 0-6-2T was recently shedded at Llandovery for banking work up to Sugar Loaf summit on the Central Wales line, but did not prove popular; Fowler 2-6-4T No 42307 was doing this work on 31/7/52, returning to the bottom of the hill as pilot to down trains to avoid light engine working. Sister engine No.42388 works the local service to Craven Arms* (October issue)...*What is probably the first appearance of "Castles" on the Central Wales line occurred on 23/10/52, when Nos 7030/36 double-headed the Royal train from London into Llandrindod Wells for HM The Queen's visit to open the Claerwen Dam* (The train had travelled via Wolverhampton, Shrewsbury and Craven Arms, and was stabled overnight on 22/23 October between Marsh Farm Junction and Harton Road. The locomotives were serviced and turned at Llandovery before returning to

Shrewsbury on 24 October)...*On 27/9/52 the 5.30pm Shrewsbury-Swansea Victoria had an unfortunate journey. To Builth Road 2-6-4T No 42307 lost 74mins, and then failed soon after leaving that station. It was assisted by 2-8-0 No 48732 on to Llandovery, where the train stood until its lateness had increased to 3¼ hours; finally "5MT" 4-6-0 No 44673 appeared to resume the journey, and brought the weary passengers into Swansea at the witching hour of 1.45am — 4 hrs 5 mins late'.*

One of those items generated further correspondence and comments. A '*TT*' reader who was aboard the delayed 7.55am ex-Swansea on 2 January 1952 excitedly wrote to the magazine about No 75004's efforts to regain time: *'We flew round the curves high up on the hillside down the falling gradient from Llangunllo to Knighton...the 12.3 miles from Knighton to Craven Arms were covered in 15 mins, start to stop...the train passed Bucknell at about 75mph* (the official speed limit on that section was 55mph), *and the 19.9 miles from Craven Arms to Shrewsbury took 21 mins!'*

On 19 April 1953 the locomotives allocated to Swansea, Shrewsbury and their sub-sheds were officially transferred to WR stock. One result of the transfer was that Swansea's ex-LNWR 'Coal Tank' 0-6-2Ts were gradually withdrawn — No 58911 went in March 1954, No 58880 in April, No 58899 in May, No 58921 in July, and Nos 58888 and 58924 (which had been sent as replacements in July) and No 58915 in September.

During 1954, '*TT*'s' enthusiastic correspondents reported that:

'Much of the track governed by Llandovery No 2 box was recently track-circuited, and at Llandilo construction has begun of a new brick signal cabin which will replace the three existing boxes early next year...On the Central Wales line the standard "5MT" 4-6-0s now at Shrewsbury shed have taken over the principal passenger workings (January issue). *On 3/11/53, however, No 73018 was noted shunting at Llandovery prior to departure on a northbound goods...2-6-2T No 40105 has been observed at Swansea (Paxton Street)* (April issue)...*The winter timetables appear to include a mile-a-minute working on the Central Wales line — the 12.25pm Swansea Victoria-Shrewsbury is allowed 1 minute to cover the 1 mile 6 chains from Pantyffynnon to Tirydail!* (November issue)'.

Shrewsbury's '5MT' 4-6-0 No 73024 pulls into Builth Road (High Level) on 21 April 1962 with the 10.25am Swansea (Victoria)–Shrewsbury train, the carriages being (G)WR stock. *Michael Mensing*

Allocation list for Swansea (Paxton Street) shed — 27 February 1954

P&M 0-4-0ST:	1153
GWR '5700' class 0-6-0PT*:	5761, 5773, 6720, 6734, 8706
GWR '7400' class 0-6-0PT:	7439
LMSR '3MT' 2-6-2T:	40105
LMSR '4MT' 2-6-4T*:	42305, 42307, 42385, 42387, 42390, 42394
LNWR '1P' 2-4-2T:	46616
LMSR '8F' 2-8-0*:	48330, 48525, 48706, 48724, 48730, 48732, 48735, 48737, 48761, 48768
LNWR/LMSR '7F'/'8F' 0-8-0*:	49033, 49035, 49117, 49148, 49177, 49358, 49376
LNWR '2F' 0-6-2T:	58880, 58899, 58921

Total: 35 plus 14 0-6-0Ts sub-shedded at Upper Bank, Gurnos and Llandovery
* Of the above, one 0-6-0PT was usually out-stationed at Upper Bank and another at Gurnos, while two '4MT' 2-6-4Ts, two '8Fs' and three 0-8-0s were usually at Llandovery.

Fowler 2-6-4T No 42390 became a Central Wales line regular in 1942. When Paxton Street shed closed in 1959 the engine was transferred to Landore, thereby continuing its association with the line for a little longer. It is seen here entering Llandovery with the well-loaded 6.25am Shrewsbury–Swansea train on 8 September 1951.
H. C. Casserley

Shrewsbury shed received a substantial allocation of '5MT' 4-6-0s in 1953, and they were soon put to work on the Central Wales line. On 4 June 1964, No 73090 arrives at Builth Road (High Level) with the 11.45am Shrewsbury-Swansea (Victoria). Note the 'Way Out' sign on the left, which has had 'And for trains to Brecon' (etc) painted out after the closure of the Low Level station.
B. J. Ashworth

Table 144 — **SWANSEA, LLANELLY, CARMARTHEN, BUILTH ROAD, CRAVEN ARMS and SHREWSBURY**

Miles from Swansea (V.)		Week Days only																		
		pm	am	pm	am	am	am ❸	am	am	am	am	am	am	pm	am	pm	am	am	am	am
						Saturdays only. Runs 23rd July to 27th August inclusive						To Brynamman West arr 11 53 am (Table 141)		Saturdays only. Runs 16th July to 27th August inclusive			Saturdays only; also runs each weekday during August	Saturdays only; also runs each week day during August. To Brynamman West arr 3 46 pm (Table 141)	Except Saturdays	Saturdays only
	104London (Pad.) .. dep	**9h25**	..	**9h25**	..	..	..	**1 0**	**1 0**	..	..	..	..	..	..	..	**5 30**	**8 55**	**10 55**	**10 55**
	104 Cardiff (General) . „	2a44	....	2a44	....	....	....	5 43	5 43	....	8†47	8†47	....	....	9 55	....	1025	12e0	1 30	2 30
	104 Swansea (High St.) ¶ arr	4d13	..	4a 7	..	..	..	7 25	7d45	..	9A55	d10N20	..	..	1122	..	1222	1e35	2 40	3 50
—	**Swansea** (Victoria) .. dep	....	....	**6a15**	**7 20**	....	....	**7 45**	....	**8 30**	**10 25**	....	....	....	**12 5**	**12 25**	**1p 5**	....	**4p15**	**4p15**
1	„ (Bay)	..	..	**6 18**	**7 23**	..	..	**7 48**	..	**8 33**	..	..	..	..	**12 8**	**12 29**	**1 8**	..	**4 19**	**4 19**
3	Mumbles Road	....	....	6 23	7 28	....	....	7 53	....	8 38	10 32	....	....	....	1213	12 34	1 13	....	4 24	4 24
4¾	Killay	..	..	6 28	7 33	..	..	..	..	8 43	..	..	..	..	1218	..	1 18	..	4 29	4 29
5¾	Dunvant	....	....	6 30	7 37	....	....	....	....	8 46	....	....	....	....	1220	....	1 20	....	4 32	4 32
7¼	Gowerton South	..	..	6 35	7 42	..	..	..	..	8 50	..	..	..	..	1226	12 44	1 26	..	4 37	4 37
8¾	Gorseinon **A**	....	....	6 40	7 47	....	....	....	....	8 58	....	....	....	....	1230	12 49	1 30	....	4 42	4 42
12¼	**Pontardulais W** .. arr	..	..	**6 49**	**7 56**	..	..	**8 11**	..	**9 7**	**10 49**	..	..	..	**1240**	**12 58**	**1 40**	..	**4 50**	**4 50**
—	Mls **Llanelly** .... dep	5a37	....	....	....	....	**7 48**	....	**8 30**	Stop	....	**11 5**	....	....	....	....		**2p50**	....	....
—	2¾ Bynea	5 43	..	..	..	..	7 54	..	8 36	..	..	11 10	..	..	..	..		2 55	..	..
—	4¾ Llangennech	....	....	....	....	....	7 58	....	8 40	....	....	11 16	....	....	....	....		3 0	....	....
—	7 **Pontardulais W** arr	**5 51**	..	..	..	..	**8 3**	..	**8 45**	..	..	**11 20**	..	..	..	..		**3 7**	..	..
—	**Pontardulais W**.... dep	**5 53**	....	**6 50**	....	**7 57**	....	**8 12**	**8 48**	....	**10 50**	**11 22**	....		....	**1 0**		**3 9**		
17	Pantyffynnon ...... arr	6 0	..	6 58	..	8 4	..	8 19	8 55	..	..	11 29	..		..	1 8		3 17		
	Pantyffynnon ...... dep	6 3	....	7 0	....	8 5	....	8 20	8 58	....	10Y58	11 30	....		....	1 9		3 25		
18	Parcyrhun Halt	6 6	..	..	..	..	..	..	9 1	..	..		..		..	..		..		
18¼	Tirydail **H**	6 10	....	7 3	....	....	....	8 23	9 4	....	11 0		....		....	1 10		....		
20	Llandebie	6 16	..	..	..	..	..	..	9 10	..	..		..		..	..		..		
24¼	Ffairfach	6 27	....	....	....	....	....	....	9 24	....	....		....		....	....		....		
25	**Llandilo** .. .. .. arr	**6 30**	..	**7 25**	..	**8 23**	..	**8 37**	**9 28**	am	**11 15**		..		..	**1 27**				
—	**104**Fishguard Harbour..dep	..	..	..	..	..	..	..	..	7 50	..		10N20		..	..			..	..
—	**104**Pembroke Dock .. „	....	....	....	....	....	....	....	....	7 30	....		10 20		....	....			....	....
—	**104**Tenby .. .. .. „	..	..	..	..	..	..	..	..	8 3	..		11 0		..	..			..	..
—	Mls **Carmarthen** ... dep	....	**6 30**	....	....	....	....	....	....	**1015**	....		**12p30**		....	....	....		....	....
—	2 Abergwili	..	6 36	..	..	..	..	..	..	1020	..		12 36		..	..	..		..	..
—	5½ Nantgaredig	....	6 43	....	....	....	....	....	....	1028	....		12 43		....	....	....		....	....
—	8 Llanarthney Halt ..	..	6 48	..	..	..	..	..	..	1034	..		12 49		..	..	..		..	..
—	9¼ Dryslwyn	....	6 53	....	....	....	....	....	....	1039	....		12 53		....	....	....		....	....
—	11¾ Golden Grove	..	6 59	..	..	..	..	..	..	1044	..	..	12 58		..	..	..		..	..
—	14½ Llandilo Bridge	....	7 7	....	....	....	....	....	....	1049	....	....	1 3		....	....	....		....	....
—	15 **Llandilo** .. .. arr	..	**7 12**	..	..	..	..	..	..	**1054**	..	..	**1 8**		..	..	..		..	..
—	**Llandilo** .. .. .. dep	**6 31**	....	**7 28**	....	**8 24**	....	**8 38**	**9 29**	....	**11 17**	....	....	**1 10**	....	**1 29**	....		....	....
30½	Llangadock..	6 49	..	7 37	..	..	..	8 49	9 43	..	..	..	..	..	..	1 38	..		..	..
32½	Llanwrda	6 54	....	7 40	....	....	....	8 53	9 48	....	....	....	....	....	....	1 42	....		....	....
36	**Llandovery** .. arr	**7 1**	..	**7 48**	..	**8 42**	..	**8 59**	**9 56**	..	**11 36**	..	..	**1 29**	..	**1 49**	..		..	..
	Llandovery .. dep	....	....	**7 50**	....	**8 44**	....	**9 3**	....	....	**11 40**	....	....	**1 33**	....	**1 54**	....		....	....
40¾	Cynghordy..	..	..	8 0	..	..	..	..	..	..	..	..	..	..	..	2 4	..		..	..
47½	Llanwrtyd Wells	....	....	8 15	....	....	....	9 28	....	....	12 5	....	....	1 57	....	2 20	....		....	....
51	Llangammarch Wells ..	..	..	8 20	..	..	..	9 33	..	..	12 10	..	..	..	..	2 26	..		..	..
52¾	Garth	....	....	8 24	..	9 18	....	9U38	....	....	....	....	....	2 7	....	2 30	....		....	....
56	Cilmery Halt	..	..	8 30	..	..	..	..	..	..	..	..	..	..	..	..	..		..	..
58¼	**Builth Road,** H.L. .. arr	....	....	**8 35**	....	**9 29**	....	**9 47**	....	....	**12 23**	....	....	**2 16**	....	**2 43**	....		....	....
—	**185**Brecon .. .. .. dep	..	..	6 30	..	..	..	..	..	..	10 32	..	..	..	..	1 25	..		..	..
—	**Builth Road,** H.L. .. dep	....	....	**8 39**	....	**9 33**	....	**9 50**	....	....	**12 26**	....	....	**2 18**	....	**2 44**	....		....	....
64	Llandrindod Wells **D** ..	..	..	8 53	..	9 45	..	10 3	..	..	12 39	..	..	2 29	..	2 57	..		..	..
67½	Penybont	....	....	9 1	....	....	....	10 9	....	....	....	....	....	2 37	....	3 4	....	....	....	....
70½	Dolau	..	..	9 10	..	..	..	..	..	..	..	..	..	..	..	3 11	..	..	..	..
74	Llanbister Road **F**	....	....	9 20	....	....	....	....	....	....	....	....	....	2 54	....	3 19	....	....	....	....
77	Llangunllo	..	..	9 27	..	..	..	..	..	..	..	..	..	3 9	..	3 26	..	..	..	..
80¾	Knucklas	....	....	9 34	....	....	....	....	....	....	....	....	....	....	....	3 33	....	....	....	....
83½	Knighton	..	..	9 43	..	1020	..	10 37	..	..	1 12	..	..	3 23	..	3 44	..	..	..	..
87¾	Bucknell	....	....	9 50	....	....	....	....	....	....	1 18	....	....	3 29	....	3 52	....	....	....	....
90¾	Hopton Heath	..	..	9 55	..	..	..	..	..	..	..	..	..	..	..	3 58	..	..	..	..
93¼	Broome	....	....	10 0	....	....	....	....	....	....	....	....	....	....	....	4 4	....	....	....	....
95¾	**Craven Arms and Stokesay** arr	..	..	**10 8**	..	**1040**	..	**10 55**	..	..	**1 30**	..	..	**3 42**	..	**4 17**	..	..	..	..
	Craven Arms and Stokesay dep	....	....	**10 22**	....	**1042**	....	**10 56**	....	....	**1 32**	....	....	**3 43**	....	**4 20**	....	....	....	....
102½	Church Stretton. .. arr	..	..	10 40	..	..	..	..	..	..	1 45	..	..	3 56	..	4 35	..	..	..	..
115¼	**Shrewsbury** .... „	....	....	**11 4**	....	**1117**	....	**11 30**	....	....	**2 4**	....	....	**4 17**	....	**5 2**	....	....	....	....
158	**152**Chester (General). arr	..	..	..	..	..	..	1z11	..	..	3gg45	..	..	5 34	..	7 13	..	..	..	..
173	Birkenhead **G** ... „	....	....	....	....	....	....	2 5	....	....	4gg25	....	....	6 37	....	7 50	....	....	....	....
147¾	Crewe .. .. .. „	..	..	12f19	..	1219	..	12C37	..	..	3zz33	..	..	5 37	..	6L20	..	..	..	..
183	Liverpool (L. St.).. „	....	....	1f25	....	1 25	....	2C58	....	....	4k50	....	....	6 44	....	7n20	....	....	....	....
178½	Manchester (L. Rd.) „	..	..	f1P24	..	1P24	..	1 37	..	..	4rr20	..	..	7 3	..	7cc24	..	..	..	..
157½	**152**Birmingham (S.H.). „	....	....	12θ41	....	1 7	....	2c55	....	....	3 55	....	....	5 53	....	7 15	....	....	....	....
172¾	„ (N.St.) „	..	..	2S16	..	2 16	..	2g51	..	..	5 34	..	..	..	..	9hh3	..	..	..	..
268	**152London** (Pad.).... „	....	....	4bb45	....	3 25	....	5bb15	....	....	6‡ 0	....	....	8 35	....	10 25	....	....	....	....
278	„ (Euston) . „	..	..	3D 5	..	3 36	..	4B12	..	..	6kk52	..	..	..	..	B9y20	..	..	..	..

LOCAL TRAINS and intermediate Stations between Craven Arms and Shrewsbury, see Table 166.

For Notes, see page 354

Western Region public timetable, 13 June to 18 September 1955. *Courtesy: Malcolm Took*

Table 144— SWANSEA, LLANELLY, CARMARTHEN, BUILTH ROAD, CRAVEN ARMS and SHREWSBURY
continued

Week Days only—*continued*

Station	pm	pm	am	am	am	am	pm	pm	pm	pm	pm	pm	
	Except Saturdays	Saturdays only		Except Saturdays	Saturdays only	To Brynamman West arr. 7 7 pm (Table 141)		TC Swansea (Victoria) to York, arr. 3 40 am (3 37 am on Sundays)	To Brynamman West arr. 8 26 pm (Table 141)	Saturdays only; also runs daily during August To Brynamman West, arr. 9 33 pm (Table 141)	Saturdays only	Saturdays only To Brynamman West arr. 10 54 pm (Table 141)	
104London (Pad.) .. dep	..	..	11F55	1155	1155	11S55	..	12Z55	1S50	3 45	4 15	4 15	..
104 Cardiff (General) . ,,	....	....	2F55	2 55	3 8	4aa5	....	4dd5	4§30	6 46	7 50	7 50	....
104 Swansea (High St.) ¶ arr	..	..	d4F20	4 16	4 37	d5b20	..	5dd15	6§15	7 55	9 8	9d30	..
Swansea (Victoria) .. dep	....	....	....	5p35	5p35	....	....	6 30	7 15	8 25	9 45	....	....
,, (Bay)	..	..	..	5 39	5 39	..	..	..	7 18	8 28	9 48	..	..
Mumbles Road	....	....	....	5 44	5 44	....	....	....	7 23	8 33	9 53	....	....
Killay	..	..	..	5 49	5 49	..	..	..	7 28	8 38	9 58	..	..
Dunvant	....	....	....	5 52	5 52	....	....	....	7 30	8 40	10 0	....	....
Gowerton South	..	..	..	5 57	5 57	..	..	..	7 36	8 46	10 6	..	..
Gorseinon **A**	....	....	....	6 2	6 2	....	....	....	7 40	8 50	1010	....	....
Pontardulais W .. arr	..	..	..	6 10	6 10	..	..	6 53	7 50	9 2	1020	..	..
Llanelly .... dep	....	....	5p 0		....	6p20	....	....	....	....	....	10 5	....
Bynea	..	..	5 6		..	6 26	..	..	..	..	..	1010	..
Llangennech	....	....	5 14		....	6 30	....	....	....	....	....	1018	....
Pontardulais W .. arr	..	..	5 18		..	6 35	..	..	..	..	..	1023	..
Pontardulais W .... dep	....	....	5 20		6 12	6 37	....	6 55	7 52	9 3	....	1024	....
Pantyffynnon .. .. arr	..	..	5 27		6 19	6 44	..	..	7 59	9 10	..	1030	..
Pantyffynnon .. .. dep	....	....	5 29	....	6 20	6 46	....	....	8 4	9 12	....	1033	....
Parcyrhun Halt	..	..	5 32	..	6 25	..	..	..	..	..			..
Tirydail **H**	....	....	5 36	....	6 28	....	....	7 4	....				....
Llandebie	..	..	5 42	..	6 35		..	..					..
Ffairfach	....	....	5 56	....	....		....	....					....
Llandilo .. .. .. arr	..	..	6 0	..			..	7 21					..
104 Fishguard Harbour..dep	..	..	..	..			4N10	..			..	..	..
104 Pembroke Dock .. ,,	....	....	....	....			3J50	....			....	....	....
104 Tenby .. .. .. ,,	..	..	..	..			4J29	..			..	..	..
Carmarthen ... dep	....	....	....	....	....		6 20	....		....	....	....	....
Abergwili	..	..	..	..	..		6 28	..		..	..	..	..
Nantgaredig	....	....	....	....	....		6 40	....		....	....	....	....
Llanarthney Halt ..	..	..	..	..	..		6 46	..		..	..		..
Drysllwyn	....	....	....	....	....		6 50	....		....	....		....
Golden Grove	..	..	..	..	..		6 55	..		..	..		..
Llandilo Bridge	....	....	....	....	....		7 0	....		....	....		....
Llandilo .. .. arr			..	..	..		7 5	..		..	..		..
Llandilo .. .. .. dep			6 2	....	....	....	....	7K32	....		....		....
Llangadock..			6 16	..	..	..	..	7K41	..		..		..
Llanwrda			6 21	....	....	....	....	7S41	....		....		....
Llandovery .. arr			6 30	..	..	..	..	7K52	..		..		..
Llandovery .. dep	6 5	6 5	....	....	....	....	....	7K58	....		....		....
Cynghordy..	6 15	6 15	..	..	..	..	..	..	..		..		..
Llanwrtyd Wells	6 30	6 30	....	....	....	....	....	8K25	....		....		....
Llangammarch Wells ..	6 37	6 37	..	..	..	..	..	8K30	..		..	..	..
Garth	6 42	6 42	....	....	....	....	....	....	....	....	....	....	....
Cilmery Halt	6 50	6 50	..	..	..	..	..	..	..	..	..	..	..
Builth Road, H.L.....arr	6 55	6 55	....	....	....	....	....	8K44	....	....	....	....	....
185 Brecon .. .. .. dep	5 5	5 5	..	..	..	..	..	..	..	..	..	..	..
Builth Road, H.L. .. dep	7 4	7 4	....	....	....	....	....	8K47	....	....	....	....	....
Llandrindod Wells **D** ..	7 23	7 23	..	..	..	..	..	9K 1	..	..	..	..	..
Penybont	7 29	7 29	....	....	....	....	....	9S 5	....	....	....	....	....
Dolau	7 36	7 36	..	..	..	..	..	9S12	..	..	..	..	..
Llanbister Road **F**	7 43	7 43	....	....	....	....	....	9S17	....	....	....	....	....
Llangunllo	7 49	7 49	..	..	..	..	..	..	..	..	..	..	..
Knucklas	7 57	7 57	....	....	....	....	....	....	....	....	....	....	....
Knighton	8 5	8 15	..	..	..	..	..	9 35	..	..	..	..	..
Bucknell	8 12	8 22	....	....	....	....	....	**X**	....	....	....	....	....
Hopton Heath	8 18	8 27	..	..	..	..	..	..	..	..	..	..	..
Broome...............	....	8 33	....	....	....	....	....	....	....	....	....	....	....
Craven Arms and Stokesay arr	8 31	8 40	..	..	..	..	..	10 1	..	..	..	..	..
Craven Arms and Stokesay dep	8 56	8 56	....	....	....	....	....	10 2	....	....	....	....	....
Church Stretton. .. arr	9 13	9 13	..	..	..	..	..	..	..	..	..	..	..
Shrewsbury .... ,,	9 35	9 35	....	....	....	....	....	10 36	..	..	..	..	..
152 Chester (General). arr	1135	1135	..	..	..	..	..	12B40	..	..	..	..	..
Birkenhead **G** ... ,,	1220	1220	....	....	....	....	....	7B‖5	....	....	....	....	....
Crewe .. .. .. ,,	1050	1050	..	..	..	..	..	11 31	..	..	..	..	..
Liverpool (L. St.).. ,,	....	....	....	....	....	....	....	1a27	....	....	....	....	....
Manchester (L. Rd.) ,,	..	..	..	..	..	..	..	1a28	..	..	..	..	..
152 Birmingham (S.H.). ,,	1210	1210	....	....	....	....	....	....	....	....	....	....	....
,, (N.St.) ,,	am	am	..	..	..	..	..	2xx2	..	..	..	..	..
152London (Pad.).... ,,	5t10	5 10	....	....	....	....	....	....	....	....	....	....	....
,, (Euston) . ,,	..	..	..	..	..	..	..	3yy32	..	..	..	..	..

A 1½ miles to Loughor
A Arr 9 44 am on Saturdays
aa Dep 3 8 pm on Saturdays
a am
B Via Crewe
bb Arr 3 25 pm on Saturdays
b 10 minutes *earlier* on Sats.
C Arr Crewe 12 33 and Liverpool (Lime St.) 1 25 pm on Saturdays
cc Arr 7 3 pm on Saturdays
c Arr 1 7 pm on Saturdays
D 4½ miles to Newbridge-on-Wye Station
D Arr 3 36 pm on Saturdays
dd Dep Cardiff (Gen.) 4 20 and arr Swansea (High St.) 5 40 pm on Saturdays
d Departure time
E Except Saturdays
e On Saturdays dep Cardiff (General) 12 35 pm and Swansea (High St. 1 58 pm
F 5 miles to Llanbister
F Dep London (Paddington) 11 35 am, Cardiff (Gen.) 2 40 pm and Swansea (High St.) 4 4 pm on Saturdays
f Saturdays only. Runs 25th June to 3rd September
G Woodside
gg Arr Chester (Gen.) 4 10 and Birkenhead (Woodside) 4 48 pm on Saturdays
g Arr 2 54 pm on Saturdays
H ½ mile to Ammanford
hh Arr 8 7 pm on Sats. (9 0 pm on 18th and 25th June)
h Sunday to Friday nights
J Dep Pembroke Dock 3 55 and Tenby 4 35 pm on Saturdays
K 4 minutes *earlier* on Saturdays
kk Via Crewe. Arr 7 10 pm on Saturdays (6 35 pm on 16th July to 3rd September)
k Arr 4 25 pm on Saturdays 16th July to 3rd Sept. inclusive
L Arr 6 1 pm on Saturdays
N Third class only
n Arr 7 6 pm on Saturdays
P Mayfield Station
p pm
Q On Saturdays 2nd July to 27th Aug. incl. arr 12 18 pm
rr Arr 4 48 pm on Saturdays. On Saturdays 16th July to 3rd September arr Mayfield Sta. 4 0 pm. Passengers can arr Victoria Sta. 4 22 pm on Sats. 25th June to 27th August incl.
S Saturdays only
t Arr 4 5 am on Saturdays 23rd July to 13th August
TC Through Carriages
U Calls to take up for beyond Shrewsbury. Notice to be given at the Station on the *previous* day
W Station for Hendy
X Set down from Llandovery or beyond on informing guard at Llandovery
xx Via Crewe; arr 2 6 am
Y Calls at Pantyffynnon on Sats. only to take up
yy Via Crewe. Arr 3 19 am on Saturdays (3 39 am on 18th June) and 3 25 am on Sundays
y Arr 9 0 pm on Saturdays
Z Saturdays only. Runs 16th July to 20th August

zz Arr 3 50 pm on Saturdays (3 2 pm 16th July to 3rd September inclusive). *z* 5 minutes later on Saturdays. ❸ Third class only. § Dep Cardiff (Gen.) 5 10 and arr Swansea (High St.) 6 40 pm on Saturdays. ‖ Arr 8 4 am on Sundays. ¶ Distance between Swansea (High St.) and Swansea (Vic.) ½ mile. Passengers cross the town at their own expense. † Dep 7 50 am on Saturdays ‡ Arr 7 40 pm on Saturdays.

Table 144— SHREWSBURY, CRAVEN ARMS, BUILTH ROAD, CARMARTHEN, LLANELLY and SWANSEA
continued

Week Days only

Miles from Shrewsbury																				
		pm	am	am	am	am	am	am	pm	pm	pm	pm	pm	pm	am	am	pm	am	pm	pm
	Notes	TC York dep 9E50 pm to Swansea (Victoria)			From Brynamman West dep 7 55 am (Table 141)				Saturdays only	From Brynamman West dep 12 15 pm (Table 141)		From Brynamman West dep 1 15 pm (Table 141); Saturdays only; also runs each week day during August	Saturdays only; also runs each week day during August		Saturdays only. Runs 16th July to 27th August inclusive	Except Saturdays	Runs Mondays to Fridays; also runs Saturdays 16th July to 27th August inclusive	Saturdays only	Saturdays only	Except Saturdays and School Holidays ❸
	London (Euston) . dep	10T45																		
	152 „ (Pad.) .... „						12 5											7J10		
	Birmingham (N.St.) „	11c10													8B20	8B25				
	152 „ (S.H.). „	am					3 50								8 32	8 32		11J0		
	Manchester (L. Rd.) „	12 35													9 25	9 25		9 25		
	Liverpool (L. St.) . „	12 10													9 15	9 10		9 15		
	Crewe .. .. .. „	2 15													1040	10 30		1040		
	Birkenhead **G** .. „	11u10													9 30	9 20		9 30		
	152 Chester (General). „	12L10													1010	9 56		1010		
		am	am	am	am	am	am	am	pm	pm	pm	pm	pm	pm	am	noon	pm	pm	pm	pm
—	**Shrewsbury** .... dep	3 45					6 25								1155	12 0		1228		
12¾	Church Stretton .. „						6 59								1222	12 30		1255		
19½	**Craven Arms and Stokesay** arr	4 17					7 13								1232	12 43		1 8		
	dep	4 22					7 40								1234	12 50		1 15		
22	Broome..............						7 46													
25	Hopton Heath						7 51													
28	Bucknell	4 35					7 57									1 5		1 31		
32¼	Knighton	4 48					8 5								1 9	1 14		1 41		
35	Knucklas						8 12													
38¾	Llangunllo						8 24									1 28		1 58		
41¾	Llanbister Road **F**						8 30									1 33		2 4		
45¼	Dolau						8 36									1 38		2 10		
48¼	Penybont	5§18					8 43									1 45		2 17		
51¾	Llandrindod Wells **D** ..	5 26					8 50								1 42	1 51		2 27		
57½	**Builth Road,** H.L. .. arr	5 38					9 1								1 53	2 2		2 40		
84½	**185**Brecon .. .. .. arr	7 57					10 21													
—	**Builth Road,** H.L. .. dep	5 40					9 4								1 55	2 3		2 42		
59½	Cilmery Halt						9 10											bb		
62¾	Garth						9 17								2 5	2 13		2 50		
64½	Llangammarch Wells ..	5H55					9 22									2 18		2 55		
68	Llanwrtyd Wells	6 2					9 30								2 20	2 25		3 2		
74¾	Cynghordy						9 45									2 40		3 16		
79½	**Llandovery** ...... arr	6 24					9 59								2 40	2 47		3 24		
	dep	6 32				8 30	10 0							2 15	2 43	2 52		3 28		4 10
83	Llanwrda	6 38				8 40	10 8							2 22	2 49	2 59		3 34		4 18
85	Llangadock..	6 46				8 50	10 13							2 27	2 53	3 3		3 38		4 21
90½	**Llandilo** .. .. .. arr	6 57				9 2	10 23							2 40	3 2	3 12		3 48		
—	**Llandilo** .. .. dep		7 30					1115									3 23		4 5	
91	Llandilo Bridge		7 34					1119									3 28		4 9	
91½	Golden Grove		7 40					1124									3 33		4 14	
93½	Dryslllwyn............		7 45					1129									3 38		4 19	
95¼	Llanarthney Halt		7 50					1134									3 43		4 24	
97¾	Nantgaredig		7 56					1140									3 48		4 32	
101¼	Abergwili		8 2					1148									3 54		4 38	
103¼	**Carmarthen** ..... arr		8 10					1154									4 0		4 45	
133½	**104**Tenby .. .. .. arr		10 22					3F29									6X30		6 50	
144¾	**104**Pembroke Dock .. „		10 55					4F 7									7X12		7 21	
145¼	**104**Fishguard Harbour. „		10N26					4C 1									6X55		7 15	
—	**Llandilo** .. .. .. dep	7 3				9 7	10 25							2 42	3 8	3 18		3 50		
91¼	Ffairfach					9 10								2 50						
95¼	Llandebie					9 20	10 37							3 5						
97	Tirydail **H**	7 20				9 25	10 42							3 9	3 22	3 32		4 5		
97½	Parcyrhun Halt..					9 28								3 12						
98¼	Pantyffynnon ...... arr	7 25			8 17	9 30	10 47			1236		1 35		3 15		3 36		4 9		
	dep	7 27			8 19	9 33	10 48			1243		1 37		3 16		3 38		4 11		
103	**Pontardulais W**.... arr	7 35			8 26	9 40	10 55			1250		1 44		3 24	3 33	3 45		4 18		
—	**Pontardulais W**.. dep				8 27	9 41				1252		1 45		3 25						
105¼	Llangennech				8 33	9 47				1258		1 51		3 30						
107¼	Bynea				8 37	9 52				1 2		1 56		3 35						
110	**Llanelly**.. .. .. arr				8 43	9 58				1 8		2 2		3 41						
—	**Pontardulais W** .. dep	7 36		8 18			10 57		1210		1 0		1 55		3 35	3 47		4 20		
106½	Gorseinon **A**	7 44		8 24			11 5		1216		1 6		2 0		3 40	3 54		4 26		
108	Gowerton South			8 28			11 9		1220		1 10		2 5		3 46	3 58		4 30		
109½	Dunvant			8 32			11 13		1224		1 14		2 9							
110½	Killay..................			8 35			11 17		1228		1 18		2 13							
112¼	Mumbles Road			8 39			11 20		1232		1 22		2 17		3 56	4 8		4 40		
114¼	**Swansea** (Bay)	8 0		8 44			11 27		1237		1 27		2 23		4 0	4 13		4 46		
115¼	„ (Victoria) .. arr	8 6		8 49			11 32		1242		1 32		2 28		4 6	4 17		4 51		
—	**104**Swansea (High St.) ¶dep	8 45		9Y35	9d28	10d26	1y30		1†10	1d49	2 30	2d43	3 50	4dd40	4 40	5 30		5 30		
—	**104**Cardiff (General).. arr	9 53		10Y53	1053	11 52	2y52		2†44	3 36	3 52	4e55	4 55	6 28	6 28	6 52		6 52		
—	**104London** (Pad.) .. „	1p 0		2t40	2t40	3t10	5b50		6g 0	7 20	7 20	7Q45	7Q45	10 0		10 0		10 0		

For Notes, see page 356

Table 144— *continued*

SHREWSBURY, CRAVEN ARMS, BUILTH ROAD, CARMARTHEN, LLANELLY and SWANSEA

Week Days only—*continued*

Station	pm	am	am	pm	am	pm	pm	pm	pm	noon	pm	pm	pm	
London (Euston) . dep	..	..	..	..	..	..	..	..	..	**12aa0**	..	..	**2 30**	..
152 „ (Pad.) .... „	..	**9 10**	**11 10**	..	**11 10**	..	..	..	..	**11x45**	..	..	**4 10**	..
Birmingham (N.St.) „	..	..	12 10	..	12 10	..	..	..	..	K2B 0	..	..	4 50	..
152 „ (S.H.). „	..	1145	1 14	..	1 42	..	..	..	..	3k27	..	..	6 50	..
Manchester (L. Rd.) „	..	..	11 55	..	11 55	..	..	..	..	3f 5	..	..	4 35	..
Liverpool (L. St.) . „	..	..	11 40	..	11 40	..	..	..	..	3 0	..	..	4 17	..
Crewe .. .. .. „	..	..	1 7	..	1 7	..	..	..	..	4f 9	..	..	6 10	..
Birkenhead **G** .. „	..	..	11 45	..	11 45	..	..	..	..	2 40	..	..	5 37	..
152 Chester (General). „	..	11N5	12 23	..	12 23	..	..	..	..	3 20	..	..	6 25	..
	pm	pm	pm	pm	pm	pm	pm	pm	pm	pm	pm	pm	pm	
Shrewsbury .... dep	..	**1 15**	**2 40**	..	**3 0**	..	..	..	..	**5 30**	..	..	**8 22**	..
Church Stretton .. „	..	1 38	3 5	..	3 30	..	..	..	..	5 52	..	..	8 54	..
Craven Arms and Stokesay arr	..	**1 51**	**3 17**	..	**3 43**	..	..	..	..	**6 3**	..	..	**9 10**	..
Craven Arms and Stokesay dep	..	**2 20**	**3 20**	..	**3 50**	..	..	..	..	**6 6**	..	..	**9 15**	..
Broome	..	2 26	..	..	..	..	..	..	..	..	..	..	..	..
Hopton Heath	..	2 31	..	..	..	..	..	..	..	6 15	..	..	9 26	..
Bucknell	..	2 37	3U32	..	4 5	..	..	..	..	6 21	..	..	9 32	..
Knighton	..	2q47	3 41	..	4 12	..	..	..	..	6 31	..	..	9 42	..
Knucklas	..	2 54	..	..	..	..	..	..	..	..	..	..	..	..
Llangunllo	..	3 6	..	..	..	..	..	..	..	6 46	..	..	9 58	..
Llanbister Road **F**	..	3 12	..	..	..	..	..	..	..	6 51	..	..	10 3	..
Dolau	..	3 18	..	..	..	..	..	..	..	6 57	..	..	10 9	..
Penybont	..	3 25	4U 8	..	4U41	..	..	..	..	7 4	..	..	1016	..
Llandrindod Wells **D** ..	..	3 32	4 16	..	4 45	..	..	..	..	7 10	..	..	1022	..
Builth Road, H.L. .. arr	..	**3 43**	4 27	..	**4 56**	..	..	..	..	**7 21**	..	..	Saturdays only	..
185 Brecon .. .. .. arr	..	5 24	..	..	8R30	..	..	..	..	..	..	..		..
Builth Road, H.L. .. dep	..	**3 46**	4 30	..	**4 58**	..	..	..	..	**7 24**	..	..		..
Cilmery Halt	..	3 52	..	..	..	..	..	..	..	..	..	..		..
Garth	..	4 0	4 38	..	5 7	..	..	..	..	7 35	..	..		..
Llangammarch Wells ..	..	4 5	4 43	..	5 12	..	..	..	..	7 40	..	..	..	..
Llanwrtyd Wells	..	4 10	4 50	Except Saturdays	5 19	Saturdays only	..	..	..	7 49	..	..	..	..
Cynghordy	..	4 26	..		..		..	..	..	..	..	..	..	..
Llandovery arr	..	**4 35**	**5 12**		**5 39**		..	..	..	**8 17**	..	..	..	..
Llandovery dep	..	—	**5 14**		**5 42**		..	..	**6 55**	**8 20**	..	..	..	..
Llanwrda	..	Stop	5U20		5 48		..	..	7 3	8P26	..	..	..	..
Llangadock	..	..	5U23		5 52		..	..	7 9	8 30	..	..	..	..
Llandilo .... arr	..	..	**5 34**	..	**6 1**	..	..	..	**7 21**	**8 40**	..	..	..	..
Llandilo .. .. dep	From Brynamman West, dep 4 35 pm (Table 141)	..	Except Saturdays	**5 50**	Saturdays only	**6 15**	..	..	..	..	..	**9 0**	..	..
Llandilo Bridge		..		5 55		6 19	..	..	..	..	..	9 4	..	..
Golden Grove		..		6 0		6 24	..	..	..	..	..	9 9	..	..
Drysllwyn		..		6 5		6 29	..	..	..	..	..	9 14	..	..
Llanarthney Halt		..		6 10		6 34	..	..	..	..	..	9 19	..	..
Nantgaredig		..		6 15		6 39	..	..	..	..	..	9 25	..	..
Abergwili		..		6 22		6 46	..	..	..	..	..	9 30	..	..
Carmarthen ..... arr		..		**6 30**		**6 53**	..	..	..	..	..	**9 38**	..	..
104 Tenby .. .. .. arr		..	..	9 5	..	9 15	..	Saturdays only	..	..	..	..	..	..
104 Pembroke Dock .. „		..	..	9 35	..	9 46	..		..	..	..	..	..	..
104 Fishguard Harbour. „		..	..	9 55	..	9 55	..		..	..	..	..	..	..
Llandilo .... dep		..	**5 38**	..	**6 3**	..	..		**7 27**	**8 41**	Saturdays only	..	..	..
Ffairfach		..	..	..	..	..	..	..	7 30	..		..	..	..
Llandebie		..	..	..	..	..	..	6 40	7 45	..		..	..	..
Tirydail **H**		..	5 52	..	6 18	..	..	6 44	7 50	8 55		..	..	..
Parcyrhun Halt		..	..	..	..	..	..	6 47	7 52	..		..	..	..
Pantyffynnon arr	4 55	..	5 57	..	6 21	..	..	6 49	7 55	..		..	..	..
Pantyffynnon dep	4 57	..	5 58	..	6 23	..	..	6 52	7 58	..	9 8	..	..	..
Pontardulais W .... arr	**5 4**	..	**6 6**	..	**6 30**	..	..	**6 59**	**8 6**	**9 6**	**9 15**	..	..	..
Pontardulais W .. dep	**5 5**	..	..	..	..	..	Except Saturdays	..	**8 9**	..	**9 16**	..	..	..
Llangennech	5 10	..	..	..	..	..		..	..	..	9 22	..	..	..
Bynea	5 16	..	..	..	..	..		..	..	..	9 27	..	..	..
Llanelly .. .. .. arr	**5 21**	pm	..	..	..	..		..	**8 28**	..	**9 33**	..	..	..
Pontardulais W .. dep	..	**5 20**	**6 7**	..	**6 31**	..	**6 40**	**7 0**	..	**9 8**	..	..	..	..
Gorseinon **A**	..	5 26	..	..	..	..	6 47	7 6	..	9 15	..	..	..	..
Gowerton South	..	5 30	6U16	..	6U40	..	6 50	7 10	..	9 19	..	..	..	..
Dunvant	..	5 35	..	..	..	..	6 56	7 14	..	..	..	..	..	..
Killay	..	5 40	..	..	..	..	7 0	7 20	..	..	..	..	..	..
Mumbles Road	..	5 45	6 26	..	6 50	..	7 5	7 25	..	9 30	..	..	..	..
Swansea (Bay)	..	**5 50**	**6 31**	..	**6 55**	..	**7 10**	**7 30**	..	**9 35**	..	..	..	..
„ (Victoria) .. arr	..	**5 55**	**6 36**	..	**7 0**	..	**7 15**	**7 35**	..	**9 40**	..	..	..	..
104 Swansea (High St.) ¶dep	6d32	6 55	7 40	..	7 40	..	7 40	9 10	9d28	..	..	..	..	..
104 Cardiff (General) .. arr	8 37	8 37	9 36	..	9 36	..	9 36	1032	1045	..	..	..	..	..
104London (Pad.) .. „	..	..	4A25	..	4A25	..	4A25	4A25	4a25	..	..	..	..	..

A 1½ miles to Loughor
A am. Dep Swansea (High St.) 9 35 pm
a am
aa Dep 12 7 pm on Saturdays
B Via Crewe
bb Calls to set down passengers only
b On Saturdays arr 6 0 pm (18th June 6 10 pm)
C Arr 4 11 pm on Saturdays
c Via Crewe on Sunday nights
D 4½ miles to Newbridge-on-Wye Station
d Arrival time
dd Arrival time. On Saturdays arr 4 32 pm
E Except Saturdays
e Arr 4 12 pm on Saturdays 2nd July to 10th September incl.
F 5 miles to Llanbister
F On Saturdays arr Tenby 3 40 pm and Pembroke Dock 4 15 pm
f Dep Manchester (Lon. Rd.) 3 10 pm and Crewe 4 17 pm on Fridays and Saturdays
G Woodside
g On 18th June arr 6 10 pm
H ½ mile to Ammanford
H Calls when required to take up
J Will not run after 3rd Sept.
K Dep 2 40 pm on Saturdays
k Dep 3 40 pm on Saturdays
L Dep 11 3 pm on Sundays via Crewe
N Sats. only. Third class only
P Calls to set down from Craven Arms and beyond on notice being given to the Guard
p pm
Q On Saturdays 2nd July to 10th Sept. arr 7 55 pm; on other Saturdays arr 8 25 pm
q Arr 3 minutes *earlier*
R On Saturdays arr 8 11 pm
T Via Crewe; dep 10 50 pm on Sundays
t On Sats. 15 minutes later
TC Through Carriages
U Calls to set down from Shrewsbury and beyond on notice being given to the Guard
u Dep 10 0 pm on Sundays, via Crewe
W Station for Hendy
X On Sats. 16th July to 27th August incl. arr Tenby 5 34, Pembroke Dock 6 12 and Fishguard Harbour 6 5 pm
x Dep 1 10 pm on Saturdays
Y Dep Swansea (High St.) 9 20 am and arr Cardiff (Gen.) 10 46 am on Saturdays, 25th June to 27th Aug. inclusive
y Dep Swansea (High St.) 12 10 pm and arr Cardiff (Gen.) 1 46 pm on Saturdays

③ Third class only
† Dep Swansea (High St.) 1 30 pm and arr Cardiff (Gen.) 2 52 pm on 18th June only.
¶ Distance between Swansea (Vic.) and Swansea (High St.) ½ mile. Passengers cross the town at their own expense
§ Sets down only on notice to the Guard at Knighton

For LOCAL TRAINS and intermediate Stations between Shrewsbury and Craven Arms, see Table 166.

It appears that the *TI's* spies might have been on holiday throughout much of 1955 and 1956, the solitary report of Central Wales matters during those two years appearing in the October 1955 issue: *'Fowler 2-6-4T No 42388 has returned to Swansea* (after a stint at Whitland), *and on 17/8/55 was seen heading a freight in the direction of Llandilo'.* Soon after, No 42388 had a spell at Llandovery shed for banking duties.

One subject which appears to have escaped the observers' attention was engineering works at Sugar Loaf Tunnel. Between 2 May and 22 July 1955 the tunnel was closed from Mondays to Fridays so that essential maintenance work could be undertaken, and a bus service was provided between Llanwrtyd Wells and Llandovery. Through freight workings were diverted via Newport. In April 1956, drainage work in the tunnel required the temporary reintroduction of the bus service.

During the closure of the tunnel in 1955 a shuttle service was maintained between Craven Arms and Llanwrtyd Wells, and although Standard '3MT' 2-6-2Ts Nos 82030/31 were transferred to Shrewsbury shed for that purpose, No 82037 and LMSR '3MT' 2-6-2T No 40097 (both of Paxton Street) were more frequently used. At the time, No 40097 was one of three LMSR '4MTs' on Swansea's books, the others being Nos 40105 and 40141 — two were usually employed on passenger work and the third as the Victoria station pilot.

The '*TI*' correspondents were somewhat more observant in 1957, although they missed 4-6-0 No 45190 working a special naval train from Shrewsbury to Haverfordwest via Carmarthen on 26 November. Forgiving them that omission, they provided us with the following:

'There is to be an extensive transfer of tanks between the LMR and the WR. In exchange for 2-6-2Ts Nos 4120/22/23-29 and 5176 of Birkenhead, the LMR is taking 2-6-2Ts Nos 40105/41/45 and 0-6-0Ts Nos 47320/58/59, 47477/80, and 47655/81 from Swansea Victoria. To make good its loss, Swansea Victoria is getting "67XX" pannier tanks, two from Cardiff East Dock and five from Duffryn Yard (April issue)...*On April 9, presumably as a result of a failure, the 2.40pm from Shrewsbury reached Swansea behind 0-8-0 No 49196 (85C)..."Crab" 2-6-0s have worked twice over the Central Wales line, while the latest newcomers at Swansea (Victoria) have been Shrewsbury's Caprotti standard "5" 4-6-0s on freight work* (June issue)'.

From 1952, pannier tanks were in regular use on pilot duties at Swansea (Victoria), and they eventually took over most of the local workings from the station as well. On 27 July 1962, No 9637 waits at the terminus with the 4.15pm to Pontardulais. *Leslie Sandler*

The Llandovery–Llanelly locals were traditional GWR workings and, on 19 May 1964, 0-6-0PT No 8474 is seen entering Ffairfach in charge of the 6.55pm from Llandovery. The spur to the left of the last vehicle led to the Gas Works siding, and had fallen out of use in September 1961. *Hugh Ballantyne*

The pannier tank take-over, mentioned above, was not effected for some time. Indeed, in April 1957 the Pontardulais locals were regularly worked by 'Jinty' 0-6-0Ts (usually Nos 47478/79/81), while the ex-GWR '6700' class 0-6-0PTs were actually prohibited from the Gwaun-cae–Gurwen line, which sent traffic via Pantyffynnon.

In 1958, significant changes were observed on the Central Wales line.

'The new Swindon-built three-car cross-country diesel units, incorporating a small buffet, have already made trial runs from Craven Arms to Swansea (Victoria), where one was noted on February 4...All the ex-LNW 0-8-0s at Swansea Victoria have been removed and replaced by WR pannier tanks and two Stanier 2-8-0s, Nos 48419/63 (June issue).

During 1959 the railway press was often preoccupied with reports of new diesel locomotives, but traditional motive power still reigned on the Central Wales line. *Trains Illustrated*'s correspondents reported that:

'An unusual combination setting out for the Central Wales line on February 8 was 0-6-0 No 2220 and 2-8-0 No 48760, which took over at Shrewsbury one of a stream of excursions returning from the Scotland-Wales rugby international in Edinburgh; their train was the 9.5am Edinburgh-Pantyffynnon.

Another service for the Central Wales route left with 2-6-4T No 42385 and Class "5" 4-6-0 No.45145 ...Paxton Street depot, Swansea, was closed on August 31. (It had 29 engines prior to closure.) *Of its sub-depots, Llandovery now pays allegiance to Llanelly, and Gurnos and Upper Bank are sub-depots of Swansea East Dock. The Fowler 2-6-4Ts at Paxton Street have gone to Landore'.*

Proposed economies

The closure of Paxton Street shed in August 1959 could easily have been interpreted as the beginning of the end for the Central Wales line as, in June 1959, the threatingly-titled Committee for Unremunerative Railway Services had met at Paddington to discuss economies on the line. The committee's remit, however, had NOT been to consider total closure but to look into possible savings by the withdrawal of facilities at certain stations. Its report was published in August 1960 and, as if to give the impression that it was a cloak and dagger affair, its cover was stamped 'Not to be released to the public until 1991'

Above: More ex-GWR motive power on the Central Wales line — this time 0-6-0PT No 4693 in the loop at Llandebie on 4 September 1963.
Andrew Muckley

Below: The Fowler 2-6-4Ts maintained a presence on the Central Wales line until the 1960s. No 42385 takes on water at Builth Road (High Level) before continuing its journey from Swansea (Victoria) to Shrewsbury. *Hugh Davies Collection*

Above: Of the various '4MTs' which worked the Central Wales line in 1963/64, No 80069 seems to have been the one which appeared whenever photographers were around. On 2 June 1964, it was captured taking water at Knighton before continuing with the 2.40pm Shrewsbury–Swansea train.
B. J. Ashworth

Below: The motive power on the Central Wales line might have changed over the years, but the scenery remained as impressive as ever. Amid glorious countryside on 26 May 1962, the driver of '5MT' No 73024 transfers the token before commencing the descent from Sugar Loaf. The train is the 12 noon Shrewsbury–Swansea (Victoria) service.
R. O. Tuck

The report included comprehensive details of the special factors at the stations under scrutiny:

BROOME: Cart weighbridge — agreement made 1 November 1955 and operative for 7 years, that the Radnorshire Company Ltd pay a minimum of £50pa (less other receipts) for use of the weighbridge. No weighings have been performed since December 1957 as the Company, on their own initiative, transferred their coal to a concentration at Bucknell. We suggest that the agreement is terminated and the weighbridge recovered.

HOPTON HEATH: Siding connection was removed April 6th 1958, but freight facilities not officially withdrawn.

CILMERY HALT: Closure of halt previously submitted to TUCC for Wales and Monmouthshire, and an enquiry was held at Cardiff on 29th May 1959. The TUCC unanimously recommended that the 7.40am train from Craven Arms should continue to call at Cilmery halt ...The permanent withdrawal of freight facilities was endorsed by the Committee, and these were officially withdrawn on 3 August 1959.

It has been recommended that additional 'conditional' stops are made in the 6.15am, 12.25pm and 6.30pm Swansea, and 12.5pm Shrewsbury trains which commenced with the Summer Service 1960.

SUGAR LOAF SUMMIT PLATFORM: This was provided for the use of staff and their families, and no public facilities are available.

LLANGADOG: (spelling changed from Llangadock in 1958) *The CWS Milk Factory which is rail connected now regularly forward liquid milk by road, but an occasional tank is forwarded by rail. Their premises are being extended for the purpose of increasing the capacity for producing dried milk products.*

LLANDILO: This is the junction station with the Carmarthen–Llandilo line, and is a terminal station for the local passenger services on that line.

FFAIRFACH: The CWS Milk Factory was closed on 1st October 1959, and the local Gas Works ceased production in March 1958. Both private siding agreements will require to be terminated.

To effect immediate savings, a recommendation that this station be reduced to an unstaffed halt and freight and parcels facilities withdrawn was submitted on June 29th 1960. This recommendation was based on the Accountant's estimated loss of receipts of £37 on the revenue of £91 for the 12 months ending 30th June 1959, which indicated that the station, if unstaffed, would be profitable to the extent of £23, but the originating revenue for the period 1st October 1959 (date CWS Milk Factory closed) to 31st July 1960 was:-

Local services bookings	*£10.19s.1d*
Long distance bookings	*£10.10s.8d*
Special trips (Clifton Down)	*£25. 1s 6d*
Total:	***£46.11s.3d***

If unstaffed, the local bookings would be 100% lost, and as the Engineer's maintenance figure for passenger services only is £14pa, the economic position does not now merit retention of the station as an unstaffed halt.

LLANDEBIE: This station would be staffed by a Leading Porter from Ammanford & Tirydail between the hours 8.15am to 10.37am for the purpose of booking passengers joining Main Line trains (the only two trains involved are the 7.45am Swansea Victoria and the 7.40am Craven Arms) and to cover all other commercial duties. Some trains are already dealt with at this station when there is no staff on duty, and it is proposed to extend this arrangement.

AMMANFORD & TIRYDAIL (formerly Tirydail — renamed 13 June 1960)*: This station became the alternative station for the passenger and parcels traffic dealt with at Ammanford when that station closed on 18th August 1958. Parcels traffic for areas served by stations on the Pantyffynnon-Brynamman branch has been concentrated at Tirydail since the closure of the branch. Although it is proposed to withdraw facilities for dealing with freight traffic in full truck loads in the station sidings, it would be necessary to retain a short length of the siding to accommodate the "Siphon" which conveys parcels traffic detached from the 5.37am ex-Llanelly. Freight traffic will continue to be dealt with at Ammanford on the Brynamman branch.*

PANTYFFYNNON: The station platform duties are carried out by the Crossing Keepers whose services would be required irrespective of whether or not the passenger facilities were retained. No freight traffic has been dealt with in the station for some years.

PONTARDULAIS: Tinplate works in the area have been closed in recent years, but it is known that Messrs Teddington Aircraft Controls Ltd have taken over the premises previously occupied by the Teilo Tinplate Co, and Messrs Evans & Williams (Llanelly) Wagon Repairers now occupy the old Clayton Tinplate Works.

GORSEINON: Steel and tinplate works in the area have closed in recent years, and apart from the fact that Messrs Richard Thomas & Baldwins Ltd have reopened a Pressed Steel and Fabricating Works, it is not known what further developments are likely to take place. The new NCB Colliery at Brynlliw (which is served by rail from Grovesend on the Swansea Direct Line) commenced production in December 1959, and it is understood that in consequence the Mountain Colliery at Gorseinon will be closed in a few years' time.

GOWERTON SOUTH: This station is situated approximately 250yds from Gowerton North (on the Swansea High St–West Wales line)

STATIONS GORSEINON TO SWANSEA BAY: Concurrently with the report on individual stations, a report has been submitted (July 1958) on the operation of Shrewsbury-Swansea services — other than the through trains from and to York — by multiple-unit diesel sets. The diesel schedules include local trips (in replacement of the existing local trains between Swansea and Pontardulais) which could be operated by the units required for the through services. In the light of the proposal to withdraw passenger facilities between Pontardulais and Swansea, there would be no purpose in continuing the local service'.

Some of the financial statistics contained in the report would, had they been made available at the time, have made alarming reading for the line's supporters. Partly on the basis of the statistics, the committee submitted proposals to:

- Close stations and halts at: Broome, Hopton Heath, Knucklas halt, Cilmery halt, Ffairfach, Dunvant*;
- Reduce to status of unstaffed halts and withdraw parcels and freight facilities at: Llangunllo, Llanbister Road, Dolau, Garth, Llangammarch Wells, Cynghordy;
- Reduce to status of freight mileage sidings and withdraw passenger and parcels facilities at: Gorseinon*, Gowerton South*, Killay*, Mumbles Road *, Swansea Bay*;
- Increase the period without staffing and restrict parcels facilities at: Llandebie;
- Withdraw freight facilities from: Ammanford & Tirydail, Pantyffynnon (Freight facilities to remain at Ammanford, ½-mile from Ammanford & Tirydail)
- Partially unstaff and restrict the number of passenger trains calling at: Llanwrda, Llangadog

* These stations were on the Pontardulais-Swansea section of line, for which there were separate proposals concerning abandonment and diversion of services.

Business as usual
While the future format of the Central Wales line was under discussion, services still had to be operated. The heyday of steam traction on Britain's railways was beginning to draw to a close, but how many of us realised how quickly the end would come? As BR's fleet of diesel and electric locomotives and multiple-units increased, steam locomotives were displaced

On 16 May 1964 — the last year of steam on the Central Wales line — '5MT' 4-6-0 No 73036 approaches Llangunllo with the 12.10pm Swansea (Victoria)–Shrewsbury train. *B. J. Ashworth*

Above: During the 1950s and early 1960s ex-GWR '2251' class 0-6-0s were regularly used as bankers at Knighton, although No 2222 was in the area for only a month or so. In this impressive (nay, plucky) close-up, it puts in some hard work at the rear end of a Swansea-bound goods on 10 June 1960. *Colin P. Walker*

Right: The ex-GWR '5600' class 0-6-2Ts were used sparingly on the Central Wales line. In September 1963, No 5602 enters Mumbles Road station with a one-coach Swansea (Victoria)–Pontardulais local. *Andrew Muckley*

from their traditional haunts and efforts were made to find alternative duties for the less-senior members. Inevitably, the Central Wales line had its share of fresh faces.

At the end of October 1960 Standard '3MT' 2-6-2T No 82042 was transferred to Landore for a trial on the Central Wales line, but its bunker capacity proved insufficient and it was replaced by Fairburn 2-6-4T No 42182. The dietary demands of steam locomotives working the line were, of course, not a new problem! During the summer of 1960, incidentally, most of the passenger services on the line had been worked by the Fowler 2-6-4Ts while the Saturdays Only 9.30am Pembroke Dock-Shrewsbury train was usually hauled as far as Llandovery by a Whitland-based '2251' class 0-6-0 — often No 2220. Furthermore, it was not unknown to see '5600' class 0-6-2Ts on local passenger duties.

Two other interesting manifestations during the period were, however, not a result of locomotive displacement. Excursions returning from the Scotland–Wales Rugby Union international in Edinburgh on 12 February 1961 provided two eye-catching motive power combinations on trains routed via the Central Wales line. One was '5MT' 4-6-0 No 73024 of Shrewsbury and 0-6-0 No 3206 of Fishguard at the head of the 8.55am Edinburgh–Swansea Victoria service. The other was Sheffield's '5MT' No 73074 and Landore's 2-6-4T No 42397 with the 9.5am train from Edinburgh to Port Talbot via Morlais Junction East.

Since the demise of Paxton Street shed at Swansea in 1959, the ex-GWR depot at Landore (87E) had serviced the Central Wales line. However, Landore shed closed on 12 June 1961 and all shunting and Central Wales duties were transferred to Swansea East Dock shed (87D). These duties provided East dock's first passenger turns since 1936.

By September 1961 Shrewsbury had a significant allocation of 'Jubilee' class 4-6-0s, but they were officially prohibited from the Central Wales line until April 1963. After the prohibition was relaxed, they regularly took charge of the 11.45am Shrewsbury-Swansea train and returned with the 6.25pm 'York Mail' from Swansea. About the same time, Standard '4MT' 2-6-4Ts, which had been made redundant on the London, Tilbury & Southend line, also started to be seen on the Central Wales Line.

'Jubilee' class 4-6-0s started to appear on the Central Wales line in 1963, but three-coach loadings were a far cry from the work they had originally been designed for. On 5 June 1964, No 45577 *Bengal* heads a Swansea (Victoria)–Shrewsbury train near Bucknell. *Derek Cross*

If No 80069 seemed to be the most photographed of the Central Wales line's '4MTs', No 45577 *Bengal* performed a similar role for the 'Jubilees'. The 4-6-0 was photographed (again!) on 12 June 1964 in charge of a Shrewsbury–Swansea (Victoria) train near Knighton. *Derek Cross*

Renewed threats

The Central Wales line's interest value to enthusiasts was not, of course, viewed as justification for continuing its life indefinitely. Since the doom-laden report of 1960, traffic figures had continued to decline and this did not escape the attention of one Dr Richard Beeching. However, even before the publication of the infamous Beeching Report, the future of the entire line had been questioned, a report in the January 1963 issue of *Modern Railways* noting that:

'The fate of the Central Wales line passenger service has now been passed to the Minister of Transport (Mr Ernest Marples) for decision. There was an unexpected development at the TUCC hearing of objections at Llandrindod Wells on 10 November, when the WR's Commercial Officer admitted that the withdrawal of the service between Llandovery and Craven Arms would occasion considerable hardship. But he pointed out that of the intermediate stations between these two points only two — Llandrindod Wells and Knighton — were taking more than £5 a day in receipts. The TUCC findings accepted that no hardship would result from closure between Swansea Victoria and Pontardulais, and said that any inconvenience caused by withdrawal between Carmarthen and Llandilo could be overcome by establishing two daily bus services between Carmarthen and Llanarthney, the locality which would suffer most. But they could see no way of alleviating the hardship that would ensue between Llandilo and Craven Arms, and referred this problem to higher counsel'.

The Beeching Report was published on 27 March 1963 and it included preliminary proposals to close the entire Central Wales line. However, the Minister of Transport intervened and agreed only to the closure of the Pontardulais–Swansea section. The execution officially took place on Monday 15 June 1964, but in the absence of Sunday services the last revenue-earning trains between Pontardulais and Swansea operated on Saturday 13 June.

The last train to leave Swansea Victoria was the 'York Mail', hauled by 'Black Five' No 45406. It did not go unremarked that many of the passengers on that last northbound train had not used the railway since they were children — '...one of the reasons why Victoria station closed on Saturday night,' admonished the *South Wales Evening Post* the following Monday.

The last train to arrive at Victoria was the 6pm ex-Shrewsbury, scheduled to reach the terminus at 10.20pm, which was hauled on the last leg of its journey into Swansea by a WR 0-6-0PT. That very un-LMR style of motive power was not, however, a deliberate WR insult. In 1963 Wind Street Viaduct at Swansea had been declared unsafe and large engines had subsequently been prohibited from passing over the viaduct *en route* to East Dock. Consequently, it had become normal practice for the tender engines on Swansea-bound trains to be changed for smaller engines (usually 0-6-0PTs) at Pantyffynnon.

The goods yard next to Victoria station remained open until October 1965, access being by means of the high level line from High Street station, but the demise of Victoria station itself marked the end of passenger services on the city's ex-LMSR lines. The end of an era indeed.

Above: In 1963, a number of Standard '4MT' 2-6-4Ts were transferred from the London, Tilbury & Southend line to the Central Wales line. Among them was No 80069, seen here with a Swansea-bound train at Pontardulais. *Andrew Muckley*

Below: On 4 June 1964 — less than a fortnight before the cessation of Swansea–Shrewsbury workings — '5MT' 4-6-0 No 73095 leaves Builth Road with the 9.45am Swansea–Shrewsbury service. *B. J. Ashworth*

Chapter 6
Reprieved

Author's note: *As explained in the introduction to this book, this chapter uses the contemporary Welsh spellings of place names, although some of the locations did not adopt the Welsh spellings until well into the period under discussion.*

Although Dr Beeching's prescribed medicine — namely the complete closure of the entire Central Wales line — was avoided, the closure of the section between Swansea and Pontarddulais in June 1964 necessitated a revision of working practices at the southern end of the line. Craven Arms–Swansea trains were subsequently diverted to Llanelli. It is somewhat ironic that the Pontarddulais–Llanelli section is, in fact, the oldest of the various components of the present-day Central Wales line.

Pontarddulais-Llanelli

To recap briefly, the 6¼ mile-long line between Pontarddulais and Llanelli was built by the Llanelly Railway & Dock Co and opened to mineral traffic on 1 June 1839. In 1853 the LR obtained permission to build a ¾ mile-long spur to the South Wales Railway station at Llanelli, but as the LR was a standard gauge concern and the SWR a broad gauge company, the former had to use a separate platform alongside the SWR premises. Part of the LR's eventual network was taken over by the GWR in 1873, the SWR having become GWR property in 1863 and converted to the standard gauge in 1872.

The closure of the Pontarddulais-Swansea (Victoria) section in June 1964 brought an end to the traditional working pattern on the Central Wales line. On 20 May — just weeks before that irreversible change — 'Jubilee' No 45577 *Bengal* pulls away from Builth Road (High Level) with the 9.45am Swansea (Victoria)-Shrewsbury train. The engine's shedplate (6D) denotes Shrewsbury. The painted-out section of the station nameboard once advised passengers about changing for the Mid-Wales line, but that facility had been dispensed with at the end of 1962. *Hugh Ballantyne*

Above: After the closure of the Pontarddulais–Swansea section, Central Wales line trains were diverted at Pontarddulais to Llanelli. There were only two intermediate stations on the 'new' part of the route, and, although both were officially open to passengers, neither provided a welcoming sight for prospective travellers. One of the two stations was Llangennech, where a Pontarddulais–Llanelli local (hauled by an unidentified 0-6-0PT) was photographed on 4 September 1963.
Andrew Muckley

Below:
A down passenger/parcels train, hauled by an unidentified 'Hymek' diesel, passes through the still-open station at Bynea, on the Pontarddulais–Llanelli section, in 1964. *Andrew Muckley*

The Pontarddulais-Llanelli section has only ever had two intermediate stations, Llangennech (2¼ miles from Pontarddulais) and Bynea (4¼ miles), both of which lost their public goods facilities on 12 July 1965. On the approach to Llanelli, part of the original LR route now forms a freight loop which is used by the British Steel Trostre Tinplate Works. Until 4 May 1970 Central Wales trains started and terminated at Llanelli, but the services were then extended to Swansea (High Street) station.

To continue from Llanelli to Swansea, Central Wales trains reverse at Llanelli's modern station and then retrace a short section of their route before taking the South Wales main line to Swansea. The only intermediate station remaining on the Llanelli-Swansea section is at Gowerton, those at Loughor and Cockett having closed on 4 April 1960 and 15 June 1964 respectively. Interestingly, immediately to the west of Gowerton station the bridge under the long-disused ex-LNWR route into Swansea (the original Central Wales line) still stands.

The Central Wales line's two appendages — the Carmarthen and Llanmorlais branches — also met their doom in the BR era. The Gowerton South–Llanmorlais branch, which had lost its passenger services as early as January 1931, closed completely on 2 September 1957, having been worked by ex-GWR 0-6-0PTs during the final years. The Llandeilo–Carmarthen branch soldiered on until 9 September 1963, the trains being steam-hauled until the end.

Devotees of the Central Wales line might, perhaps, draw a smidgin of comfort from the fact that all but one of the intermediate stations between Craven Arms and Shrewsbury — on the supposedly much-grander main line from Hereford — were closed to passenger traffic on 9 June 1958. The only one to escape closure was Church Stretton, which is still open today.

New motive power

Immediately after the closure of the Swansea section of the Central Wales line in June 1964, there was a major revision of the timetables. A service of four through trains in each direction was advertised (five each way when the journey was extended in 1970 from Llanelli to Swansea).

On 2 April 1964, prior to the closure of the Swansea section, a three-car DMU made a trial trip between Llanelli and Craven Arms. When regular services commenced on 15 June, the through workings were provided exclusively by DMUs, with Swindon-built cross-country sets taking over in the late summer. These units lasted until May 1982.

Diesel locomotives were uncommon on the Central Wales line. The appearance of Landore's Class 37 No D6862 on 3 July 1964 did not herald the

Llanelli station, showing the Pontarddulais branch bay in the days before Central Wales line trains were diverted to Llanelli. *Andrew Muckley*

Diesel multiple-unit set No C603 emerges from the short tunnel on the approach to Pontarddulais with a Central Wales line working from Llanelli in May 1972. *Andrew Muckley*

Prior to 1964 Pontarddulais station was an expansive four-platform affair, but by June 1972 it was a shadow of its former self. A Llanelli–Shrewsbury working is given the right away from Pontardulais (with one 'd'!), the disused Swansea line platforms being just about visible behind the dilapidated station building. *Andrew Muckley*

Diesel multiple-units took over on the Central Wales line on 15 June 1964. Here, a Shrewsbury–Llanelli train emerges from Llangunllo Tunnel in the autumn of 1966. *Michael Mensing*

start of something new, as it was in charge of a special inspection train from Llanelli to Shrewsbury. Later, in 1967, WR 'Warship' No D602 was occasionally seen with a local goods working, but that did not last. The engine had been transferred to Pantyffynnon for goods and mineral workings, but being found unsuitable for the local mineral branches its potential usefulness was negligible. That was something of a reflection of the type's life stories, as they had regularly been moved around in a vain attempt to find something they could do satisfactorily.

Through freight workings on the Central Wales line lasted only until 10 August 1964, freight trains subsequently being diverted via Cardiff. However, a local pick-up goods continued working as far as Llandrindod Wells until 22 May 1965, when it was truncated at Llandovery. It ceased altogether on 26 May 1983, when the last wagons left Llandovery.

After the closure of Swansea (Paxton Street) shed in 1959, several of the depot's '8F' 2-8-0s had been transferred to the small shed at Llandovery, not only for goods and banking duties but also summer Saturday passenger workings. The switch to diesel traction for passenger services and the cessation of through freight workings rendered Llandovery's impressive stud of locomotives redundant.

Llandovery shed closed on 10 August 1964, the same date as the cessation of through freight workings on the Central Wales line. Prior to the shed's demise, it had accommodated no less than 17 engines — three Standard '4MT' 2-6-4Ts and 14 '8F' 2-8-0s. Of the 2-6-4Ts one (No 80069) was transferred to Nine Elms, the other two (Nos 80133/34) going to Feltham. Of the '8Fs', nine were placed in store at Llanelli, two were transferred to Neath (87A), and three to Bath (82F) for duties on the equally delightful Somerset & Dorset line. Neath shed, incidentally, had taken over the duties of Swansea East Dock shed on the latter's closure in June 1964.

The changes in the working of the Central Wales line brought an end to the brief reign of the 'Standard' 2-6-4Ts on the route. In September 1963 — nine months before the changes — No 80069 was photographed taking water at Llandovery. *Andrew Muckley*

The three small sheds towards the northern end of the Central Wales line — at Craven Arms, Knighton and Builth Road — had, along with their parent depot of Shrewsbury, been transferred to the Western Region after Nationalisation. Shrewsbury was initially coded 84G under WR auspices, but in September 1960 was recoded 89A. In the last days of steam, the Knighton banker was usually an ex-GWR '2251' class 0-6-0.

Above: Standard '5MT' 4-6-0 No 73003 enters Garth station with a Shrewsbury-bound train on 3 September 1963. Although swingeing economies were soon to be introduced on the Central Wales line, Garth station retains a well-maintained air.
Andrew Muckley

Below: At Llandrindod Wells the up platform was taken out of use in 1955 and the line singled in 1966, but in April 1986 the up line and platform were reinstated. On 25 April 1970 — in 'single-track' days — a two-car set enters the station with the 14.57 Shrewsbury–Llanelli train.
John A. M. Vaughan

Since the closure of the ex-GWR shed at Builth Wells in November 1957, Builth Road shed had assumed the former's responsibility for stabling and servicing the engines engaged on the Mid Wales line between Moat Lane and Brecon. This was a somewhat late flurry, as Builth Road shed itself closed at the end of 1962.

A new awareness

Having fended off closure once, and having had its route altered in 1964 and singled in 1964/65 as an apparently necessary economy, the Central Wales line continued to face an uphill battle against the accountants. Complete closure was proposed again in 1967, but a reprieve was granted. This time the reprieve was accompanied by the long-overdue realisation that the line was, for many, a social

CRAVEN ARMS, LLANELLI AND SWANSEA. WEEKDAYS PB213

Until 2 October

DOWN
SINGLE LINE
Craven Arms to Morlais Jn.
CROSSING PLACES
Llandrindod Crossing Ground Frame, Llanwrtyd, Llandovery and Llandeilo.

Mileage M.C.	Station		No.	2V83	2V83	2V83	2V83	2V83	2V83
								14 20 from Crewe	
	TIMING LOAD			D2	D3	D3	D3	D3	D3
						SX	SO		
	SHREWSBURY	dep	1	03 46	06 22	10 40	10 40	15 43	18 40
0.00	CRAVEN ARMS	arr	2	04 13½	[illegible]	11 17½	11 17½	16 11½	19 16½
	CRAVEN ARMS	dep	3	04 15	[illegible]	11 18½	11 18½	16 13	19 17½
2.61	Broome		4		07 01	11R27½	11 27½	16pR22	[illegible]
5.24	Hopton Heath		5		07pR05	11pR31½	11pR31½	16pR26	[illegible]
8.19	Bucknell		6	04b 31½	[illegible]	11qR36	11qR36	16R36½	19rR36
			7	[1]					
12.38	Knighton		8	04e 41½	07e 16½	11b 43½	11b 43½	16e 37½	19 41½
15.04	Knucklas		9		07R21	[illegible]	[illegible]	16pR42	[illegible]
18.72	Llangynllo		10		07pR29½	[illegible]	[illegible]	[illegible]	[illegible]
21.70	Llanbister Road		11		07qR34½	12qR01½	12qR01½	[illegible]	[illegible]
25.41	Dolau		12		[illegible]	12rR07	12rR07	17rR01	[illegible]
28.36	Pen-Y-Bont		13	05 06½	[illegible]	12rR11½	12rR11½	[illegible]	[illegible]
			14	[1]					
31.51	Llandrindod Crossing G.F.	arr	15		07 40½	12 16½	12 16½	17 10½	
	Llandrindod Crossing G.F.	dep	16	06 12	07X57	12X19	12X19	17X13	20 14½
32.08	LLANDRINDOD	arr	17	06 13½	07 58½	12 20½	12 20½	17 15	20 16
	LLANDRINDOD	dep	18	06 27	08 11	12 21½	12 21½	17 16½	20 18
37.55	Builth Road		19	06b 37	08R19½	12 30½	12 30½	17pR25	20R26½
39.54	Cilmeri		20		[illegible]	12pR34½	12pR34½	17qR29	[illegible]
43.04	Garth		21	06e 46	[illegible]	[illegible]	[illegible]	17rR34	[illegible]
44.62	Llangamarch		22	06e 50½	08rR32	12rR43	12rR43	17rR37½	20rR38
			23	[1]					
48.12	LLANWRTYD	arr	24	06 57	08 37½	12 48½	12 48½	17 43	20 43½
	LLANWRTYD	dep	25	[illegible]	08 39	12 49½	12 49½	17 43½	20X48
			26	[1]					
54.70	Cynghordy		27		08R50½	13rR01	13rR01	17pR55	20R59½
58.45	LLANDOVERY	arr	28	[illegible] 19	[illegible] 57½	13 06	13 06	18 02	21 06½
	LLANDOVERY	dep	29	[illegible] 23½	[illegible]	13 08	13 08	18 03½	21 07½
63.29	Llanwrda		30	[illegible]	[illegible]	13R14½	13R14½	[illegible]	21R13
65.10	Llangadog		31	[illegible] 33½	[illegible]	13pR18	13pR18	18pR11½	21pR16½
70.62	LLANDEILO	arr	32	[illegible] 42½	[illegible] 17	13 27	13 27	18 20½	21 25½
	LLANDEILO	dep	33	[illegible]	[illegible] 18	13 28	13 28	18 21½	21 27½
71.50	Ffairfach		34		[illegible]	13R30½	13R30½	18pR24	21R30
75.65	Llandybie		35	[illegible]	[illegible]	13pR36	13pR36	18pR31½	21pR37½
77.48	Ammanford		36	07pR02	[illegible]	13pR41½	13pR41½	18qR36	21pR41
			37	[1]					
78.61	Pantyffynnon		38	07e 07	[illegible] 34½	13 44	13 44	18e 38	21e 44
83.43	Pontarddulais		39	07 14½	[illegible]	13pR51	13pR51	18pR46	21R51
84.13	Hendy Jn.		40	07 16	09 43	13 52½	13 52½	18 46½	21 52½
85.21	Morlais Jn		41	07 17½	09 44½	13 54	13 54	18 48	21 54
85.66	Llangennech		42	07R19	[illegible]	[illegible]	[illegible]	[illegible]	[illegible]
87.62	Bynea		43	07R22½	[illegible]	[illegible]	[illegible]	[illegible]	21 59
88.69	Llandeilo Jn.		44	07 24½	09 51½	14 01	14 01	18 55	22 01
			45	[1]	[1]	[1]	[1]	[1]	[1]
90.40	LLANELLI	arr	46	07 28	[illegible] 55	14 04½	14 04½	18 58½	22 04½
	LLANELLI	dep	47	07 43	[illegible]	14 06	14 06	19 10	22 06
			48						
	SWANSEA	arr	49	08 03	10 17	14 28	14 28	19 30	22 28
			50						
			51						
			52						
			53						
			54						
			55						
			56						
			57						
			58						
			59						
			60						
			61						

Above: Extract from the WR working timetable for 17 May to 3 October 1982.

Below: The evening Shrewsbury–Llanelli train enters Builth Road station on 10 June 1983. Until the mid-1980s, when some £600,000 was invested in the line, Builth Road rather typified the neglect which had become painfully apparent at many places along the route. The 'uneven surface' sign part way along the platform says it all. *Andrew Muckley*

necessity. That was particularly true of the section between Knighton and Llandrindod Wells, where the roads were often too narrow to accommodate buses — the railway was the proverbial lifeline to the residents of several villages.

BR's newfound awareness of the line resulted in services being increased from four to five trains each way and the extension of the services from Llanelli to Swansea. It was proudly announced that journey times had been cut by up to 24min, but the revised and accelerated schedules did not always provide good connections at Shrewsbury for those wishing to travel on to Crewe or beyond.

Despite a grant of £370,000 in 1970, economies were still sought to offset the extra expenditure on the Central Wales line. An inspired piece of thinking resulted in a Light Railway Order being granted on 29 March 1972 for the Craven Arms–Pantyffynnon section of the line. The Order enabled many operational procedures to be simplified, with consequent economies.

The first Light Railways Act of 1896 had been intended to encourage the construction of rural branch lines, and a number of existing railways also had their powers transferred to those of Light Railways Orders. However, the Light Railway Commissioners of the 1890s could surely never have foreseen an LRO being applied to a 78¾ mile-long stretch of line; nor could they have envisaged a *bona fide* light railway having a speed limit as high as 60mph — the current maximum on the Central Wales line.

In 1975 the line was subsidised by a Government Public Service Obligation (PSO) grant, but even that didn't offer the long-term security for which the line's users had hoped. Essential repairs to the line were required, and BR's estimate for the necessary work was a frightening £1,000,000. In an attempt to postpone the work locomotive-hauled trains were prohibited on the line, and that effectively brought an end to special excursion trains upon which local hoteliers and other business people relied extensively. The last recorded locomotive-hauled train of the period was the return trip to Leeds of a Llandrindod Wells weekend excursion on 21 December 1980.

The local concern about the line's future resulted in the formation on 7 November 1981 of the Heart of Wales Line Travellers' Association — HOWLTA for short. The inaugural meeting of HOWLTA was held at Llandrindod Wells and, in order to transport the large party to the meeting, a LMR three-coach Class 120 DMU was used to augment the usual WR Class 120 set. The LMR sets had not previously worked the line due to their lack of spotlights. From May 1982, incidentally, the regular services were taken over by Metro-Cammell DMUs; trials with a Class 140 railbus in June 1981 and January 1982 (and also in June 1982) had proved unsatisfactory.

The 10.46 service from Shrewsbury to Swansea passes the fixed distant signal near Llandybie on 10 September 1979. The train is formed by Swindon-built Class 120 two-car set No C611. *Brian Morrison*

Above: By the early 1970s, the Central Wales line was in dire need of investment. This was evidenced by Hopton Heath station — once a proud twin-platform affair — in October 1971. *Andrew Muckley*

Right: At the risk of seeming repetitive, the countryside through which the Central Wales line passes remains unchanged. Despite the appeal of steam-hauled trains, dare it be suggested that DMUs offer Central Wales' passengers a better view of the scenery? On 10 September 1979, Swindon-built Class 120 two-car set was photographed emerging from Sugar Loaf Tunnel on the 09.59 Swansea-Shrewsbury service. *Brian Morrison*

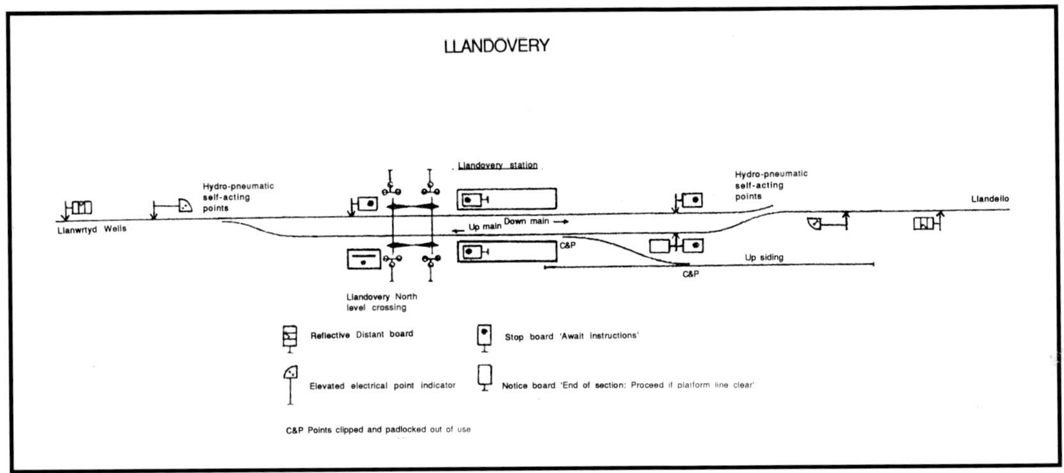

HOWLTA has, arguably, been one of the most successful of Britain's transport users' groups. It has worked closely with British Rail to promote cheap fares and excursion traffic, the latter including the summer Sunday 'Rambler' trains. Nowadays, Sugar Loaf platform — the one-time unadvertised stopping place for railway staff only — is opened on 10 Sundays each summer principally for the benefit of ramblers. To repeat a much-asked question, is there any other station in Britain which is served only on summer Sundays?

In the mid-1980s some £600,000 was invested in the Central Wales line and the train control system was modernised so that, by 28 September 1986, the signalbox at Pantyffynnon controlled the entire section between there and Craven Arms. The system of working is known as 'No Signalman Token on Single Lines with Remote Crossing Loops', or, a little less tongue-twistingly, NSTR for short.

South of Pantyffynnon, matters are controlled by the modern signalbox some distance away at Port Talbot. Under the terms of the Light Railway Order, the manning of level crossings between Craven Arms and Pantyffynnon was dispensed with and all but four of the crossings on that section are now ungated.

Much of the resignalling work was undertaken in 1986. Llandrindod Wells signalbox was closed in June that year and a temporary cabin was installed on the up platform for a month until the new system between there and Llanwrtyd Wells was installed. The boxes at Llanwrtyd Wells, Llandovery North and Llandeilo closed in August/September 1986 and all existing signalling equipment at those sites was taken out of use.

Above: The new signalling arrangements at Llandovery, July 1986.

Below: On 25 August 1990, the 09.30 Paddington–Llandrindod 'Heart of Wales Limited' charter arrives at its destination headed by InterCity long-range fuel tank Class 47/4 No 47803 *Women's Guild.* Who said that the LNER Pacifics had a monopoly of daft names? The signalbox on the right houses a small but interesting museum. *Brian Morrison*

In case the scenic delights of the Central Wales line haven't been adequately emphasised so far, how about this gem? The return 'Heart of Wales Limited' charter from Llandrindod to Paddington crosses Knucklas Viaduct on 25 August 1990, hauled by Class 47/4 No 47803 *Women's Guild. Brian Morrison*

The line's ability to accept tourist specials was improved by the alteration of the station layout at Llandrindod Wells and the installation in June 1990 of a passing loop at Knighton station. More recently, Regional Railways converted some of its two-car diesel units to single cars (Class 153s), and some £300,000 was spent on altering several of the platforms along the route so that they could accommodate the longer-bodied cars.

Although the line has enjoyed a high public profile in recent years — largely due to the efforts of HOWLTA — there has been one particularly sad black-spot. On 19 October 1987, after a prolonged period of very heavy rain, the bridge over the River Tywi at Glanrhyd collapsed into the flood waters, taking with it the front carriage of the 05.20 DMU from Swansea. The driver and two passengers died. Furthermore, a BR official was taken ill at the scene of the accident and died before he could reach home.

While the line was severed, passengers were conveyed between Llandeilo and Llandovery by bus. The replacement of the bridge was, however, remarkably swift, a pre-assembled structure being swung into position less than a year later. Ballasting was undertaken in October 1988, Class 37 No 37146 being in charge of the ballast train on 26 October. On the day before the reopening of the line the new bridge was tested by No 37212. The line reopened throughout on Monday 31 October 1988, the first train being a Class 101 two-car DMU from Swansea to Shrewsbury.

The reopening of the line coincided with the cessation of the regular use of Sprinters. They had not been particularly popular with the line's administrators, as their inability to accommodate bicycles and bulky luggage had been viewed as a deterrent to some tourists.

And now....

At present, the basic service on the line usually comprises four through trains between Shrewsbury and Swansea on weekdays and five on Saturdays. Two trains normally run each way on summer Sunday afternoons. In October 1987 a Saturdays Only shoppers' train from Llandovery to Swansea and return was introduced — the first 'extra' train south of Llandovery for over 20 years. Most trains call at all stations, although many stations are now request stops. The only freight traffic now seen on the line is coal from the Gwaun-cae-Gurwen branch, which is taken south via Pantyffynnon, usually by Class 37s.

Most of the services are now worked by Canton-based Class 153s. After the passing of the early DMUs, lightweight Class 108s based at Landore (Swansea) had taken over and these were followed by Class 150s. In recent years locomotive-hauled specials have started to appear on the line once again, whilst on 29 January 1994 an HST worked through to Llandrindod Wells on a circular tour that had started at Bedford. This was believed to be the first HST ever to venture on to the line.

The icing on the cake was, arguably, the appearance of steam-hauled specials in the summer of 1993. On 16 May preserved '4MT' No 80079 worked between Craven Arms and Carmarthen and the following weekend 'Black 5' No 44767 was used. Those two engines worked together on a northbound-train on 6 June. Further steam specials operated on the line in October (with 2-6-4Ts Nos 80079 and 80080) and the exercise was repeated in 1994.

By 1993/94, however, the Central Wales line's future was again looking dodgy. The reduction of PSO grants resulted in Sunday services being reduced for the summer of 1993 — only a few years after they had been introduced and despite BR's insistence that radio signalling would remove the obstacles to Sunday running. The 1993/94 winter timetable advertised four through trains each way instead of five and no Sunday services.

At the end of 1993 it was announced that £10 million of European Union funding would be injected into Radnorshire to create jobs and support community projects such as the railway. Among the projects considered for the EU funding is a goods facility at Crossgates, north of Llandrindod Wells where four arterial roads meet. If it comes off, it will provide the first public freight traffic for the northern section of the line since 1964.

Llandrindod station has benefited from some excellent restoration work, although when this photograph was taken on 25 August 1990 the work on the up platform was still in progress. Class 150/2 Sprinter No 150269 enters Llandrindod with the 12.08 from Crewe to Tenby. *Brian Morrison*

Singling of Central Wales line

11.12.1955	Llandrindod Wells up platform taken out of use
21.6.1964	Llanbister Road to Penybont Junction
11/12.12.1965	Penybont to Llandrindod Wells
12.12.1965	Craven Arms to Knighton
31.12.1967	Pantyffynnon South to Pontarddulais Junction

Central Wales line stations — economies and changes

Station	Closed for goods	unstaffed	'Halt' added	'Halt' dropped	Request stop now	New spelling/ name
Craven Arms	6.5.68[1]	-	-	-	-	
Broome	1.3.65	28.9.64	-	-	Yes	
Hopton Heath	1.3.65	28.9.64	-	-	Yes	
Bucknell	28.6.65	6.9.65	6.9.65	5.5.69	Yes	
Knighton	1.3.65	6.9.65	6.9.65	5.5.69	-	
Knucklas	21.10.57	1.2.56	1.2.56	5.5.69	Yes	
Llangunllo	20.4.64	6.9.65	6.9.65	5.5.69	Yes	Llangynllo (1980)
Llanbister Road	28.9.64	28.9.64[2]	28.9.64	5.5.69	Yes	
Dolau	22.6.64	6.9.65	6.9.65	5.5.69	Yes	
Penybont	24.5.65	6.9.65[2]	-	-	Yes	Pen-y-bont (1980)
Llandrindod Wells	6.5.68	30.12.68[5]	-	-	-	Llandrindod
Builth Road	5.4.65	6.9.65	-	-	-	
Cilmery	3.8.59	31.8.36	31.8.36	5.5.69	Yes	Cilmeri
Garth	28.9.64	28.9.64[2]	-	-	Yes	
Llangammarch Wells	28.9.64	28.9.64[2]	-	-	Yes	Llangammarch
Llanwrtyd Wells	7.6.65	-	-	-	-	Llanwrtyd
Cynghordy	28.9.64	28.9.64[2]	-	-	Yes	
Llandovery	26.5.83	-	-	-	-	
Llanwrda	1.3.65	6.9.65	6.9.65	5.5.69	Yes	
Llangadock	14.6.65	6.9.65	6.9.65	5.5.69	Yes	Llangadog (1958)
Talley Road	2.11.64[3]	2.6.41	-	-	-	
Llandilo	26.5.83	-	-	-	-	Llandeilo
Ffairfach	1.5.61[1]	1.5.61	1.5.61	5.5.69	Yes	
Derwydd Road	14.3.66[3]	?	-	-	-	
Llandebie	3.5.65[1]	3.5.65[2]	-	-	Yes	Llandybie (1971)
Tirydail	2.11.64	6.9.65	-	-	-	Ammanford (1973)
Pantyffynnon	14.6.65[1]	-	-	-	-	
Pontardulais	7.6.65[1]	6.9.65	6.9.65	5.5.69	Yes	Pontarddulais
Gowerton South	15.6.64[4]	-	-	-	-	
Dunvant	15.6.64[4]	31.12.56[2]	-	-	-	
Killay	15.6.64[4]	31.12.56[2]	-	-	-	
Mumbles Road	15.6.64[4]	-	-	-	-	
Swansea (Victoria)	4.10.65[3]	-	-	-	-	

Notes:

[1] Retained private siding after date shown

[2] Partially unstaffed earlier: Llanbister Road — 2.1.1956; Penybont — 5.12.1955; Garth and Llangammarch Wells — 30.12.1957; Llandebie — 17.9.1956; Cynghordy — 16.2.1959; Dunvant and Killay (on date shown)

[3] Closed to passengers earlier

[4] Closed completely on date shown (last public trains two days earlier)

[5] Staff restored 4.5.1970

Above: In the last few years, steam-hauled specials have brought a new dimension to operations on the Central Wales line. On 16 May 1993, preserved '4MT' 2-6-4T (a type which saw regular action on the line in 1963/64) No 80079 worked between Craven Arms and Carmarthen and is seen here crossing Knucklas Viaduct. *B. J. Ashworth*

Despite the line's rejuvenation, things are not all sweetness and light. At the time of writing, it is estimated that the line is losing some £2½million annually. Despite the recently announced EU grant the line's future cannot be considered totally secure given the present climate of uncertainty which hangs over many of Britain's railways. Another fly in the proverbial ointment is that, prior to the privatisation of British Rail, the spectacularly acquisitive bus operator, Badgerline, started to show an interest in the Central Wales line.

For those of us who have come to know the Central Wales line, it is unthinkable that it would ever disappear. That said, and putting realism above sentiment, did any of us really think that many of Britain's delightful rural railways would actually close in the 1960s — even after Beeching had spoken? And, even in the early 1960s, didn't we think that the projected elimination of the beloved steam locomotive couldn't really happen?

Below: The steam-hauled special of 16 May 1993, with 2-6-4T No 80079, was photographed leaving Builth Road. The cars in the foreground are parked on the site of the old Low Level station, which closed to passengers at the end of 1962. *B. J. Ashworth*

Preserved '4MT' 2-6-4T No 80079 reappeared on the Central Wales line on 6 June 1993, this time with 'Black Five' No 44767. The dynamic duo were photographed entering Llangunllo station, 950ft above sea level. *B. J. Ashworth*

On 9 October 1993, '4MTs' Nos 80079/80 worked together on the Central Wales line. They are seen here entering Knighton station. *B. J. Ashworth*

A fine study of the return to steam over the Central Wales line — '4MTs' Nos 80079/80 take on water at Knighton on 23 October 1993. *B. J. Ashworth*

Above: Knucklas halt was never the best-equipped of stopping places, but at least it was, at one time, kept in a presentable condition. By October 1971, however, it had lost its precariously-leaning platform buildings, and what little remained was in dire need of a great deal of attention. This sort of view was, unfortunately, not totally unique on the Central Wales line during the 1960s and 1970s, but in more-recent years the stations along the route have been treated to a little more respect. *Andrew Muckley*

Below: After Swansea (Victoria) station closed to passengers on 15 June 1964, the site was redeveloped. However, nothing earth-shattering happened overnight, as this picture of 9 July 1966 clearly shows. *R. O. Tuck*